Dr. Dre

Dr. Dre

The Biography

Ronin RO

THUNDER'S MOUTH PRESS
NEW YORK

Dr. Dre
The Biography

Published by
Thunder's Mouth Press
An Imprint of Avalon Publishing Group, Inc.
245 West 17th Street, 11th Floor
New York, NY 10011

AVALON
publishing group incorporated

First Printing, April 2007

Library of Congress Cataloging-in-Publication Data is available.

ISBN-13: 978-1-56025-921-3
ISBN-10: 1-56025-921-3

Interior design by Maria E. Torres

Printed in the United States of America
Distributed by Publishers Group West

For Rachel. (Daddy still loves you.)
For Lissette. (Thank you for being there.)
And for my readers. (Without you I'm nothing.)

"There is hardly any money interest in art, and music will be there when money is gone."

—Duke Ellington

Contents

1

D r. Dre wonders what he'll do with his life. It's 1981, he's not called Dre yet, and he's not a producer. He's Andre Romelle Young, he's sixteen, he's still in high school, and he's reportedly gotten a woman pregnant. He doesn't ever talk about this situation—she's due to give birth in December, which is only three months away—but he won't be staying with her. He's swamped enough just trying to get through high school. It's the dawn of a new decade. In Compton, California, forty or so gangs have carved every inch of the city's ten square miles into various territories. And he's trying to figure out what to do with his life.

He could join the gangs if he wants. He gets on well with many members. But unlike them, he wants more than to spend his entire life focusing on what's happening, or who's rolling through the neighborhood. He wants more than this street with its private homes, tiny lawns, and bar-covered windows. He doesn't want to always see the same guys serving vials to the crackheads, or an O.G. with fading tattoos wasting his days playing dominoes or trying to customize or repair some old car. Nor does he want to be the one spray painting some future victim's name on a wall, or seeing that someone has tagged his name and drawn a thick decisive slash through it.

He can get a job flipping burgers if he wants to, but feels he's worth more than that. That won't bring in any real money. He'll be taking orders, slaving away, wearing some uniform that embarrasses him, and will probably be seen by many of the girls he's constantly flirting with. He worries about the future sometimes, then reminds himself he's still young. He has time to figure it all out.

With his mom working a full-time job, he keeps being shuttled among relatives' homes. If he's with his grandmother, around Bloods, or in school near Crips, he avoids blue or red and sticks to neutral black. He makes it a point to be cool, friendly, but knows at heart he has little in common with many of them besides a love of parties and girls and being raised by single moms in Compton. Unlike them, he's had his mom forcing him to be disciplined, to develop a strong work ethic, and to respect human life. He's sometimes crippled by self-doubt but ultimately knows he has to be positive about the future. He won't have fights to preserve a rep and won't resort to dealing or robbing somebody to get some ends. He can easily join a set but thinks, "If you ain't gonna make money out of it, don't do it. It's just gonna get you motherfucking shot at; you gonna shoot at some motherfuckers; you gonna end up in jail; dead; something like that."

So he keeps going to school, dabbling in subjects that catch his attention and seeing people around him get paid. Guys his age carry beepers and drive new cars. They rock custom-made clothing. They battle other gangs for the right to serve cluck heads. They describe their latest arrest and carry guns and stop whatever they're doing if a strange car rolls through the tree-lined hood.

Meanwhile, Andre does so well with drafting that his teacher wants to enroll him in an apprenticeship program at Northrop Aviation Company. He's excited by the idea—he can potentially have a well-paying career and a stress-free adulthood—until he learns his poor grades make him ineligible. So he keeps drifting through school, chatting up girls, hanging with friends, and immersing himself deeper into this relatively new rap music.

It's been around since the early 1970s in New York, but the rest of the country, including Cali, only heard about it after The Sugarhill Gang's 1979 single, "Rapper's Delight." Andre—already a visionary—likes nothing better than to listen to some of the newest songs. The music's released on singles so he can afford a few, and he takes them to his room and spends hours analyzing every note, picturing every word these rappers describe, like a movie. The music transports him from his mundane life in a secluded hood. When in the middle of a song, he's not the tall, skinny father-to-be with no prospects for the future and little interest in most of his classes. He's not the guy many ladies reject since his clothes aren't as fancy as those of some of the dealers and Gs hanging outside the school. He can pretend to be the tough-talking guys on the records, surviving every obstacle the ghetto throws their way.

With Sugarhill enjoying unprecedented success with the new music, other adventurous labels create their own singles, so Andre has more to choose from. And he gets to hear these labels' house bands cover the latest rhythm and blues or disco records. One week, he'll hear Gwen McRae's single "Funky Sensation." The next, Afrika Bambaataa & the Jazzy 5's instant cover, "Jazzy Sensation." Soon after Tanya Gardner's "Heartbeat," he'll hear The Fearless Four's "Feel the Heartbeat," and Sweet G's "A Heartbeat Rap."

He still loved his mom's oldies (Marvin Gaye, Sly Stone, Parliament-Funkadelic, and more), but rap allowed him to develop his own musical identity, and to hear lyrics he could relate to. In the two years since "Rapper's Delight" the music had evolved to the point where Grandmaster Flash created his seven-minute opus, "Grandmaster Flash on the Wheels of Steel," with nothing but two turntables and old songs. By scratching funky drum solos or bass lines from old records that DJs called "break beats," Flash had finally captured the undiluted sound of the streets. The sound of Flash mixing "Apache," "Good Times," Queen's "Another One Bites the Dust," Blondie's "Rapture," and other Sugarhill house-band singles moved sixteen-year-old Andre so much, he went home and told his brother Tyree—three years younger, and more involved with gangs—that he wanted to become a dancer. "That was my favorite shit," Dre recalled. With his mom and Tyree looking on, he quickly encouraged his fellow rap fans Darrin and June Bug to join him in forming a new dance crew.

Tall, and pretty athletic when he wanted to be, Andre quickly picked up a few of the pop-lock moves The Lockers—another dance crew formed by kids living over in Crenshaw—had done on *Soul Train* since the early 1970s. He struggled to find his own identity when his mother, Verna, insisted on involving herself in his latest venture, this time saying she'd help design their flashy costumes and drive them to various dance competitions. With frantic dance music playing, the normally reserved Andre got out in front of crowds, waved his arms, bent his knees, pretended to collapse, then jerked back up to his full height—he was over six feet tall—to perform more robotic moves. His mother looked on with pride. "Everybody thought that they should have won first place but somebody always beat them," Verna recalled. Ultimately, coming in second proved too crushing a blow to his already fragile ego. "Really and truly," his mom noted, "he doesn't like to talk about that!"

Andre next decided to remake himself in the image of a Flash-like DJ. He assembled his friends as his new music crew, The Freak Patrol. He sat with old stereo components, tearing them apart and reshaping them into home-made mixers. He spent every waking moment thinking of ways to combine old records. There was little reason to believe this latest venture would amount to anything, but Andre was determined to see how far he could get. Soon, he confidently carried his turntables and speakers out to the park around the corner from his house to spin records for neighbors.

At the time, other local residents were doing the same. Some had been at it for years and were now making the leap into their new genre now that their meal ticket—string-filled disco—was on the wane. So when he wasn't dee-jaying himself, if he wanted to, Dre (as he was soon nicknamed) could catch shows by crews like Unique Dreams, who played everywhere from Culver City to Pomona; The Dream Team, who rocked South Central; and promoter Lonzo Williams' The Wreckin' Cru who were playing Compton nightclubs. Or, if he happened to wander into a park or on the street at the right time, he could watch other young hopefuls like Eric Wright rock barbecues, house parties, and street festivals.

At home, Dre kept recording tapes with his homemade mixer or listening to the latest records. After releasing early singles with call and response themes (shouting out zodiac signs or birthdays), Grandmaster Flash & the Furious 5's rapper Melle Mel filled "The Message" with a harrowing portrait of ghetto life. Dre could picture the roaches and rats, junkies urinating in alleys, bill collectors, stickup kids, prison rapes, and suicides Mel described. But he also liked lighter fare, such as the progressive dance music Afrika Bambaataa and the Soul Sonic Force created with drum machine and synthesizer for "Planet Rock."

By the time Christmas rolled around, Dre felt he wasn't getting far with that crummy homemade mixer. He asked his mom and stepfather, Warren Griffin, for a real one. To his surprise, they got it for him. And from that moment his life changed forever. "That was it for me," he said. No sooner had he unwrapped the package than he ran to get dressed. Outside, he showed it to all his pals in the Freak Patrol and said they'd really be able to do something now. Then, while his parents and their guests gathered around the tree and dinner table, he holed up in his room, plugging it in, slipping headphones on, and placing records on his matching turntables. He spent the entire day working to master the speed and precision he heard on Flash records.

He was getting the hang of it when his mom came in and said he had to come eat. In frustration he did, but he chewed quickly and got back to his music, actually playing records at this point. He worked to the point of exhaustion, his mom told him the next day. When she came in later that night to check on him, she found him sleeping on the bed with his headsets on and the music blasting. "I took the headsets off, turned off the music, and threw a blanket over him, trying hard not to disturb his sleep," she recalled.

Since then, entire days passed like minutes as Dre practiced his mixes. At school, sensing that his talent gave him authority among his classmates, he based his public image around that of an aspiring, hungry young DJ. Then after school, on the way home, he invited neighborhood kids up to the house to hear him mix, giving him an audience. Eventually, neighbors complained about the noise, and his mom started feeling he turned the house into "party central." But when she came to the door, yelling to be heard over the music, he'd lower the volume long enough to hear what she said. Once she was done, and had gone, he'd raise it again, and get back to what really mattered, his music.

◆ ◆ ◆

Music had been a constant in Dre's life since his birth on February 18, 1965, in L.A. County General. For one, his parents were aspiring singers when they met. Verna, born in 1950, had wanted to be an entertainer herself, but her dreams of making it big with The Four Aces ended once her seventeen-year-old boyfriend Theodore Young got her pregnant. Until then, she said, "We practiced at my house every chance we got if my mom allowed it." But once their parents learned she was with child, they quickly arranged a nice wedding for the fifteen-year-old in Theodore's mother's living room. The newlyweds moved in with her mom. She had Dre two weeks after her sixteenth birthday and called him Romelle in honor of Theodore's own unsigned group, The Romells.

With her music career over, Verna looked for something to fill the void and found it in lavishing attention on Dre. "It was like I had a live doll," she later said. A diaper change suddenly became a fashion show, as she changed it two or three times during one sitting to try different ways of dressing him up. She also loved showing him off to his four uncles, two aunts, and various neighbors in the community. "Everyone wanted to hold him and bounce him around." She loved to hear them say he was big for his age, and so smart. She in turn regaled his admirers with tales of how he seemed to love music (since, when she left him on a bed with a radio playing, he'd doze off).

On August 18, 1966, when Dre was a year and a half old, he saw his mom give birth to another son. For weeks beforehand, his grandmother had told him he'd soon have a new playmate. When his mom got home with his new brother, Jerome La Vonte, Dre lingered near the crib, watched Jerome move around, and soon called him "Bubby." For two months, he was happy and intrigued by his baby brother. But then one morning, everything changed. As usual, his mom woke up and went to get Bubby's bottle. After she fed him, she'd dress Dre and head to work. But this time when she pulled Bubby's blanket back she saw blood on his crib sheet. Rolling Jerome over, she saw more blood coming from his nose. In horror, she lifted him. "His head dangled like a loosely filled rag doll." She screamed at the top of her lungs and Theodore leaped out of bed. Running over, he took Bubby from her and tried to give the baby CPR. Since they didn't have a phone, Dre's mom ran down to the pay phone on the corner in bare feet to call her mom. Within minutes,

Dre saw his grandmother arrive. His mom was still crying uncontrollably and his father was holding Bubby and numbly repeating, "He's going to be alright." They ushered Dre and Bubby into a car and sped over to Bon Air Hospital, where doctors pronounced Bubby dead on arrival, of intestinal pneumonia.

At home, Dre noticed the mood become uncommonly grim and seemed to wonder why Bubby wasn't in his crib. His mom meanwhile struggled to move past the paralyzing loss. "My whole world went numb when my baby died," recalled Verna. In an unbelieving daze, she helped arrange the funeral. "I had never before seen such a small casket." Once it was over, Dre couldn't help but notice his mom was a little withdrawn. "Andre really missed him," she remembered, noting that as Andre seemed to realize Bubby was somehow gone, he reverted to crying for a bottle and wetting his pants. Even more heartbreaking, for months he kept running to the crib, forgetting Bubby was gone, peering in, and yelling, "Bubby! Bubby!" His mother could relate. "For months afterwards I could hear a baby crying in the distance."

By March 19, 1968, Verna split with Theodore and had another son by a new man, Tyree Du Sean Crayon. And as soon as she arrived from the hospital with him, Andre ran to get his ball. He was about to toss it, to play catch, when she said Tyree had to grow before they played. Dre was glum until she let him help feed, change, and even hold the new baby.

The Young family experienced hard times economically but never let them dampen their spirits. If anything, they started throwing parties with music so loud it shook the walls. And Verna let four-year-old Andre stand near her little turntable. While changing records—tiny vinyl 45s—Andre felt like part of the action. People drank, danced or chatted about life's problems while he determined what they'd hear next. He couldn't read but he recognized the colors on the labels, so he busily created stacks (play lists), and made sure when one record ended, the next was ready to go.

His mom helped prepare him for school by teaching him the entire alphabet; how to count to 100; how to remember his address and phone number and spell and write his name. She taught him how to tell time and tie his own shoes. If he couldn't get the hang of something, she "pushed him beyond normal limits" and encouraged him to keep trying. "Like my mother did with me, I didn't allow Andre to say, 'I can't.'"

By 1972, however, his father was gone. His mom divorced Theodore and married Curtis Crayon. Since he was looking for work, Curtis was there to take care of Andre and Tyree while his mom worked for the phone company. But she soon lost that job and they again experienced money woes that led to moving from one small apartment to another, all within the same vicinity in Compton. But through it all, Andre noticed his mother never stopped trying to improve their lives. When she got laid off from the credit department at Sears and Roebuck and they moved into an even smaller place on Eighty-Second, she tried to earn a few dollars by sewing things for neighbors. Right before Andre started school, "I made plans to sew all of his clothes. He was going to be the best dressed boy in the whole school." In her hands, remnants from a nearby fabric store became an assortment of stylish vests and suits. "I made so many clothes that Andre was able to wear a different suit to school every day."

When Verna learned bigger kids from a nearby house bullied Andre and Tyree, she immediately planned another move. Instead, she found a job, and Andre had to spend his afternoons with his grandmother in another part of town. He and Tyree shared a room in their new larger apartment in the Wilmington Arms housing project in Compton while his mother turned the third bedroom into a den. Along with music, he always heard his mom stay on them about their behavior, their grades, and their chores. "I expected nothing less than the best from them in whatever they did." And when she and Curtis had guests over she let him play records.

By 1976, Andre enrolled in Vanguard Junior High School and started slacking off. His mom had just given birth to his sister Shameka but made it a point to work with his teachers to get him on the right track. By now, she sensed that he didn't react well to orders. "Instead of hollering at him I remained calm so that I could determine the cause."

She also helped him get over the fact that a burglar broke in and stole a new bike he only rode once (even though the same burglar took her prized, irreplaceable record collection). When new kids moved into the complex and started picking fights with her sons, she quickly scheduled another move. Andre and Tyree could have probably fought their own battles, but by now gangs were on the rise. And, she explained, "My sons meant everything to me. I was not going to reside in an atmosphere that was uncomfortable for them."

Things were finally looking up for the family. Andre felt safer on Mayo Street, and made many new friends at Roosevelt Junior High. Verna found a great new job as an Operations Control Analyst at the McDonnell-Douglas plant in Long Beach. When he and Tyree asked for karate classes, she said no problem. Every night after work, she took them to class and asked them to not mention it to Curtis. Since he was against the idea, she recalled, she asked them to sneak their uniforms into the house, wash them quickly, then hide them until the next day. Curtis did not explain why he was so dead set against the karate classes.

Before long, Dre heard his mom say she wanted to move to a better house in Carson. The place needed renovations but a few coworkers—including Warren Griffin, a father of four in upper management at her job—spent three weeks helping her fix the place up. Shortly after their move, Andre saw his mom and Curtis divorce.

It was at this point that his mom decided—after weeks spent hanging with eleven-year-old Andre and Tyree, then eight—to accept an invite to a party. Dre's grandmother was driving her back to their apartment when they were involved in a car accident. His grandmother began making a left turn at an intersection when another car ran a red light and slammed into them so hard, their vehicle spun a few times then landed on the curb across the street.

Andre, napping in the backseat with his head against a window, flew across the backseat and slammed face-first into a closed window, which shattered. As he fell into darkness under the seat, he could hear his mom yell, "Momma, momma, momma," and Tyree (in the backseat) scream, too, since he had a cut in his head. Soon, a police officer opened the back door and loaded Andre and Tyree into a patrol car. At nearby Dominguez Valley Hospital, the cuts in his face began to hurt but Andre didn't cry, even when a doctor started sewing his face.

He went home that night but quietly suffered from pain in his chest and on one side of his body. Andre never mentioned it until one day when the pain became too much. His mom rushed him to a doctor, where they learned he'd spent months silently nursing a broken collarbone.

Despite this, things were looking up. Verna and Warren Griffin grew so close they wanted to get married and buy a home on Thorson Street in Compton. As Warren's wife, she was much happier. Andre and his siblings Tyree and Shameka meanwhile made more new friends in a new neighborhood and were soon having a great time whenever Griffin's only son, Warren III (or Little Warren), spent weekends with them. Little Warren had just as much fun; when he had to leave, he'd actually start crying. During the summer, Andre's mom and Warren discussed having Little Warren move in with them. By September, Griffin's ex let it happen but soon complained of wanting more money for Warren's three daughters. She barged into the home one night, and scared the children to the point where Tyree tried to shield Shameka and Little Warren (who burst into tears) from her. Verna meanwhile calmly asked the ex, who was by now holding a knife, to leave since she was frightening the children. The ex said she didn't care.

Verna walked to the porch, grabbed a heavy iron, then returned to the kitchen in time to see the ex slice Warren Senior's hand with the knife. "I swung the iron at her, hitting her in the head," Verna recalled. The woman dropped the knife and fell. Verna came to her senses "and didn't hit her again," and saw the woman finally leave.

Incidents like this were rare as Andre prepared to start freshman year at Centennial High. Thanks to his mother, he now possessed the intelligence, the work ethic, and the love of music that would all play a part in his future success.

2

At Centennial High, the tall, slim, upbeat student with an Afro spent his time hanging with pals, chasing girls, and playing hookey. Andre's grades plunged to the point where his mom, to separate him from his friends, suggested he transfer to Fremont High. On December 15, 1981, a young woman in nearby Paramount, California, gave birth to Andre's son, Curtis Young, but whether Andre knew this happened is unknown (only later would the son emerge as a rapper named Hood Surgeon and say he met his father when he was twenty-one).

Andre quickly made friends at his new school and, during the early months of 1982, was interested in dating sixteen-year-old Lisa Johnson, from Culver City. This led to even worse grades as he began cutting class to be with her. Like him, Lisa was attending Fremont out of her district. He interested her enough to inspire an invitation to her home for an Easter celebration. In his best clothes, his Afro picked to the hilt, he had his mom drive him over and met her parents.

On another day, Lisa called his house to ask his mom if she could come over for a visit. His mother said yes but minutes later received another call from Lisa's mom, who opined Lisa was too young to be involved with someone. Andre, however, didn't let this stop him from sneaking over to her home when her parents were out and before long, Lisa's mom was on the phone again, wringing her hands over the fact that Lisa was pregnant. When Andre's mom asked if she were sure her son was the father, Lisa's mom "got very upset. 'If I had come home and caught that nigger in my house you would have been picking him up in a box,'" Andre's mom quoted her as saying. In response Verna said that if the woman touched Andre, there'd be nowhere she could hide. "My son didn't break into your house and rape your daughter," she added. "She let him in, which makes her just as much at fault as he is."

Andre, after the call, sat with his mom for a talk. She asked what happened. Embarrassed, he kept evading the issue. Finally, he admitted that he'd been sneaking over there and having sex with Lisa. She urged him to do right by the baby but didn't suggest marriage "like my parents forced me to do. After all," she adds, "he was only seventeen and Lisa was only sixteen."

With Lisa pregnant, and his grades slipping, Andre sought escape in rap music. When he learned local promoter Alonzo Williams was playing some in a new nightclub called Eve's After Dark on the corner of Avalon and El Segundo, he went over to see what was happening. After paying admission, he approached a curtain. It was packed and hot inside, but he enjoyed the music and watching ladies dance. He decided to return another night but Lonzo wouldn't let him in since the place had a dress code (dresses for ladies and slacks and ties for the fellas).

Eventually, Andre became a regular. At Eve's, he finally felt a sense of belonging. Around him, the same people he might otherwise see in all blue or red now wore ties, slacks, and shoes. Instead of colored handkerchiefs to promote their gang affiliation, many sported Jheri curls as slick and sculpted as Michael Jackson's or some of the guys creating rap singles. The girls meanwhile were just as done up, in tight dresses, heels, jewelry, and bright red lipstick. Even the DJs were impressively dressed.

From his place in the crowd, Andre watched the DJs get behind state-of-the-art turntables and turn a gig into so much more than just playing records. Some were even more meticulous about their Jheri curls than he was; and instead of cheap sweatshirts, jeans, khakis or sneakers with worn heels, Lonzo had his performers in matching lavender outfits, performing choreographed dance moves. During those halcyon Friday nights, along with the usual R&B, disco, and funk singles Andre heard them play new electronic rap singles like "Planet Rock." Everything was well organized at the club, right down to the technical crew (Lonzo had them in fancy jackets with the name Wreckin' Cru on the back) and Andre soon started to wish he could be part of the group. When he practiced his mixes at home, he did so with the hope that Lonzo would somehow get to hear him mix.

Like Andre, Alonzo Williams was a dancer-turned-DJ looking to earn money by throwing parties. He'd been attending Compton High School when he started playing disco records at house and block parties. He formed a DJ group, Disco Construction, and joined his pal Roger Clayton in promoting parties that attracted over 1,000 people to the Alpine Village club out in Torrance. But after two years as Disco Lonzo, he and Clayton split. Clayton went on to form his own group, Uncle Jam's Army, while Lonzo reacted to disco's fading by changing his nickname to Grandmaster Lonzo, forming a new group, The Wreckin' Cru, and promoting events at Eve's After Dark. When Clayton's rival group, Uncle Jam's Army, started wearing costumes on stage—like those worn by Afrika Bambaataa and the Furious 5—Lonzo wouldn't be outdone. He coaxed his DJs into wearing their own garish outfits. After every night at Eve's, Andre was more inspired to pursue his own budding deejay career. With his friends, he drove his equipment around town in a van to play "a lot of P-Funk stuff," and rap singles at house parties and high schools.

He had to slow down a little in January 1983, since on the nineteenth, Lisa gave birth to his daughter, La Tanya Danielle Young. Whatever excitement Dre may have felt was dampened by the fact that his relationship with Lisa's mother had deteriorated. Because of their parents' previous argument, Lisa's mom didn't want him present during the birth. Soon, however, he made his way to her hospital room, his mother recalled. "I bought an assortment of baby items and sent them to Lisa." He held his daughter that day and beamed with pride. And when Lisa said she'd bring La Tanya by the house he felt even better.

◆ ◆ ◆

If Andre Young didn't know what to do with his life, he at least wanted to do something. Tall, slim, boyish, with an Afro and infectious grin, he kept haunting the street outside Eve's After Dark. "People came out in droves," Lonzo recalled. "It was a constant party." From his place in the crowd, the ambitious young father dreamed of being up on stage. Though seventeen and still in high school, he had three years' experience as a deejay and a collection of obscure old records that could easily fill a dance floor.

One night, he learned one of Lonzo's Wreckin' Cru DJs didn't show up. Andre's distant relative Tim urged Lonzo to give Andre a shot. Inside, with Lonzo looking on, Andre challenged Yella, one of Lonzo's DJs, to a battle. And to his surprise, Yella accepted. While Yella did his routine, Andre waited, psyching himself up. Finally, Yella stepped away from the turntables.

Andre couldn't believe he was actually mounting the stage and had people facing him with anticipation. He reached for the headphones, slipped them on, and found a copy of "Planet Rock." Next, he put a copy of The Marvelettes' Motown classic "Please Mr. Postman" on the second turntable. They had different beats, tempos, and moods and even Lonzo looked skeptical. But Andre adjusted the tempos—having them meet halfway—and the crowd loved it. Lonzo had already noticed the many looks Andre drew from the ladies in the crowd. Now he thought, "Hmm, what do we have here?" He realized Andre could help him compete with Uncle Jam's Army, who wore leather boots, skintight parachute pants, and lace gloves. They were huge fans of Prince and Morris Day, and believed New Wave–patterned clothing (black and white checkerboard patterns) combined with their onstage personas would lure women to their shows. It was corny, but it did the trick as Egyptian Lover, a stocky guy with dripping Jheri curls, a mustache and beard, and a ladies'-man image emerged as one of the scene's most popular draws. In Andre, Lonzo saw someone that could outdo Egyptian Lover. Besides being tall, skinny, and soft-featured, he was as visually non-threatening and clean-cut as Michael Jackson. "He's absolute magic with women, man," Lonzo later said. "Ladies fucking love him."

That night at home, Andre told his mom about the show. Emboldened by the positive response, he called himself Dr. Dre, the Master of Mixology, after basketball superstar Julius Erving. He didn't exactly know what to do next but soon Lonzo approached him near his grandparents' home to offer a regular deejay gig for fifty dollars a night. Dre listened in disbelief. The Cru was one of the city's premier deejay groups; they were paying him and already preparing a jacket with a logo.

Now, when playing records and performing a few cool dance moves on stage, Dre faced the audience and saw Tyree watching. He was relieved. Where Dre was mesmerized by rap music, Tyree was embroiled in a variety of gang-related fights at Roosevelt Junior High. Crips didn't like his red pants and Dre urged him not to provoke them, but Tyree kept wearing crimson until the day a group of Crips chased him up the driveway. Even when his mom opened the door and Tyree ran inside, his opponents tried to gain entry. She had to swing a sturdy brass umbrella stand to keep them out. She secretly threw the offending slacks away that night, but Tyree kept getting into it with gang members. However, with Dre making progress in the local music scene, his kid brother was hanging around, staying, at least for a while, off the streets and away from gangs. His mom was just as supportive. When Tyree wanted to attend a show, she'd fill her car with his friends, drive them to the club by nine p.m., then head home, set the alarm clock for one a.m. and pick them up, to make sure they got home safely.

Joining the Cru allowed Dre to travel in different circles. Soon he bonded with fellow member Antoine "Yella" Carraby. Born and raised in Compton, Yella got his stage name from The Unknown DJ, who heard The Tom Tom Club's "Mr. Yellow," and said, "That's what your name should be." Yella was shorter, older, and unmarried, and favored facial hair (he had a thick frowning mustache) but enjoyed the same records Dre did. He could relate when Dre described his money woes. More important, Yella helped Dre develop his turntable skills since he was the one who helped bring full-scale scratching— the rhythmic variety Flash and DJ Davy D performed on East Coast singles— to the region. (Kurtis Blow had performed a few hits at Eve's, and Blow's skillful DJ, Davy D, taught Yella the technique.)

The club could get a little rough sometimes, but Dre didn't worry about his safety. Not with about fifteen street-hardened young men around the stage and his brother Tyree and his friends out in the crowd. So Dre could focus on his act and improving his skills. He quickly embraced the visual side of performing, buying a doctor's coat and stethoscope. There was already another self-proclaimed doctor in the club (his pal Doctor Rock) and already a rap doctor in the recording group UTFO (Doctor Ice), not to mention Dr. Fink in Prince's group The Revolution, but Dre didn't care. He felt he had the right to this image, and that he was differentiating himself from everyone on stage with him by filling his set with breakbeats and surprising oldies. If anything, he soon believed, his well-designed shows made him better than these regular DJs. "People would come from everywhere just to see Dr. Dre on the wheels of steel." He was just getting used to all the attention when, as quickly as it began, his new career was in danger of ending.

♦ ♦ ♦

With the sheriff's department looking to shut the club down, Lonzo said, "I was looking for something else." Noting how popular rap had become in the East, he figured it'd inevitably hit the West Coast. One day, Dre heard him tell the group, "We're going to put together a little package real quick, and we'll be ready to roll." Fifteen people were enthusiastic, but only a few made the cut. Yella was one. Then Lonzo picked Dre. Since both could deejay, they merited automatic inclusion. That Lonzo couldn't deejay or rap didn't stop him from thinking, "I'm just gonna be a member of the group, and finance everything."

Plans to record gave Dre another excuse to ignore school. In Eve's After Dark during the day, when the place was empty, he and Yella turned on some of the fancy recording equipment Lonzo stored in a back room. Yella could work the drum machine so they spent many a day playing records and re-creating their melodies or drum solos on an old four-track recorder. While hearing some old songs, Dre would think, "I would have done this different."

By this stage, Dre was recording tapes and analyzing them afterward. He was most comfortable when in the middle of a mix. When he shut his equipment off, he loved listening to the radio, noting that stations were starting to play more and more rap music. Eventually, two college students in black fedoras changed the course of his life.

They were called Run-DMC, a clean cut duo from Queens, New York, who yelled insults and boasts over sparse beats and some turntable scratching.

"Sucker MC's" floored him to the point where he got a copy and listened closely to every mesmerizing note. Soon he had all their singles in his room, listening to them over and over, trying to understand why they worked and what elements made them so memorable.

Once he got the hang of the drum machine, he'd bang out patterns that echoed those perfected by Run-DMC's producers. Eventually, he started taping their work so he could analyze it later. With each listening, he became even more intrigued by the possibilities offered by recording. He experimented with scratches, counter melodies, and increasing a song's power by piling beats onto each other. He and the rest of the group auditioned a few demos in the club at night, then passed tapes to friends or neighbors. In addition to giving Dre a public persona as a producer, they brought in a little spending money and attracted the interest of a local radio station.

Greg Mack, KDAY's new music director, wondered how he could help the small radio station in nearby Echo Park compete with ratings leader KFGF. In his mother's home in South Central, Mack had heard rap music and Dre's mix tapes blaring from passing cars. A street-smart cousin then said everyone liked KFGF because they were the only station playing rap. When Mack further researched the local scene to learn which crews were making the most noise, he kept hearing about The Wreckin' Cru. Before long, he got hold of one of Dre's tapes and loved it enough to arrange a meeting. That day, Mack pitched Dre and Yella on the idea of creating original mixes for a new five o'clock rush-hour program, The Traffic Jam.

The duo immediately set about planning a fifteen-minute routine and got the sample into Mack's hands. Dre kept his fingers crossed and tried to calm his fear of rejection. To his surprise, Mack not only enjoyed the tape, but in early September 1983 he aired it on KDAY and asked for more. Dre was happy to see listeners embrace his musical ideas and at the start of his senior year made music even more a part of his public image. Mack was just as delighted. Thanks to Dre's and Yella's mixes, the radio show "really took off." KDAY's ratings soared until one episode scored a tremendous 22 percent share of the audience, making it number one in its time slot.

Lonzo was already making arrangements to get the group into a recording studio, but Dre was nervous. He was thrilled to go from fan to artist in such a short time but couldn't sing, rap, or play instruments. Then Lonzo booked Run-DMC into the club. While watching the duo and their DJ rock the crowd, Dre was awe-struck. They wore hats, jeans, sweatshirts, and sneakers. They yelled at the audience. They pointed at people's faces and sneered. They marched around the stage as if they owned the joint. They didn't care who liked it or not. Dre thought this was the freshest thing he'd ever seen. This shit was hard. "That was just it for me."

Yella was just as astounded. He'd been just as anxious about recording original material. But after seeing the performance by a group that was nothing but guys in regular street clothes, he faced Dre with relief. "This is it? It's not even a ten-minute show. We can do this!" Their confidence grew even more after Jam Master Jay gave them advice about how to be stronger, more commanding rappers on stage.

In 1984, Dr. Dre joined Lonzo and the other members of The Wreckin' Cru at Audio Achievements, a Torrance studio run by engineer Donovan Smith. Lonzo invested a hundred bucks to record "Slice," and "Cru Groove." But instead of the tougher style Dre preferred, Lonzo called for more "Planet Rock"–inspired dance beats and scratches. Dre and Yella shrugged and filled a reel tape with drum tracks and scratching.

With tape in hand, Lonzo traveled to Santa Monica Boulevard in Hollywood, where a pressing plant named Macola would, for a few hundred dollars, press hundreds of vinyl records, let him credit the song to his Kru-Cut Records, and let him keep publishing rights. They sold copies of the double-sided, twelve-inch dance single out of the trunk of his Mazda RX-7. "We sold five thousand of them," Lonzo said. "Five thousand. That's like ghetto gold." Dre was just as encouraged. "Everybody was digging it, so I decided that this was the job I was going to take."

The decision came at a good time. With tapes on radio, and crowds coming to see him spin, Dr. Dre had become even less involved with school. His mom urged him to get his diploma to avoid facing the sort of hardships that characterized her own life, but he kept skipping class at Fremont, inspiring another round of battles at home. When he did attend school, he did exceedingly well in the classes he enjoyed. His swim teacher called him the best diver on the team and begged his mom to help raise his grades since anything less than a C meant he couldn't compete anymore. His English teacher was just as dismayed by his low grades. "I know he's not a dummy," the teacher told his mom. "I watch him play chess at lunch time and he beats everybody. Students line up to challenge him yet he remains undefeated."

At home, Verna told Dre he could choose another school. "I even threatened him. Yet nothing seemed to work." She wondered if her relationship troubles had affected him, but Dre was just getting deeper into music. After February 1984, he was nineteen and now too old to attend Fremont. His mom demanded he find a job, another school, or both so he enrolled in Chester Adult School in Compton. When she asked how he'd do well there when he hadn't in other schools, he said, "The people who go to this school don't act crazy."

He surprised his mother by applying himself, then signed up for a radio broadcasting school. But after orientation, he felt it wasn't teaching him anything he didn't already know, and he didn't want her wasting hard-earned money on it. But she stayed on him about finding work until he couldn't take it anymore. "He never liked being amongst confusion, and there was so much of that in our house, especially concerning money," she said.

He packed and moved, first finding peace at his grandparents' home but he moved again when he learned where his father, Theodore, lived. He was happy there, but when Theodore was arrested on a drug charge, his sister drove Dre back to his mom's house. This time, Verna said, "I tried hard to keep the peace in my home so that Andre would not leave again."

3

Lonzo focused on another single but Dre was even more desperate to turn their pop music sideline into a paying career. After two years of middling effort he left Chester Adult School with no real plan for what to do next. He didn't want a job at a fast-food place or store. He could barely support himself, he still lived at home, he quickly spent what little money his shows brought in, and he was now a father of two—La Tonya, and Curtis, whose paternity was as yet unconfirmed. But he wanted to be his own boss.

In Eve's, he and Yella kept creating ideas for what would be about forty-nine other radio mixes. They were wild, Dre said, "each like a little record." They were also making him one of the most famous DJs in town. One day, he was working on a mix when Steve Yano showed up for a meeting with Lonzo. Yano was an affable Japanese former high school guidance counselor, as well as the owner of a popular record shop stall at the Roadium, an outdoor swap meet that catered to a mostly black clientele. He was there to meet with Lonzo, from whom he frequently bought new rap singles, but watched in awe as Dre scratched over one of Yella's drum machine beats. "Is that how you do it?" he asked.

Yella said yeah, and offered a tape.

Yano played it at the swap meet, where everyone in the huge crowd around his table asked, "Who did that tape? Can I get that?" Dre now had another outlet for his music and soon popped up at the stall with Yella to cut beats up for a live crowd to spur sales. Soon, people began playing his tapes during parties. Others loved what they heard and asked, "What's that?" Dre finally asked Yano, "Why don't you make a label?" Yano rejected the idea since he was busy enough running the stall.

♦ ♦ ♦

When Dre arrived at the club now, he was treated like a star. Even better, Lonzo wanted to cut another single (the returns on the first were good) and to move closer to the sound Dre liked on New York rap singles by including a rapper. But to Dre's chagrin, Lonzo resisted changing the group's basic sound now that they had settled into the Kraftwerk style heard on "Planet Rock" and continued to draw crowds.

Many people wanted to join the group but Lonzo chose the winner of a weekly talent contest at Eve's After Dark. His name was Marquette "Cli-N-Tel" Hawkins. Along with his cousin the easygoing rapper had made the rounds at talent shows and house parties in Compton. For a week before the contest, he practiced various routines. But on stage that Saturday night he improvised chants that riled up the crowd. "Yes, yes, motherfuck it!" he yelled. After Cli's victory, Lonzo sidled up to him. "Hey man, come on back later this week."

Dre was performing in his white doctor's coat and stethoscope when he saw Lonzo and Cli in the crowd. Lonzo pointed at him on stage, asking Cli—whom Dre recognized from junior high—to write a song about him. Dre was pleased and even more so when he heard the results of Cli's writing session.

Cli had considered what doctors were best known for, and created a routine that wasn't as rough as those of Run-DMC or LL Cool J, but did get Dre's name out there even more. Cli dutifully threw in a few buzzwords: Dre was "on call" seven days a week; he "operates" on his turntables; he "prescribes" good beats; and he holds "a Ph. D. in mixology." He also included the sort of call-and-response chants their audience now expected from the group.

In the studio, for 1984's "Surgery," Dre took a stronger hand in the music. "Surgery" featured a crawling bass, an electronic beat with hard snares, and a synth line that evoked "Planet Rock." After some heavy breathing ("Ahh"), Cli's lyrics described L.A. and how great Dre was ("L.A. is the place to be for you to witness Dr. Dre in surgery"). A second later, he continues, "Seven days a week, he's on call/to get the party people up off the wall." It was decent, fun-loving dance music that fit the mood and market at the time. During the break, Dre was able to add a hardcore edge with a scratch solo using the same record UTFO did on their many hits (a voice saying "Fresh"). Even better, most of the song featured a robotic voice simply repeating his name, "Dr. Dre." Then he actually entered the recording booth with Yella.

"Dr. Dre," Yella began.

"Yo," Dre responded, in as deep a tone as he could muster.

Then he tried to rap. "I'm Dr. Dre, gorgeous hunk of a man," he said, "Doing tricks on the mix like no others can." The rest of the lyric claimed nurses found him irresistible; he'd blow people's minds; he'd lure ladies into his car or home and feel them up; and he'd get them in the sack and make them scream.

The record was tame compared to Run-DMC, but "Surgery" sold 50,000 copies, ten times as much as their debut, and inspired Lonzo to plan another single. Though thrilled by their latest success Dre and Yella were "getting tired of the Wreckin' Cru 'cause the money situation wasn't right and we were always broke," recalled Yella.

◆ ◆ ◆

The music industry Dre hoped to enter was dominated by major labels that viewed rap as a fad, and independent labels churning out singles. At the same time, MTV, the music video cable channel catering to an under-25 crowd, helped a number of black crossover musicians sell more albums worldwide. Michael Jackson's 1982 album, *Thriller,* got the ball rolling. Jackson's slick videos, sequined jackets, trademark white glove, and crossover singles "The Girl Is Mine" (a duet with former Beatle Paul McCartney) and "Beat It" (which included blazing guitar work by Eddie Van Halen) helped him sell forty million copies of *Thriller*. He released seven of its ten songs as singles and all reached the Top Ten. He won 150 gold and platinum awards and a record-breaking eight Grammys and inspired *Time* to write, "Jackson is the biggest thing since the Beatles. He is the hottest single phenomenon since Elvis Presley."

Various licensed products—posters, buttons, sequined gloves—flew off the shelves and at one point, the album sold an outrageous one million copies every four days. "It inspired black artists not to look at themselves in a limited way," said Quincy Jones. "Before Michael, those kinds of sales had never happened for a black artist. Michael did it. He did it for the first time."

Since then, Motown's Lionel Richie reached number one with his single "Truly." His videos on MTV—featuring Richie in Jheri curls and sequined jackets—spurred sales of his solo debut and led to *Billboard* naming him top artist in 1984. Prince, a short, slim guy from Minneapolis who set sexual lyrics to soul, funk, and a few Van-Halen–like guitar riffs, also wore curls and sequined outfits and had videos on MTV. As a result, his double album, *1999*, emerged as a hit and his movie soundtrack *Purple Rain* sold fourteen million copies and won an Oscar and a Grammy. And this was just the tip of the iceberg. So Lonzo felt a flashy Michael Jackson style could boost sales and draw crowds. But Dre disagreed. He didn't see Run-DMC in Jheri curls, flashy costumes, or cooing over techno and marching in tandem like The Temptations, and their albums were selling well. And since that show at Eve's, the young Queens group was selling even more albums on a national level with harder music (including metal guitar on "Rock Box"). But whenever Dre tried to take the stage in sneakers, Lonzo put his foot down. "Fuck that," said Lonzo.

While Lonzo continued to have his own views of the market, away from the Cru, Dre met another ardent Run-DMC fan, O'Shea Jackson (born June 15, 1969). Nicknamed Ice Cube by his older brother (since he kept trying to steal his brother's girls and "thought I was too cool"), he lived two houses down from Dre and was recording demos with Dre's cousin Tony Wheatob, who called himself "Sir Jinx" (sort of like "Sir Nose," a character on P-Funk songs).

Like Dre, Cube avoided joining local Crip sets. "A lot of the people who were deep into the gangs were motherfuckers who didn't have fathers or older brothers to set them straight," Cube said. But Cube had both, and spent five years playing Pop Warner League football. He also heard his older brother say, "Man, you don't have to do that. You don't have to be out there fucking up to show these motherfuckers that you're down when they don't give a fuck about you." As many of his peers joined the Neighborhood Crips ("N-Hood") and emerged with reputations as killers, Cube became fascinated with hip-hop, content to be a fan until Kiddo, a friend in typing class, asked, "Did you get the new Run-DMC?" Cube had in fact enjoyed the group's landmark "Sucker M.C.'s." Kiddo nodded, then challenged him to a battle. "You write one and I'll write one, and we'll see which one comes out the best." Cube said his was better, and "from then on I never stopped."

He had enjoyed singles by Egyptian Lover, the L.A. Dream Team, rapper Ice-T, and The Cru's "Surgery." Cube and Jinx were working in Jinx's garage since Dre's aunt didn't want the music in the house, but Jinx's dog "would shit in the garage," Cube recalled. "We'd be in there smelling dog shit, stepping over dog shit, rapping in the garage."

Dre was staying with Jinx for a while, standing with Cli-N-Tel in Cube's backyard when he first heard Cube rap. After the performance, Cli pulled Dre to the side. "Hey man, that dude right there got a little something. We should just take him under our wings and do something with him." Dre wasn't ready to act yet. He had to promote "Surgery," record another single, and create tapes for KDAY. But he saw Cube again during a show at Skateland, a roller rink with a crowd as temperamental as the one at amateur night at the Apollo. But where the Apollo crowd was content to boo and jeer, the Skateland crowd hurled insults and items at groups they hated. "The place was rowdy as a motherfucker," Dre said. "You had to get up there and get busy."

Since Cube was near the turntables, Dre asked, "Why don't you perform?" Cube had never rapped publicly but was brimming with confidence. "What kind of shit do you want?" Dre considered the success of Slick Rick's bawdy "La-Di-Da-Di." He also remembered X-rated comedy albums by Dolemite and Richard Pryor (including Pryor's 1974 classic, *That Nigger's Crazy!* which included his routine "Niggers vs. the Police") that he loved during his upbringing. "People like shit that is funny, with a little bit of cursing in it," he said. Cube, himself a Richard Pryor fan, mentioned Brooklyn crew

UTFO's single "Roxanne Roxanne," in which the Brooklyn quartet insulted a stuck-up girl. By now, it had inspired over twenty similar records. "Why don't we do a parody of that?"

Dre felt that was fine but warned they'd better sound good when they got up there; if they didn't the crowd would lob full cups at them. He cued up an instrumental on a rap record and started cutting it up on two turntables while Cube did the obscene lyric, "Dianne Dianne." "We tore the place up," Cube said. "They loved that shit." When the group was invited to come back, Dre felt he was on the right track and asked the young rapper to ride with him to the store. "I was like, oh shit, I'm gonna hook up with Dre," Cube recalled.

Dre retreated to the four-track in Lonzo's garage to experiment with heavier drums, slower tempos, and angrier riffs. Eager to show off his ever-improving production abilities he worked with his core group—Cube, Jinx, and K.D.—to polish a repertoire of parodies and street raps, with the verbal gymnastics of the Beastie Boys, Ice-T, and Schoolly D serving as a template. He threw these on mix tapes, kept learning how to use the mix board, and managed to make a little money on the side. And when Lonzo kept getting better equipment—a bigger board, an eight-track, and soon a twelve-track—Dre kept teaching himself the dynamics of song-writing and production, amassing a collection of beats and searching for a way out.

Eager to find success apart from The Cru, Dre figured the rap group C.I.A. might do the trick. Already their tapes sold well at the Roadium, and to get them out there even more, he convinced Lonzo to include them on the bill during shows at Eve's After Dark, World on Wheels (where the Rolling 60 Compton Crips hung out), and Skateland (favored by Bloods). With C.I.A. continuing to thrill tough crowds, Dre could have shopped them around at various labels for a deal. Instead, the group wound up signing to Lonzo's Kru-Cut label.

For their single, Dre produced tracks that mimicked a few by white New York producer Rick Rubin for The Beastie Boys' hell-raising Columbia debut *License to Ill*: big beats, lots of scratches and samples, irreverent lyrics, and complex arrangements. Cube, just as inspired by the white group, tried to yell as loud as they did on his numbers "My Posse," "Ill-Legal," and "Just 4 the Cash," and later said, "We were out there on that shit."

But they were also tapping into the rap genre's latest new direction. Since Run-DMC and LL Cool J the emphasis became showing audiences how hard you were. Philadelphia's Schoolly D rose to the occasion on self-released singles "P.S.K." and "Gucci Time." By rapping about hanging with his old gang the Park Side Killers, shooting someone in the head, and pummeling a few sucker MCs and bitches he managed to give the Run-DMC set serious competition. In Compton, meanwhile, rapper Toddy Tee was personalizing rap hits on local tapes (chiding crack heads, rapping about dealers, and complaining about how the LAPD's new armored tank kept busting into crack houses). At the same time, other rappers were presenting tougher lyrics: Los Angeles' Ice-T rapped as a dealer on "Six in the Morning" while South Bronx rapper KRS-One did the same on his chilling, "My 9MM Goes Bang."

But Dre's bread and butter, his source of stability, continued to be the Cru—now called The World Class Wreckin' Cru. When Lonzo summoned him to the studio for another single, he came running. Where "Surgery" merely evoked "Planet Rock," "Juice" actually sampled it. They used the heavy breathing ("Ah") gimmick again, but spiced up their beat with eerie chimes and a computerized voice that sounded exactly like one on a popular single called "It's Time." Each verse bragged about their fame and "vicious beat" and ended with the line, "Give me some juice." During the break, instead of scratches, they included another "Planet Rock"–style melody, this time with dramatic horns. Dre had no objection to the sound. Privately, he was embarrassed and stressed about being so broke. But with music like this and his costume, he kept seeing many women try to get close to him. And when he turned on KDAY, 1580 on the AM dial, he'd hear "Juice" playing. Every time KDAY played it, retailers nationwide called Macola to order anywhere from ten to thirty thousand copies.

Lonzo was frenzied by the success of "Juice" and leapt right into planning an album. Dre was even deeper into the hardcore New York sound by now but Lonzo filled their 1985 debut, *World Class*, with songs like "Planet," "World Class," and "Horney (Computer)." He included the topical "Gang Bang You're Dead," but Dre still felt the album was wack. It started eating away at him. While others recorded, he sat in the studio resentfully, thinking it sounded dated and soft. He wanted more of a say and tried to speak up to add his two cents, only to hear Lonzo and sometimes Cli-N-Tel reply, "Yo man, we don't want to do that." They viewed him as an inexperienced kid— he was the youngest—and kept dismissing his ideas. Instead of battling them, he passively thought, "Okay, fuck it. I'll go with the flow." He'd fill space on an album cover and on stage and make what money he could until he was finally in a position to do something on his own.

Yet when he returned to sessions with the Cru, where Lonzo and Cli would call for a rap ballad called "Lovers," he found it difficult to give in and do what they wanted. "Lovers" was a mid-tempo beat with clacking snares, a melancholic minor key piano, sampled sounds of wind, and a moody Prince-like keyboard. Cli-N-Tel spoke the lyric about being with the crew at a club and meeting a girl that looked "exceptionally well." While claiming he'd take her to Wonderland, he cried, "Aw girl" and adopted the faux Victorian cadence Prince sometimes used on his records. After he told the girl they would make love all night, a woman singer crooned that she didn't want to be lovers before they were friends. Dre hated the song. And this time, Yella joined him in objecting. "Nah, man, we rappin'. We ain't doing slow records." Lonzo and Cli got their way, however; and "Lovers" appeared on the album.

Once they finished recording, Dre became just as upset with Lonzo's plan for the cover. Lonzo insisted they spend good money on uniforms he called "flashy hard like the Temptations and Soul Sonic Force." Even worse, he had a woman named Shirley ("the big fat girl Dre had the crush on," Lonzo recalled) style them, and apply eyeliner for this Prince-like shot. Lonzo and Yella were burly, with frowning gunfighter mustaches and stiff Jheri curls, but she got them into spandex jumpsuits, frilly lace, and shiny jackets. And for baby-faced Dre, a ribbed white sequined bodysuit. "I'll tell you what," Dre later griped. "I never had no motherfucking lace on! That was Yella. I was motherfucking seventeen years old. I had a motherfucking 'doctor suit.'" Obviously embarrassed by the image, he nevertheless went along with the effete cover shot, Arabian Prince recalled, "'Cause the publicist said it would be more appealing to the women."

In addition, Dre now needed money more than ever. He was used to being in the limelight and the subject of more than a few songs. He liked partying in clubs and being looked at like a star. He also reportedly had another woman about to give birth to his third child (a daughter named Manaj).

◆ ◆ ◆

During the summer of 1985, along with palm trees, the unflinching hard sun, and local gangs cruising around looking to relieve their boredom, sell drugs, or stock up on brew, Compton's streets filled with teens happy to put school-work and grades behind them for a while. They enthusiastically threw themselves into parties, parks, summer jobs, and the latest rap records. Dre himself had more time for his KDAY tapes and taking the stage with the Cru , at gang-infested roller rinks for the younger set, their home base, Eve's After Dark, or another club called Dudo's, where the local audience watched LL Cool J rap a few hardcore numbers then booed and jeered. When he wasn't pulling in some money with these shows, Dre kept making tapes Steve Yano could sell at his ever-crowded stall at the Roadium. He could not suspect that the tapes would lead him to another person that would change the course of his life.

Short, broad shouldered, and sporting Jheri curls under his ball cap, Eric Lynn Wright had stopped by the stall and bought a tall stack of 12-inch singles. Born September 7, 1963, in Compton to postal worker Richard Wright and school administrator Katie, Eric was a tenth-grade dropout who indulged in petty drug sales, drove a new car, and saved about $25,000 in six years. But at twenty-three, he wanted out of drug dealing. "My cousins got killed," he said. "I figured I could do something right for a change instead of something wrong."

Behind his tough exterior—massive shoulders, clenched jaw, and sun-glasses—Eric liked local acts The Cru, Uncle Jam's Army, and the L.A. Dream Team. But exposure to East Coast rap and underground tapes left him feeling local rappers were no longer speaking to the class many of them came from. While choosing singles to buy, Eric lingered on one by The Cru. He asked Yano where he got it from. Yano didn't answer so the no-nonsense dealer pulled a thick wad of bills from a sock, paid for his records, and told him, "Tell Dre Eric says Whassup."

A week later, Eric was back, spending more money on records and asking for Dre's number. He kept coming back to ask about Dre so Yano finally asked if he knew Eric. Dre said he did. In his neighborhood, who didn't? In his new tailored clothing and shiny car, Eric was impossible to ignore. Yano then got Dre and Eric on the phone one night after two a.m. Dre was surprised to hear Eric say he wanted to open a record store. Yano discouraged the idea. "It's a bad business. I can show you how, but don't do it." Eric was looking for a fresh start. Dre was too. "Why don't you start a label?" Dre asked.

Some who knew Dre were surprised by his new friendship with the Crip many knew as Casual. The two couldn't be more different visually but kept hanging out. While Eric wore heavy blue jackets, ball caps, and sunglasses, Dre tagged along in golf shirts (with rolled up sleeves) and slick, close-cropped Jheri curls. Then there was the fact that, publicly at least, Eric spoke little, kept a grave expression on his face, and concealed his eyes behind impenetrable sunglasses. Dre had little in common with Eric's milieu of shootouts, cluck heads offering blow jobs, and people gossiping about dismembered crack whores found in trash bags. However, they were both ambitious, both loved the ladies and had children, both loved a good party or joke, and both wanted to somehow be their own boss. And both felt Dre knew more about how to rock a crowd than Lonzo did, so Dre liked Eric even more.

Since reconnecting with Eric, also known as Eazy E, Dre joined him for parties in high schools and proms. They also performed at house parties under the name High Powered Productions. And at home, Dre described his pal Eric from nearby Muriel Street in terms one would reserve for a personal hero. He lingered on descriptions of Eric's Suzuki Samurai, his gold chains, his custom-made leather coats and hats, that fat wad of bills he kept tucked in a sock, and the respect he commanded wherever he went. His mother asked where Eric worked and Dre sounded a little too impressed when he answered that he didn't work. Sensing Dre might be lured by the streets, she chose that moment to tell him, "Fast money is not good money." It would bring madness and crazy people. Legal income that trickled in slowly was better than fast money that could get you killed.

She didn't have to worry about him dealing drugs. For one, Dre wasn't tough enough to make it out there. And he knew it. Not with kids carrying semiautomatics and killing each other in drive-bys, and the one-times always rolling through the hood, rounding black men up during yet another gang sweep. He already had a career. His music with the Cru and Cube's group C.I.A. were yielding results.

Dre felt The Cru material was beginning to sound a bit outdated and that his work with C.I.A. was a poor imitation of Run-DMC and their white protégés The Beastie Boys. But he learned that Larkin Arnold at CBS' Epic subsidiary liked what he heard and invited Lonzo to a meeting. That day, Dre and the others sat in the plush waiting area alongside crews that for years competed for the same nightclub audiences. The Dream Team— rappers in Panama hats, suspenders, pleated pants, and shades—had a three o' clock meeting. Musician Bobby Jimmy had three-thirty, The Cru were at four. Dre was stunned when he learned Arnold wanted to sign both The Cru and C.I.A.

Any thoughts of branching out on his own subsided as Dre got his cos-tume together and packed his bags and gear. He would now be joining the group on a tour outside of sunny L.A. Rick James, the funk artist behind hits like "Superfreak," wanted them to open for him. Though their Kraftwerk-like numbers—created on drum machine—had little to do with James' mix of fiery funk and seductive ballads, their costumes, synthesizers, and dance steps fit right in with the American public's newfound appetite for anything remotely resembling black chart-toppers Prince or Michael Jackson.

The tour took them to London's Wembley Stadium and Dre definitely had fun, but the crew experienced a few creative differences. Then there was the fact that Dre and Yella felt they weren't making any money despite having released a full-length album. They told people they were going unpaid for their work during the same period The Cru's manager, Jerry Heller, remem-bered seeing Macola hand Lonzo checks. Since Lonzo didn't have a checking account, Heller claimed he'd deposit them then meet Lonzo on the corner of Santa Monica and Vine when they cleared. "We'd split up the money right there on the corner, usually $20,000 or $30,000," Heller explained. Other times, $100,000.

But the group decided to join Lonzo and Cli-N-Tel on a tour bus Lonzo rented for $3,500 and played a few dates in Mississippi. They gained experience, attracted sexy groupies, and saw crowds cheer their sets. But Dre continued to despair about needing more money. Before his anger could reach the boiling point Lonzo's lawyer called to say Epic was offering a whopping $100,000 for a Cru album alone. Even Lonzo was taken aback. But he soon regrouped and yelled into the phone, "Sign the damned contract! You got power of attorney! Sign it before they change their minds!"

Dre could breathe easier. He needed new sneakers, a car, and to handle a few bills. Lonzo was just as relieved. He wanted to recoup what he'd spent on ads for shows, studio time, renting the tour bus, filling its tank, and new equipment. Rapper Cli-N-Tel, however, shocked them all by leaving the group for a solo career. Why he left is unknown. Meanwhile Dre soon gave voice to his feeling that he could use a raise. As he saw it, his music attracted Epic to the group. "One day you're cool, the next day you're not," Lonzo said. "By the time we came off the road, we were on the down slide. Something happened with those guys."

◆ ◆ ◆

Epic was definitely a step up. The label would handle recording costs, have its sales staff promote their work to radio, have a publicist arrange interviews, and if it so decided, work with the group to create a video for a single. Most important, the company was affiliated with CBS, the biggest label on earth, which guaranteed a Cru album would command precious rack space in giant national retail chains. It was a far cry from selling vinyl copies out of Lonzo's car trunk but at the same time "the worst thing that ever happened," said Lonzo. "From that point on, we had nothing but dissension over money."

After the tour, "I had some dollars," Lonzo recalled. Epic sent a $10,000 advance so he handed each member some money, then invested in equipment for a studio in his garage and had them come over to do pre-production. The sooner he booked time in a commercial studio—paying for sessions from his own pocket, Lonzo claimed—and got the finished album into Epic's hands, the sooner they'd receive the next, much larger, payment.

On January 1, 1986, Epic told them how much they should spend on recording and gave the group complete creative control. "The Wreckin' Cru decided they didn't want to do the whole electro dance thing anymore," said Arabian Prince. "They wanted to sing more R&B love songs." This would have been fine but Lonzo decided to do the album "in such a slick way it pissed 'em off." He quickly got everyone into a recording studio and had them churn out numbers like "Mission Possible," "He's Bionic," "B.S.," "Love Letter," "World Class Freak," "Wreckin Cru Blues," and "Masters of Romance."

"He's Bionic" was another song about Dre. This time, they included tinny snares, bubbling tom-toms, and the usual computerized chant. The lyrical style imitated Run-DMC's "It's Like That" but the words described how Dre had two nurses by his side and kept them satisfied, he was in control, and he was better than all the sucker DJs. And once the others yelled a chorus ("He's bionic! Yes!"), Dre scratched the word "fresh" over the latest "Planet Rock" synths.

"Love Letter" was another rap ballad, with gentle drums, harp strings, subdued synth, and spoken word lyrics about writing someone to say, "I miss you." Then a woman sang she missed them, too, they threw in some nice chord changes on synth and they spoke a few more schmaltzy lyrics about absence making the heart grow fonder. Dre didn't like it much, but Lonzo gave him free rein on "B.S." Dre filled its slow beat with a sampled crowd, a few breaks, and growling Run-DMC–styled vocals. The drums still featured cheesy bass—the sort of sound on the *Ferris Bueller's Day Off* theme—but Dre was able to rap about "rolling down the street with my mind at ease." He described seeing a freak at the bus stop looking him over. After making a U-turn, he realized he tried to get her back in eighty-three. Now she wants to give him a call. He tells her lay off the alcohol. "You didn't want me then," he adds.

"World Class Freak," meanwhile, buried Run-DMC's beat from "It's Like That" under quick keyboard riffs, chiming bells, and another lyric that positioned Dre as the group's star. This time, he calmly said, "Dr. Dre is who I am. Come with me and your body I'll exam." With the others playing second fiddle (periodically yelling backup vocals like "Who?" and "What?"), Dre told a girl not to fight him; she couldn't resist; he wanted to take her home. "'Cause I'm a bachelor that's tired of being alone." "Mission Possible" also put Dre at center stage. Over the dance beats, Bambaataa-like melodies, and computer voice, he told the listener their mission was to take black music in a new direction. The others breathed heavily while Dre kept repeating, apropos of nothing, "Book him, murder one." Then he got to shine even more in a stripped-down bridge, yelling "Rock rock rock the house," (only to hear ladies yell, "No") after which Lonzo added a sheeny rendition of the "Hawaii Five-O" theme.

By January 15 they delivered *Rapped in Romance* and Lonzo received a $75,000 check. But just as quickly, Epic heard the album and called to complain. They assumed the Prince-like troupe would record with a real band. Instead, the group got it done on the cheap with drum machines, synthesizers, turntables, and old records. "You just took $100,000 from us," one executive yelled. A number of heated conversations ensued, with Epic refusing to release the album until The Cru recorded something it could market as a single. One executive finally told Lonzo to listen to Minneapolis funk guitarist Jesse Johnson's "Free World" and record something similar. Lonzo quickly called Dre and Yella back to the studio to rush-record "The Fly," which Lonzo called "nothing but 'Free World' with some new lyrics." "The Fly" mixed chunky bass to a rock beat with cowbells; a high-pitched, bouncy keyboard; and a growled lyric about a new dance. They urged the crowd not to confuse it with "The Bird," a move seen in Prince's *Purple Rain*, and during the chorus yelled, "The fly—yeah—is what you gotta do!" And to capture the feel Epic requested, Lonzo filled the song with whiny synths that evoked the music people played during furious aerobics sessions. Only when they created this work did Epic agree to pay the group whatever other monies were due.

The new Prince-like image extended to another cover. This time, Dre stood in the center of the group. He wore his slick Jheri curls, a shiny red jacket with padded shoulders, and a white shirt with open collar (so as to show his thin chain). To his left, the taller Lonzo had a lion's mane of curls, a shiny white jacket, and a goatee. To his right, Yella stood with his bushy mustache and shiny gray suit. A fourth member in shiny gold jacket and black pants sat in profile on a couch in front of them. They obviously did not resemble the traditional rap group.

Once the rest of the Epic payment came in Lonzo recouped expenses. One

Tuesday, he handed each member $5,000. Two days later, he claimed, "They came back broke." Dre and Yella returned a month later, saw Lonzo with a new house and a BMW, and, told Lonzo that they suspected him of holding out on some of their money. Lonzo ignored this and let Dre have his old Mazda. He handed him the keys, let Dre co-sign for it, and handled payments with Dre's weekly stipend (his part of the CBS money).

During the winter of 1986, they managed to book shows in the roller rink Skateland but thanks to Crips and Bloods, these opportunities soon dwindled. In the past, gangs were content to act up only when a DJ played Zapp's "So Ruff So Tuff" or any other song they'd adopted as an anthem. While these played, gang members strutted around, did little dances, hollered a little, and threw up their set with curled fingertips. But with gangs fighting over dope spots and more guns on the streets, many music-loving gangsters started bringing their feuds, and weapons, to rap shows.

Even respected rapper Kurtis Blow watched what he said around them. The wrong words could start a fight, he knew; a gangster would run to get a gun. "They are playing for real, playing for keeps," he said. Gang violence even marred a major Run-DMC concert at the Long Beach Arena. Brooklyn trio Whodini were performing a peaceful set when one gang member threw someone over a balcony and onto the stage. Within minutes, Greg Mack told author Brian Cross, "a whole section was running, gangs were hittin' people, grabbing gold chains, beating people." A few people died at the concert. And there were other unreported incidents. Weekly events at World on Wheels, a reputed Crip hangout, now ended with a fight in the parking lot or someone getting shot. "That was the end of that," said promoter Matthew McDaniel. Promoters could still attract top talent but, Mack said, "They raised the insurance so high no one can afford it." With fewer shows, the Cru suddenly earned less money.

During the early weeks of 1987, Dre's problems with the beat-up old car led to some serious situations. He had received and ignored numerous tickets. Someone also broke his car's rear windshield and stole the radio. He didn't have enough money to get it fixed so he drove it like that even though he froze during the one-hour freeway drive to Rialto to see an aspiring female rapper (later of the group J.J. Fad) he was dating.

Back in Compton, though the car was old and battered, someone stole it. He paid to get it out of an impound lot, but ignored bills and sternly worded letters demanding payment for outstanding tickets. The notices kept coming in the mail with fines doubling and tripling but he figured it'd have to wait. Finally, things came to a head. Cops stopped him and learned he owed $500 in tickets. They impounded the car again (while Lonzo was technically paying for it) and put Dre in a cell.

Epic had now dropped the group and the group was inactive. Their singles hadn't done well and they were "just sitting at home getting fat," Lonzo recalled, "talking about what we used to do." Even so, a terrified Dre called for bail. Lonzo paid to have him freed. "What you gonna do?" he asked rhetorically. "Couldn't leave him in jail. You might have a gig that weekend."

Dre now owed half the bail and ongoing car payments but quickly got back to spending whatever money he had "on tennis shoes and motel rooms." Within two months, he racked up "another stack of warrants" and was rearrested. Once again, he called Lonzo.

"You know what? I'm gonna let your butt sit in jail for a while. Maybe you'll learn something."

Dre kept asking for help.

"Look," Lonzo remembered saying, "I'll go half with somebody but I can't afford to keep doing this."

Eric remembered it differently: He told Lonzo to bail Dre out and heard him say, "I ain't got no money." Whatever the case, Dre called and told him the bail was a steep $900. "Sure, I'll post your bail," Eric said. "But you got to do something for me." He'd have to create beats for the label Eazy now wanted to form. Held over a barrel, Dre would have agreed to anything. He assured Eazy it'd be no problem, and a bail bondsman got him out.

Dre quickly found a duo who were originally from Brooklyn but now living in Orange County. They called themselves HBO (Home Boys Only). He told Eric and his other friend Laylaw to sign and record them, then called Cube. HBO's voices were cool and they had stage presence, but Cube knew a thing or two about gangbanging and could deliver the sort of gritty lyric he wanted. Cube wrote some words about life in the hood during English class at Taft High School in Woodland Hills.

With pleasure, Dre listened to "Boyz-N-tha-Hood." It was heavy on visuals and real-life details. Like any other exclusive group, the Crips and Bloods had their own language. In their hoods, they talked about drive-bys, gats, one-times, O.G.'s, lleyo, and jack moves; smoking niggas, slapping bones, and ratpacking fools and busters. For Dre and the others, it was what they'd seen all their lives. But to the rest of the world, in 1986, it'd be cutting edge. Once Cube finished running it past him, Dre thought it was like a movie. He knocked out a Beastie Boys–style track on the four-track in Eve's After Dark, slowing the tempo, rocking hard snares, and including horn blasts. Then he scratched in Cli-N-Tel's voice from "Cru Groove."

Eric booked time in the tiny studio in Lonzo's home. When Dre brought him by, Lonzo liked him, and gave a few pointers about the industry and owning a company. But Eric was competitive. He envied Lonzo's house and BMW and wanted the same.

Dre spent an entire session loading sounds into the bulky, box-like SP-1200 sampler. The next night, he had HBO present. "They being from the East Coast, it was a big East Coast–West Coast thing," Dre said.

One member said, "This is some West Coast shit." They left.

Dre faced Eazy and Laylaw. "Yo, I'm out of here," Laylaw said.

Since he and Cube were in other groups, Dre asked Eric to record it.

"I can't do this shit!"

Dre kept nagging until Eric finally put his shades on, and read Cube's lyric into the microphone. But the results were horrible so Dre had him come back and try again.

This time, Eric said he didn't even have a rap name. Cube, present that night, quickly suggested Eazy-E. At the board, Dre tried not to feel like some sort of serf working off a debt. This time, Lonzo was there, too, watching with suspicion. He knew Dre and Yella wanted to create music as aggressive as Run-DMC and sensed, correctly, that Eric was telling Dre, "Fuck that shit! He can't even get you out of jail; you and Yella doing all the work and shit."

When Dre was ready to roll tape, Eazy rapped about girl-watching while driving his 1964 Cadillac through the hood; meeting knuckleheads shooting hoops in a park; and learning his friend J.B. was smoking freebase. Then J.B.

tried to steal his car's Alpine radio, he gave chase, and J.B. pulled a .22. He blasted him with a 12-gauge and saw the *L.A. Times* report on the shooting. After Dre had him chant the chorus, Eazy struggled through the second verse: meeting the homeboys and drinking beer; visiting his girl and hearing her say something that "made me mad"; grabbing her weave and slapping her then knocking her father out with a right cross. The song continued with more of the same: Eazy seeing his friend Kilo fight with some cops; Kilo being tried for resisting arrest; Kilo's girl trying to break him out with an Uzi and cops aiming guns at her. "Police shot the bitch but didn't hurt her," he rapped. "Both upstate for attempted murder." Obviously, none of the group was exposed to these sorts of situations; but Eazy sounded convincing, and it was as crazy as some of the stuff the Beasties were doing on *Licensed to Ill*. "It took forever to do that record," Cube remembered. "Nigga was in the studio for days, trying to do some lyrics." He felt his voice sounded stupid, he kept messing up and having Dre stop the music, and he had Lonzo in a crowd watching and joining in laughter; "'cause it was so bad," Lonzo recalled.

But Dre kept punching Eazy in, line-by-line. "He did the record," Dre said proudly. "We put it out and sold it out the trunk." Eazy quickly had Macola create pressings and carried one over to Yano's busy stall at the Roadium. Yano enjoyed the song and said, "I can sell that." So Eazy moved on to the next step. With an artist personalizing customers' T-shirts with spray-paint, he asked, "Whattya think of Ruthless? Ruthless Records?"

"That's cool," Yano answered.

Eric had the artist paint his label's logo.

Once "Boyz-N-the-Hood" achieved underground success, Eazy wanted to try something else. "He said, 'Well, I'm gonna do a record with Cube, Dre, and some other people, just put it out locally, call it N.W.A.,'" said his friend Ren. And it would present music gangsters could enjoy.

Eric became a fixture at the shows the Cru managed to book. At Eve's he'd walk up to invite DJ Yella into a group. Yella was willing to listen. "We made two albums but we never got paid," he claimed. Eric also invited Cube. With C.I.A. gone and forgotten, Cube was writing raps in his bedroom at his mom's Compton house and wondering what to do once he graduated from high school. And when Eric ran into Arabian Prince, the brilliant techno-rap writer born Kim Nazel but calling himself "Mik Lezan," he said he was welcome, too. With Egyptian Lover, Arabian had created the sort of dance music Dre did with the Cru and C.I.A. Figuring it was a sound L.A. liked, Eazy wanted N.W.A. to do some, too. Though none were actually famous yet, Eazy played to their egos, saying, "Man, N.W.A. is a all-star rap group."

He also kept working on Dre. He told him Lonzo had him and Yella doing all the work for peanuts. Their record sold so Dre shouldn't have a fucked-up car. He deserved more than $25 a week. "He used to give Cube and Jinx $25 a week between them," Eric claimed. He then included Dre's girlfriend, Michel'le, a short, curvy beauty with curly hair and full red lips who was a singer on Lonzo's label. "You can't have somebody blowing up and getting on the radio then give them a hundred dollars."

Lonzo noticed Dre catching an attitude, he said. Dre barely came around and seemed to envy Eazy's lifestyle. "He wanted to be a rapper." And where Lonzo rejected his hardcore sounds ("I loved ballads") Eazy let him have free rein in the studio. But Lonzo tried to save the group by keeping them busy. They were off of Epic, back on tiny Macola (until their contract expired in November 1987), and playing World on Wheels, tiny clubs, and Mexican joints out in Santa Ana. But they weren't earning much money. He figured another record would turn that around and invited them to the studio again. Though Dre was souring on the group, he joined them for these sessions and found Lonzo let him have more of a say in "House Calls." With Cube helping out, Dre eschewed the usual dance beat and instead threw in some 808 cowbells, an old-school break beat, and a sampled telephone ring. And once again, Dr. Dre was the star of the show. "Hello, this is Dr. Dre. I'm not in right now," he said, as if on an answering machine. After a beep, a married woman asked if she could come over now that her man wasn't around. Dre then rapped about riding in his car, "not doing anything" but knowing his phone would ring. His voice was breathy and conversational, like a calmer version of the Soul Sonic Force, and the lyric found him claiming he wasn't "your average gigolo." Lonzo included the inevitable "Planet Rock"–style strings, this time during the break, but did let Dre throw in the samples, break beats, and rap energy he'd been dying to capture.

And while Dre told everyone around him The Cru wasn't letting him record the sort of music he did with Eazy, Lonzo let him fill "Cabbage Patch" with the exact same sound and lyric style. Essentially an imitation of Run-DMC's "My Adidas," Dre filled the song with part of "The Big Beat" (rocker Billy Squire saying, "I"), a horn Jam Master Jay scratched on a few Run-DMC songs (from "Scratching"), and a record UTFO used on many hits (a voice breathing, "Ahhh").

Over a beat as bouncy as the one on "My Adidas" and a break beat Run-DMC used on that single's B-side (Bob James' chime-heavy "Take Me to the Mardi Gras"), Dre and rapper Shakespeare yelled as loud as Dre's heroes about hitting a party in West L.A., doing a few popular dances like the Wop, and finding them all lacking. "So we made this dance called the Cabbage Patch." They shared sentences, used rapper Slick Rick's trademark line ("And it goes a little something like this"), threw in some Beasties' slang ("getting ill") and described their new move, which involved moving your shoulders. But while the end result was as entertaining, catchy, and rough as anything Dre did with Eazy, the single did little to improve their fortunes. Then Lonzo informed them that Macola called to say they owed the company $65,000 for some reason, which meant no royalties anytime soon.

One night, Dre agreed to meet with everyone—Arabian, Yella, and Cube—at Eazy's house. "We were broke, we had no money, and we were getting ripped off by the people we were producing for," Arabian claimed.

Eazy faced the motley crew and said, "I'll fund you guys. I don't want to do the whole drug thing anymore. I want to stop." The others thought it was a great deal. Eazy wanted to go straight; they wanted to keep making records. "So we said we'd do the song and just start this new group and go from there," Arabian added. Since it wouldn't mean leaving the Cru, Dre agreed to join. He also hoped no one would laugh at their exaggerated lyrics or the fact that Eazy's group would include him and Yella, most recently seen in the Prince-like Wreckin' Cru.

◆ ◆ ◆

With his jalopy in an impound lot, Dr. Dre needed money to get it out and figured producing more tracks for Eazy was a way to end this period in which his pal DJ Pooh had to drive him to the studio. It was a good decision. No sooner had Eazy had the record pressed up than Dre learned it sold 5,000 copies. "Bam," Dre said. "There it was." Macola (the same pressing plant that manufactured some Cru records) got involved with distribution and Eazy helped promote it by hiring friends and people who could use a few bucks to carry his singles to local shops. Each morning, he'd pick Ren up from his mother's house and head over to Macola, where he'd ask whomever was at the front desk, "Yeah, yeah, how my record doing?"

M.C. Ren said, "They'd just look at him," but he didn't care about their opinions anyway. He was really there to head into the back room, sneak a few boxes of his record out the back door, then load them into his jeep. He'd then visit various shops and force people to sell them (sometimes at gunpoint, he claimed). "He used to do that all day," said Ren. He also had people head into violent hoods and hand free copies to the guys leading sets. And when he ran out of copies, he'd simply park his jeep behind Macola and steal a few more copies. Though he struck some people as cocky and overconfident, Eazy concealed that he was still considering a job at the post office. "He was thinking: 'This shit ain't gonna work,'" Ren later revealed. Ren was also trying to keep hope alive. He accompanied Eazy to take the written test for the job, to show support, but also said, aloud, "God, let everything happen."

"Boyz-N-the-Hood" was far from a hit but Dre was also not about to give up. He was too absorbed in his music to think of anything else, and Cube didn't have anything better to do, so they sat and wrote another song for Eazy, figuring they might as well take another shot at the hardcore hip-hop crowd. They came up with "Dope Man," and were still working on it at Audio Achievements in Torrance when Eazy asked Lonzo to introduce him to the Cru's manager, Jerry Heller. Lonzo delayed in setting it up. As he saw it, Dre was supposed to produce Eazy but stay in the Cru. Now Dre was devoting more time to Eazy's record and a side group of some sort.

Since they needed a name, Dre joined Eazy, Cube, and M.C. Ren at Arabian's home in Inglewood, and threw concepts around. At one point, Arabian suggested From Compton with Love (sort of like a James Bond film title). But the others jeered, "Hell, no." When they quieted down, Eazy leaned forward and said, "How 'bout N.W.A., Niggaz with Attitude?" He wanted to shock people and it sort of evoked C.I.A. and HBO. Everyone loved it, Ren recalled. "Hell, yeah. N.W.A. it is." During the same period, they decided that Yella, helping with production and hanging around with Dre, should be in the group, too. "We started doing shows and everybody just clicked like that."

Sensing the end was near and eager to earn the $750 Eazy now offered for an introduction, Lonzo worked to introduce him to the Cru's manager. To his credit, forty-six-year-old Jerry Heller (born October 6, 1940) agreed to help Lonzo earn this money. He was also intrigued by Eazy's actually paying for a meeting. From Cleveland, Heller obtained his MBA at USC and followed late sixties' work with Creedence Clearwater Revival by representing many of Geffen's biggest singer-songwriters. Along the way, he helped introduce Elton John in America and booked successful tours that established Pink Floyd.

On Tuesday, March 3, 1987, at 3:30 in the afternoon, Eazy arrived at Macola in his Suzuki Samurai with a friend in the shotgun seat. Short, barrel-chested, his slick curls barely tucked under his ball cap, he met Lonzo in the lobby. Lonzo faced Heller. "Hey, Jerry, this is Eric Wright." Then, facing Eazy, he said, "Jerry Heller."

Next, Lonzo said, "This is Lorenzo."

Eazy's friend said, "Lorenzo Patterson," and extended a handshake.

Bending over, Eazy pulled his wad of bills from a white striped tube sock and counted the $750 out with Heller observing. In a conference room, he got right down to business, playing "Boyz-N-the-Hood." The experienced manager asked to hear it again so Eazy rewound it. Then he played their newer songs, "8 Ball" and "Dope Man." The first was another laid-back rhyme in the Schoolly D mode, about drinking malt liquor in the hood, which included parts of William DeVaughn's "Be Thankful for What You Got" and the well-known drums on the Pointer Sisters' break, "Yes, We Can Can." "Dope Man" meanwhile was set to two other East Coast standbys: Herman Kelly & Life's "Dance to the Drummer's Beat" and the Ohio Players' squealing "Funky Worm." Lyrically, it was even more sobering than "Boyz-N-the-Hood." It started with one member yelling, "Yo Dre!" Over another big beat Cube coldly described the day-to-day business of selling crack. He describes crackheads begging for a hit; the dope man trading one for a blow job and choking a woman during the act; his car and wealth and beating anyone that doesn't pay. After they all yell "Dope man, dope man" and a crackhead begs for crack, Dre stops the track and plays the title character. "Wait a minute, wait a minute. Who the fuck are you talking to? Do you know who the fuck I am? Man I can't believe this shit." He pretends to face a dishonest female addict and threatens to slap her head with his penis. Another member yells like a Beastie Boy ("Yo Dre!! Kick in the bass!"), then Cube tells listeners they'd be stupid to smoke crack; they'd spend all their money on it; they'd be hopeless fiends groveling on the floor and searching for a crumb. "And niggaz out there messin' up people's health. Yo, what the fuck you gotta say for yourself?"

The song was sobering enough but Eazy rapped as an amoral dealer, bragging about his riches until—after switching his voice—a Mexican gangster says his crack made his sister sick. And if she dies because of his drug, "I'm puttin in your culo, a thirty-eight slug." Here, Dre threw in a resounding gunshot. When the song ended, Heller asked, "The label you want to start, it have a name?" After a three-hour talk, Heller signed on to work with him.

The next step was radio. Since Dre had a good relationship with Greg Mack of KDAY, and Mack knew Eazy's tapes were selling like crazy, Dre introduced them at La Casa Camino Real in downtown L.A. Mack, a huge supporter of local talent, once said, if given the choice, he'd play a mediocre West Coast effort over an East Coast hit since the local rapper "would say KDAY is the shit all over the streets and with the kids you gotta be a hit." After a few pleasantries, Eric cut right to the chase. "What do I need to do to make what I'm doin' radio airplayable?" Mack liked that he didn't bullshit like other aspiring artists. "Well, you just need to clean up the lyrics." Within a day, Eazy handed him a clean version of the song. "Not only that," Mack recalled, he included a rap about KDAY. Soon, "Boyz-N-the- Hood" became the station's most requested record, and Cli-N-Tel heard it on the air and thought, "Shit, that's my voice they're scratchin' in there." At the same time, Ice-T felt it sounded a little like his own "6 'N tha Morning." Cube had already called to let him know the song included a similar sound, but T felt N.W.A. was different. On his records, he rapped about crime but always said, "If you do it, you might end up in jail." N.W.A. meanwhile was "like 'Fuck it, we're going to jail," so Ice-T was not upset at all.

With "Boyz-N-the-Hood," "Dope Man," and "8 Ball" having done so well, Eazy decided to release a five-song N.W.A. EP. In the studio, Dre worked with Cube on "A Bitch is a Bitch," in which the outspoken rapper railed against women who wouldn't date him because he didn't drive the right car or dress as expensively as drug dealers. Dre programmed a loping piano and behindhand beat while Cube claimed some bitches wanted his money (when he didn't have any), and were cranky because of premenstrual syndrome. For another song, Eazy did "Fat Girl," his take on the ribald Slick Rick–style (sexually explicit story raps over swing beats) and a number credited to N.W.A. Once again, Dre gathered Eazy and his pal Ron-De-Vu around the microphone and had them mimic the Def Jam and Run-DMC school, opening with a memorable chorus, "Fat girl! You're a fat girl!"

Then, as on a Slick Rick song, he had Ron-De-Vu pop in to play the fat woman (with a comical voice) before Eazy piled on more juvenile insults about her huge chin, thunder thighs, and whale-like appearance. That was followed by "Panic Zone," Arabian's speedy Cru-like work about a rough neighborhood near Compton where thieves routinely carjacked or shot people. For this one, Dre tried to talk in a deep Bambaataa-like tone. They put it on there, Arabian said, because they loved the music. And no radio station would play the other songs with curses. "So in order to get the radio play, we had to do the electro music."

Before Dre knew it, Eazy told him and the others, "Everybody come on. We gonna take this album picture." Everyone showed up at a graffiti-covered loading dock. As might be expected, Dre sat at the center of the huge crew. He was still rocking a close-cropped Afro and looked a little out of place in his black *Thriller*-style jacket. The others meanwhile were an odd looking bunch, almost a compendium of current trends in rap. Two of the guys wore huge Flavor Flav clocks around their necks. Another had the Jheri curls, mustache, and open shirt and chain of a Kurtis Blow type. A light-skinned guy was dressed like a cholo and held a big beer bottle. Cube wore a blue and white sweatshirt and held his own huge beer while M.C. Ren, Eazy, and a few others wore the sort of Raiders hats, T-shirts, chains, and khakis you'd see on any other gangbanger, but not for dramatic effect. "We was wearing what niggas could afford, really," said Ren. "Khakis cost twelve dollars. Niggas wear khakis, T-shirts, and Raider hats 'cause niggas out here just wear hats." Some held forty-ounce bottles of beer. Others scowled. That he had just been seen wearing sequins and shoulder pads with the Cru didn't matter. Dre was happy. They were N.W.A. now.

After writing "Dope Man" and "8 Ball," however, Cube decided rap was too risky. C.I.A. had flopped and Eazy's singles were far from hits so after graduation in June, he took the train to Arizona to study drafting at the Phoenix Institute of Technology. Eazy didn't let it stop him. He soon auditioned his pal Lorenzo Patterson for a spot on his new label.

Like Dre, Eazy, Cube, and Yella, Patterson hailed from Compton. He liked sports as a kid but his mom said, "I ain't got money for that," so he joined a Crip gang and earned pocket change with petty drug sales until cops raided his homie Chip's pad. During junior high, he started calling himself Master Ren; recording demos over other artists' instrumentals ("Kick It like a Champ" and "Money to Burn") and letting Eric hear new raps whenever Eric stopped by his home to hang with Ren's older brother.

At the time, Ren said, there were no lawyers involved. Eazy offered artists an unprecedented amount of creative freedom. It was unlike the local major labels, where artists had to record soft R&B, behave in certain ways, and wear flashy outfits. "We had it all, man," said Ren. "We did everything we wanted to."

Dre soon found another artist for the roster. In Texas, his pal Dr. Rock, who'd previously deejayed alongside him at Eve's After Dark, was spinning records on local radio every Saturday night. Dre was in town to guest deejay and did a few beats in Rock's crib for Rock's amateur group The Fila Fresh Crew. But he felt one member—a light-skinned guy with a square high top, a track suit, a few rings, and tinted sunglasses—stood out. Like Cube, Doc T (born Tracy Curry) first heard rap on The Sugarhill Gang's "Rapper's Delight." He also enjoyed their subsequent single "Apache." Then, like Dre, he went from being a huge Run-DMC fan to enjoying Boogie Down Productions, LL Cool J, Slick Rick, and Eric B & Rakim. Even better was that his name was inspired by The Wreckin' Cru's "Surgery."

◆ ◆ ◆

Before Dre could work on Eazy's solo album, *Eazy Duz It,* he agreed to join the Cru in the studio in August 1987 to record "Turn Out the Lights." Originally, this was to be another in a line of "Lovers"–like ballads but, viewing it as a way to show off his production skills, Dre emphasized a hard beat. Everything ran smoothly. To Lonzo's ears the track sounded like a hit. After a church bell, some whirring bass, and a short quote of the piano from "Lovers" gave way to a plodding beat, chimes, and glossy Prince-like synths, Dr. Dre asked a girl, "What's happening, baby?" He called himself "the world class doctor" and "a master of seduction," before Michel'le sang her throaty chorus about being a hell of a woman, needing a hell of a man, and warning him he better not turn off the lights. They managed to get through the song but things came to a head.

Dre and Yella had grumbled among themselves about how they were tired of going without pay. When they saw Lonzo receive $1,000 from Macola they asked for royalties. He said it was a refund, his personal money, but they felt he was holding out on them. Dre finally said if he and Yella weren't paid, they'd leave. Lonzo tried to calm them, he said, but the cash-starved musicians kept yelling, "Fuck you, fuck you, fuck you." Finally, Dre left. "I wanted to get up outta that shit. Money wasn't right, basic reasons . . . I just felt like I wanted to be in control of my shit. I was just sitting in the studio knowing what I can do. I didn't have no input on a lot of that shit that came out."

D re's priority is an Eazy-E solo album. With "Boyz" still the most requested record on KDAY the single keeps selling thousands of copies each week. They're about to begin writing songs, with others creating Eric's verses, when Dre learns nineteen-year-old Cube is finished with school and back in his parents' home. Now, he joins Dre, M.C. Ren, Doc, and Arabian Prince in Eazy's garage to create a full-length work. They have five songs completed, including "Boyz-N-the-Hood," but it hasn't been easy. It's so cold out here some nights, Dre and Eazy have to keep a tiny portable heater near their drum machines and samplers. Further, Eric doesn't like a being a rapper. His singles "Boyz," "8-Ball," and "Dope Man" are doing well but he continues to rethink this avocation. The others tell him he has a commercial voice and has to keep going. "He sounded and looked like a little kid," says Yella. "That's why we pushed him out front; he was the image."

Another source of anxiety is that Eazy sometimes lacks rhythm. Dre sits by the board with a sheet of paper. Every time Eazy blows a take, he jots a mark on the page. Soon, there are hundreds of marks. Finally, other members say, "Let that nigga do his shit last." Or, if they're done, and Eazy's up at bat, "Alright, nigga, we gone." Dre will be there all day.

During one session, for "Ruthless Villain," Ren spends hours trying to teach Eazy the lyric but since the beat is quicker than "Boyz" and the stanza holds more words, Eazy can't master the hairpin turns of Ren's lyric. Dre watches Ren keep repeating the lyric, Eric keep failing, Ren saying, "It don't sound right." Finally, Dre says, "Fuck it; let Ren say it."

Once it's done, Dre likes what he's brought to the table. During a trip to Hollywood, where Eazy's getting a P.O. box, Dre sits in a car with them. "Man, since it's gonna take a long time for you to do your solo shit, you might as well get in N.W.A.," he tells Ren. Eazy agrees with the decision. He soon asks Ren to pen "Eazy Duz It," and "Radio."

Dre's discovery Doc, meanwhile, has moved from Tyree's place near Centennial High and into the new apartment on Paramount that Dre shares with Yella. With Eazy wanting to include curses no radio station will play and Dre wanting to cross over, Doc works to soften E's themes, keep him happy, and "use words that don't scare white people." He delivers light-hearted fare like "We Want Eazy," and "Still Talking Shit."

Some sessions find Eazy more combative than ever. He'll waste time arguing over the most trivial thing, "like a siren on the fuckin' record or somethin'" Dre quips. "It should go eight bars in instead of at the beginning." He argues for hours until he gets his way. But just as quickly, Eazy returns to the mic and affirms their friendship on his raucous "Eazy-er Said than Dunn," rapping, "My homie Dre is a doctor not a lawyer."

They're making progress just as their manager, Jerry Heller, finishes arranging their first tour, fourteen dates in November 1987. He'll make the rounds at record labels, seeking a deal, while they perform live shows. The group packs their black sweatshirts, matching jeans, L.A. Kings hats, Run-DMC–like gold chains, and in Dre and Yella's case, the tiny silver studs they wear in both ears. They join Brooklyn quartet UTFO, upbeat female duo Salt 'N Pepa, and dapper Heavy D but become the butt of a few jokes since they can't afford plane tickets and arrive in towns in rented vans, disheveled and the worse for wear. Then they notice other acts sometimes staring in confusion at Cube and Eazy's Jheri curls.

Backstage, they continue to see other artists curse up a storm. Yet, the same artists never include profanity on their records. "We was like, 'they're hypocrites,'" Ren recalls. They vowed to fill whatever they'd record with honest lyrics, even if means cursing as much as Eddie Murphy and Richard Pryor do on albums recorded during their concerts.

What the group doesn't know is that Macola's learned they want to sign with another label. "And if you left to get a bigger deal, they'd press everything you've ever done and put it out," says Arabian. While they're on tour, Macola fuses the five-song N.W.A. EP to unrelated tracks Dre did with the Fila Fresh Crew. The Fila Fresh stuff represents another early attempt to imitate, or bite, the LL Cool J sound, and it shows. Their "Toughest Man Alive" includes dull beats and horn blasts, a gravelly voiced rapper with generic themes, and group member Fresh K sounding out of step with the times when he yells, "Yeah, and if you want your beats to be def, call Dre before Monday!" "Drink it Up," meanwhile, is a Cru-styled novelty work, a cover of The Beatles' 1963 "Twist and Shout" that starts with a Richard Pryor sample ("Winos never get afraid of nothin but runnin' outta wine"). Macola adds these and similarly unfocused works to the album and rushes *N.W.A. and the Posse* into stores on November 6, 1987. "That shit was like some wack shit and that's why we never supported that record," says Ren. But to their chagrin, it starts to sell.

At the same time, back home, their manager persuades Priority Records, down the hall from his office, to meet with them. Priority's new, but has sold two million copies of a compilation credited to The California Raisins. Its owners are young and willing to try new things. Co-founder Bryan Turner loves "Boyz-N-the-Hood," and when a distributor sends Priority a copy of *N.W.A. and the Posse*, he enjoys that, too. "Almost instinctively, without a lot of experience, I wanted to be in business with these kids," Turner remembers. Meanwhile, after seeing them in concert Turner's partner, Mark Cerami, is just as enthusiastic. When they all meet, they sign N.W.A. as Priority's first real act. The six-week schedule's a little tight but Dre is happier than ever when N.W.A. enters the studio to finish their debut.

◆ ◆ ◆

Dre's away from Compton, school, the want ads, and the expectations of the past. He has a vision for the album, promoting Compton the same way

KRS-One promotes the South Bronx, Public Enemy champions Long Island, Run-DMC describes Queens, and Ice-T represents Los Angeles. "We just went in there writing shit, yelling, "Compton," talking about hoes," says Ren. They want to create an indelible image, make their name, and shock everyone by discussing the streets, cursing and hollering. They also want to show the East Coast that California rappers aren't all like those in the famous Dream Team (since Ren feels they're "wack compared to groups like Run-DMC, Whodini, LL Cool J"). But mostly they brag, rock different styles, and record music their friends would like to hear. "We [were] never tryin' to make a hit," says Yella. "We made music."

Dre starts sessions at noon and usually gets there first. He's also the last to leave. At the mix board, he comes to the fore, showing his friends how to unite their voices and beats to capture the sound they hear on East Coast albums. Dre does beats, with Yella working the recorder, board, drum machines, and other equipment. "It had on there produced by Dre and Yella but Yella was just like his assistant," Ren recalls. "Like, 'Do this for me, hand me that, push that.'" With twenty-four tracks to fill (as opposed to only eight in Eazy's garage) Dre's more ambitious. The standard 808, synthesizers, and an SP1200 come into play as do samples from break beats, but he also asks session players to cover old riffs. And if it doesn't sound right, he'll go to a record.

After pulling a break beat from his crates, he'll say, "We're gonna rap to this one." While he programs beats, M.C. Ren and Cube huddle over lyrics. Cube's the main lyricist and others come and go as needed. Doc's writing all of Eazy's parts and also, he says, "being the extra set of ears for Dr. Dre because I was the only person that he really trusted. Back in those days Dre really trusted my ears." Dre listens and stops the music if something isn't perfect. "That's terrible," he'll say, or shoot them a withering look. "Try to make it like this," he'll add. Once they get it right, he'll mutter, "Cool," and keep moving.

They have a great set-up. Ren and Cube write lyrics. Cube also brings ideas for inserts, and records to scratch. Yella's a technical assistant. Eazy handles the business side. "Dre would do the music and he would take our ideas and apply 'em and put it all together, which was what he did best," says Cube.

At Dre's new apartment on Paramount one day Cube walks over and says he has an idea for a chorus. Dre hears the words, "Fuck tha Police." He looks the lyric over. "What else you got?" He prefers music people can drink and dance to. But he soon revisits the idea after cops catch him and Eazy shooting paint balls at people near bus stops in Torrance. Now that he's personally experienced something it's worth covering. Cube wants it to be a solo number, but Dre joins Ren in saying it should include the entire group. The others gather around the equipment as Dre sits with pen and paper, mapping out an intricate work that evokes an old-time radio courtroom drama. Dre even assigns Doc a role as a hateful white cop. With convoluted bridges designed, he then turns to the milk crates that hold his ever-growing record collection. Many of the albums are break beats from Yano's booth at the Roadium. In exchange for tapes, Ren recalls, "Steve would pay Dre with records." He starts pulling albums out: James Brown's "Funky President," and "Funky Drummer," Marva Whitney's "It's My Thing," Roy Ayers' "Boogie Back" and Fancy's "Feel Good." Once he lays the tracks down, he has everyone record their vocal.

Ren, as a courtroom bailiff, says "Judge Dre" is "presiding in the case of N.W.A. vs. the Police Department." "Order, order, order," Dre says. "Ice Cube, take the motherfucking stand. Do you swear to tell the truth, the whole truth, and nothin but the truth, so help your black ass?"

"You god damn right!"

"Well, won't you tell everybody what the fuck you gotta say?"

Cube starts by saying, "A young nigga got it bad 'cause I'm brown." He describes cops in Compton as abusive, describes racial profiling, and threatens violent retribution. He also alleges that many cops are homos that want to touch his testicles while searching him, and that black cops are even more abusive in an effort to impress bigoted white partners. During the chorus, Dre scratches a phrase from an earlier single ("Fuck the police") then includes dialogue in which a white cop harasses them during a traffic stop. M.C. Ren's verse is even more angry. He says cops are weak without badges and guns and need to blind him with mace because they fear him. But without a gun, he'll fuck them up. Eazy shares this opinion. Without a gun, what have you got? "A sucker in a uniform waitin' to get shot." During the song's closing bars, listeners hear Judge Dre say the jury has found the white cop "guilty of bein' a redneck, white bread, chickenshit motherfucker!" The cop, played by Doc, screams, "That's a lie! That's a god damn lie!"

"Get him out of here!"

"I want justice!"

"Get him the fuck out my face!"

"I want justice!"

"Out, right now!"

"Fuck you, you black motherfuckers!"

"That was one of the first songs we start putting together," Cube recalls.

At Audio Achievements in Torrance, they arrive each day at twelve-thirty, and move quickly so as to not waste studio time. "We'd go in there, lock the doors, then just start working," says Ren. They keep recording songs and trying new ideas. As producer, Dre keeps creating a wall of sound as dense as any on old Phil Spector or Brian Wilson songs. During "Gangsta, Gangsta," he digs out the Jimmy Castor Bunch's "Troglodyte," The Honey Drippers' ubiquitous "Impeach the President," Kool and the Gang's equally exploited "N.T.," and The Ohio Players' "Funky Worm." But he adds something new—a guitar line from Steve Arrington's "Weak at the Knees," and some curses from Richard Pryor's routine "Prison."

On other songs, he uses obscure records (Ronnie Hudson saying "In the city of Compton") but also includes the East Coast standbys "Funky Drummer," "I Get Lifted," "Rock Creek Park," "Take the Money and Run," and The Winstons' "Amen Brother." Then to personalize it he reaches for funk records by Funkadelic, The Isley Brothers, and the Ohio Players. With acts like Eric B & Rakim covering songs like Bobby Byrd's "I Know You Got Soul," Dre decides to rap over Charles Wright's buoyant "Express Yourself." But he's not done yet.

Though the songs are already crowded enough, he adds another layer of sound—horn blasts, sirens, gunshots, and curses. He wants it all to sound great in a car. He knows California's a maze of highways and freeways, most people own at least one vehicle, and the first thing most people do when they get behind the wheel is turn the radio on. So he keeps telling recording engineer Donovan Smith to raise the bass. After each mix, he rushes to his ride to hear how it sounds.

Then he joins the others in wondering if Arabian's still a good fit. They've already given a few groups from the compilation the boot since they sounded a little soft. And Arabian's doing techno. As sessions continue, it turns out he's only done one song and "that shit didn't fit in," says Ren. They feel it's old fashioned, and consider how the harder stuff keeps getting them press coverage. They keep knocking out one street record after another. So Arabian stops coming to the studio.

Eric feels sorry for him. "Man, let him do this song."

Dre hears what Arabian has written, a dance cut called "Something 2 Dance 2" set to the classic vocal harmony from Sly & the Family Stone's "Dance to the Music" and grooves from D Train's "You're the One for Me." Arabian joins Eric and Yella on the microphone but M.C. Ren and Cube want nothing to do with it. "It was like . . . we wasn't doing that type of shit," says Ren. Arabian's had enough. He poses near them in a new cover shot— the group looking down at the camera as if upon a victim of a group beating—then leaves with dignity.

After six weeks, and about $8,000, Dre has thirteen songs that reflect what he feels rap should be. Even if he really doesn't gangbang, living in Compton put Dre in close contact with guys who did. It isn't his life at all— he's a former celebrity with the Cru, a radio DJ, and a young father of three with another kid on the way (with Michel'le)—but it was happening all around him. So "Boyz-N-the-Hood," like "Dope Man," captures the relentless pace of Los Angeles gang life, from innocents in the cross-fire to gang sweeps to being in the county with other Gs. The album describes the scene in even more detail, from drive-bys, Jheri curls and Locs (sunglasses), to 8 Ball malt liquor, customized Chevys, beef with Mexican *esés,* and the arsenals some gangsters hid in their tiny shag-carpeted bedrooms.

The first three cuts, "Straight Outta Compton," "Fuck tha Police," and "Gangsta, Gangsta," dabble with street themes. Ren calls the other ten "just filler." Ironically, they cap the album with Arabian's "Something 2 Dance 2."

After celebrating and playing it for anyone near them, Dre and the group help Eazy promote his solo album, *Eazy Duz It.* It arrived in stores September 1988, and Eazy's nervous about playing the Apollo in Harlem. Dre joins him on stage and they all get booed. Some audience members even make like the crowd at Skateland and throw things. They feel even worse downstairs, when they realize a few New York rappers saw it all happen on backstage monitors. But Eazy's debut starts outselling works by many people in that room (it would go on to sell 2.5 million copies) and later, back in Los Angeles, Dre joins the others in a jewelry store. With *Eazy Duz It* in stores and selling quickly, Ruthless and Priority have decided to prep *Straight Outta Compton* for release. At the jewelry store, the guys are gearing up for promotional appearances by picking out thick gold chains.

Doc's there too. By now, he's changed his stage name to The D.O.C. (to evoke N.W.A.). He's also wearing the same sort of black clothes, hat, and shades as the other group members do. He steps up to Eazy and says, "Yeah man, what's up? I want some gold, too."

"I'll tell you what," Eazy replies. "If you sell me the publishing on the songs that you wrote on [various projects], I'll give you whatever you want."

"Yeah, give me that chain; give me that watch and that ring. I'ma write a million more songs. You can have them, no problem." Now that he wears about $5,000 in jewelry, he more closely resembles the other group members.

◆ ◆ ◆

Dre sees Priority release *Straight Outta Compton* on January 25, 1989, but radio and MTV ignore it. The group's unknown, they figure, and even if they do give it a listen, the curses turn them off before they hear Dre's softer "Express Yourself." But even without radio play, with Priority barely promoting it, twenty-four-year-old Dre learns *Straight Outta Compton* has sold an impressive half a million copies in six weeks. He also sees many reporters wring their hands over N.W.A. lyrics and ask, "Well why did you say this? What do you mean by this word? When do they give interviews?" Ren remembers. "We'd be like 'What?' Just fucking with them." But this only inspires negative stories about how they frightened journalists.

Two weeks later, Dre hears MTV won't air their video for the title track, claiming images of them running down empty streets in the daylight (their low-budget re-creation of an LAPD gang sweep) glorify violence. But not even the embargo slows sales. "Basically, we just manufactured and shipped records," says David King of Priority. "And people kept asking for more."

Back in Compton, people harp about Dre's new image. "Dre never gang-banged a day in his life," says Lonzo. "When we had fights, he was the last person to do any swinging." They needed his help but Dre would say, "Hey, I got to mix these records," he recalls. Then there was the night he and Dre were driving through a hood. A Pinto hit Lonzo's car, knocking the muffler off. Lonzo got out to argue with the Mexican driver and soon saw ten other Mexican men lower their beers and walk toward them. "Dre's sitting in the car scared shitless," Lonzo claims. He doesn't get out to try to help. He just sits there until one of the men sees his Wreckin' Cru jacket and asks where he got it from. He says, "I'm Dr. Dre, man," which inspires these Cru fans to offer beer and fix the car. As Lonzo sees it, Dre is a lover, not a fighter. "It would take a hell of a lot to convince me that he's really the person he's claiming to be." Up and coming rapper King Tee, like many of Dre's peers, remembers his flamboyant white outfit with the Cru. Now he's rocking heavy black Carhartt jackets and jeans and pointing at cameras in newspaper photos. "It's like, damn, these niggas is the roughest gangsta rappers around and they used to sing like Prince and shit."

At home, Dre's mom tells his brother Tyree she doesn't understand the appeal of Dre's songs. Tyree defends Dre's new sound. "But Tyree, I just don't like that music."

"You should be proud of him," he replies.

"Why does he have to talk so bad?"

"Well, Mom, if he made records and rapped just normal, nobody would buy it. He's only saying what the people want to hear."

In the suburbs, and small towns, suburban white teens play *Straight Outta Compton* in their cars, and buy copies. The media believes N.W.A. poses a political threat but in reality, white fans are buying *Straight Outta Compton* because they're weary and frightened of the pro-Black political content seeping into other rapper's lyrics. The album also does well with junior high kids, one music executive says. "It was illicit, forbidden fruit." Newspaper stories dismiss their sound as "gangsta rap" (after one chorus of their song "Gangsta Gangsta"). The members of N.W.A. are furious. They prefer to call their music "Reality Rap" since the songs are describing the lives and characters who dwell around them. Either way, a young audience makes the album nothing less than a phenomenon. So Dre's more confident than ever when he gets back to work, squeezing in sessions for the female pop trio J.J. Fad but deciding to produce The D.O.C.'s album before one by his current girlfriend, Michel'le. "I was the best thing we had in that camp," The D.O.C. says.

Since The D.O.C.'s flow is as complicated as that of New York's literate Rakim, Dre sets records to sleek bass lines and eventful drums at breakneck tempos. *No One Can Do It Better* finds him once again digging into crates of records for break-beat albums, samples already used on other rappers' songs, and his favorite funk jams. He fills The D.O.C.'s songs with genre staples "Impeach the President" and "Synthetic Substitution," "Hook and Sling" (by Eddie Bo), and Lyn Collins' "Think," James Brown's "Funky Drummer" and Parliament's "Chocolate City." His drums evoke New York acts Eric B & Rakim and Public Enemy, but Dre adds a different flavor by including obscure, even eccentric, melodies by Heatwave, Sly & The Family Stone, Roy Ayers, Lou Donaldson, Yellow Sunshine, B.T. Express, and Teddy Pendergrass, among others.

The D.O.C. has his own ideas and keeps asking Dre to sample "Misdemeanor." He keeps sitting at the turntable playing the funky little tune by young, high-pitched singer Foster Sylvers but Dre says, "There's nothing I can sample. I'm not fucking with it."

Other break beats include drum or bass solos. This song has Sylvers crooning over every bar. But days later, D.O.C. plays it again and repeats his request. "There's not enough space," Dre replies. A week later, the same thing, only this time, D.O.C. pleads. "Okay, fuck it. I'll make it."

While Dre works on the backing track, D.O.C. spends the day drinking. When he sees D.O.C. enter the recording booth and slip on headphones that night, Dre asks, "Since you're in the booth, why don't you go on and give us a level on it?" Unknown to Dre, alcohol has D.O.C. believing the song sounds like reggae. D.O.C. thinks, "since the shit sound Jamaican, I'm gonna give it a Jamaican feel." Assuming they'll do another take, D.O.C.—slightly inebriated—raps with a phony accent. Dre, who enjoys Boogie Down Productions' reggae-tinged lyrics, likes what he hears. D.O.C. wants to do it again but Dre says, "fuck that; that was a 'One-Take Willy'."

For another song, he asks D.O.C. to rap over a heavy guitar. D.O.C. writes "Beautiful but Deadly" and figures Dre's tapping into Run-DMC's rock-rap audience. But it's not even real rock. Dre's using a chunky guitar from Funkadelic's old "Cosmic Slop" and the big rock-style beat on the break "Different Strokes." Then another night, Dre and his girl Michel'le get home at one-thirty or two in the morning and Dre walks over to D.O.C.'s usual bed on the floor. D.O.C. sits up in confusion. "Nigga, I was on my way home and I got caught up in a day dream," Dre begins. "It was me and you bustin' a song called 'Tha Formula' to a Marvin Gaye beat." Before D.O.C. can answer, Dre rushes to his bedroom, fetches a cassette, and plays D.O.C. this old song, "Inner City Blues (Make Me Wanna Holler)." He re-enters the bedroom and hits the sack.. The next morning D.O.C. already has a lyric ready to record that day.

With D.O.C., Dre keeps creating material in the studio, exercising more control over the final product by suggesting lyrics and themes. "He was only interested in making party songs that motherfuckers wanna get drunk and dance to," D.O.C. says. But D.O.C. doesn't mind. Later he boasts that they had no plans. "Everything was natural." Eventually, they finish another song and Dre asks, "How many is that?"

D.O.C. says, "Seventeen."

"Yeah that's enough." He nods. "Fuck it; let's move on."

He wants to get back to N.W.A.

In the spring of 1989, he learns *Straight Outta Compton* has sold 700,000 copies. White writers like Robert Hilburn and Dennis Hunt of the *Los Angeles Times* continue to heap praise on them, and during concerts, Dre notices more white kids in the crowd (with mullets, old jeans, and metal T-shirts). Even stranger, they're singing the words to N.W.A.'s songs. But a few black college radio DJs in the Bay Area in Northern California ban their songs (since they feel their image promotes negative racial stereotypes).

Some of the other group members go on the air on station KMEL to defend their music but Dre sits out the interview. He's busy creating a new single. He's gone back to "Express Yourself" and removed the curses. During the upbeat new clean version, Dre claims he doesn't smoke weed or cess, thus positioning himself as another of the day's "positive" acts (after spending the

rest of the album implying otherwise). The new single's probably the closest
to his daily reality—a calm guy that doesn't want any fights—but he quickly
gets into his black windbreaker, straight leg jeans, ball cap, and thick gold
chain to film a video, bopping through Compton streets as if he's really a
gangster, with fans behind him.

With pride, he sees Ruthless ship the single to stores on May 31, 1989,
and radio DJs start playing it. Then MTV sees the video and decides it can
air it. By the time school lets out for summer, he sees N.W.A. become the
most popular rap group in the United States of America. He's making
money, Ruthless is about to buy him a million-dollar house, he's thinking of
maybe getting a Ferrari, and he's about to go on a national tour. But clouds
are beginning to appear on the horizon.

5

Dre was already on a forty-date national tour when he heard the album sailed past the 1 million sales mark. Like the others, he was stunned. "It was like, we did the album, video got banned, next thing you know we're on the road," Ren recalled. Now, groupies yelled and reached out for him. White kids yelled his lyrics about how he didn't smoke weed or cess. And in every town, one community leader or another was up in arms. "They didn't like the word 'nigga,'" D.O.C. explained. The divisive term had existed "for fifty-thousand years," but everyone suddenly wanted to hit the street and protest because N.W.A. dared use it on a record. But the tour kept rolling and selling out venues, and in New York Dre got an idea of how much his reputation had grown. There, in a nightclub, he was shocked to learn Hank Shocklee of Public Enemy not only knew his work but was happy to meet him. Dre loved Public Enemy's single "Rebel Without a Pause," which was on KDAY and changing the genre's direction, and called the others over. But when he started introducing them, pointing at M.C. Ren and saying, "This is—," Shocklee interrupted. "Yeah I know." He laughed. "This is Ren, this is Eazy."

By July 1989, Dre was one of the genre's biggest stars. He was young, famous, and down with hip-hop's most popular upstart label. He had a new million-dollar house waiting for him, a Mercedes, a Corvette, and a million in the bank. "You couldn't tell me shit at that time." But after one show, the mood soured.

His mother had bad news. She'd been sleeping at home when Little Warren knocked on her door and woke her up. It was the middle of the night and Warren said Tyree's friend Jerry was at the door with two men in suits. At the front door she asked, what happened?

The homicide detectives said Tyree was murdered.

"He got into a fight," Dre recalled.

Tyree—who was twenty-one and had a son—was with three friends on a Compton street when it started. His opponent grabbed Tyree's head with both hands and jerked hard. "Neck got broke and all kind'a shit." Tyree fell, striking his head on the pavement, and didn't get up. And the last words he heard, Dre said, were "Fuck tha Police" from a nearby radio. "So it kinda fucked with me. My brother was my best friend. He was three years younger than me."

He went home for the funeral. He cried for days. That the police eventually caught Tyree's killer didn't relieve the pain. He either cried or sat alone, staring into space. It was like Bubby all over again. But he eventually composed himself and got back on the road to honor agreements for the tour.

Dre sensed tension among members of the group and knew it was shaping up to be another crippling problem. Between shows, Cube had seen people selling N.W.A. merchandise. He had asked if they'd get a cut of profits and heard people say mind your own business. After a hectic show in Columbus, Ohio, Cube finally voiced concerns about their manager, Jerry Heller. "'It's either him or me,'" Eazy quoted Cube as saying, to which Eazy replied, "N.W.A. is me, Dre, Yella... and Jerry Heller; here's your plane ticket home."

Cube remained with the tour, promoting the image of gang-related friendship on stage, but in Arizona, he told Ren, "Jerry Heller is coming up here and they want us to sign a new contract." Cube didn't know contracts. Neither did Ren, who thought it peculiar someone would "pop up on a nigga with contracts and no lawyers." Cube vowed not to sign it and urged Ren to help him take a stand. "I could say I ain't gonna sign it and I'm just one person and the shit can still go down, but if you say it, me and you together, then can't nothing happen."

Ren, however, needed the $70,000 his signature would bring. He had never seen this much money in his life. He also considered how "Eric grew up right around the corner," he was Ren's pal, and had brought him in. "Man, I ain't got no money," he told Cube. "I ain't got no paper, I ain't got nothing. Nigga, I been rappin' for nothing this long and nigga fittin' to give me seventy Gs?"

To Cube's chagrin, Dr. Dre signed the contract. M.C. Ren did, too. So did Yella. That he was the sole holdout inspired them all to ask, why didn't he sign it?

The tour continued, and with it, controversy over "Fuck tha Police." Dre was stunned to learn that in August 1989 Milton Aerlich, an assistant director of the FBI, sent Priority a letter that said he understood the song encouraged violence and disrespect for law enforcement. He didn't threaten any action, but opined it was wrong to advocate violence and assault; mentioned "the law enforcement community takes exception to such action"; and claimed N.W.A.'s work was "both discouraging and degrading to these brave, dedicated officers." He did everything, it seemed, but address the issues they'd raised.

Suddenly, Bryan Turner at Priority was nervous. "You kidding? It was the FBI. I'm just a kid from Canada, what do I know?" His lawyers assured him the agency couldn't do anything, so the group's handlers circulated the letter and "the thing was like a nuclear explosion." A number of media outlets leaped on the story, implying it was a free speech issue, but just as many others attacked the group. A headline in an issue of "Focus on the Family Citizen"'s newsletter screamed "Rap Group N.W.A. Says 'Kill Police.'"

Cops down south and in the Midwest faxed each other the lyrics.

Some promoters cancelled tour dates, fearing they'd cause riots (when nothing ever happened at their shows).

Cops in Toledo and Milwaukee wouldn't provide security.

All they wanted to do was grumble about how cops stopped their cars for no reason and made them sit at the curb "just because you're black, dress a certain way, whatever," Yella explained later. "Not all cops are bad," he added, "but a few bad ones make everyone look at police in a bad way." Instead of the one or two complaints they'd expected, the group now saw federal agents in Cincinnati conduct a drug search and ask if they were L.A. gang members using the tour as a front for a crack-selling business. Things got so tense out there that Eazy himself started rocking a bulletproof vest on stage even though audiences consisted mostly of supportive whites. Then promoters asked them to sign an agreement promising to leave "Fuck tha Police" out of their set. By the time they arrived in Detroit for their August 6 show, the 20,000-strong national Fraternal Order of Police was publicly complaining about the song. The group also heard preachers and city officials were working to cancel their show at the Joe Louis Arena. They had to fly in for a press conference and everywhere Dre looked someone was telling him, "Don't do 'Fuck tha Police.'" Hysteria about their lyrics was so intense, they had to meet with the city council before the show. "We sat down with the mayor of Detroit and he told us don't do 'Fuck tha Police,'" Ren remembered. "We're going to jail if we do it." They planned to leave it out of the set, then headed back to their hotel. While waiting until they had to head to the Arena they turned on a TV. The sight of people on the news denouncing the song, and them, inspired them to say, "Right, let's do the song, that'll sell more records,'" said Ren.

That night, they saw cops show in huge numbers. But they also heard the crowd chanting "Fuck the police" all night. They thought, "Fuck it" and said a few lyrics, only to hear two loud booming noises. "Sounded like gunshots and the crowd started running," said Ren. The cops rushed the stage. They all ran backstage. The cops followed, looking for every member. At least fifty of them stormed backstage with badges held high and drawn guns. They put some people up against walls and aimed guns at their heads. Eazy and Dre, meanwhile, kicked open the back door and ran out. "I had it all on video tape," said Ted Demme, a producer for *Yo MTV Raps!* "N.W.A. escapes, no one finds them, and they are arresting all kinds of managers and people." Even Demme wasn't immune. Cops saw him filming, grabbed his video camera, and destroyed the tape. Then some went to the group's hotel and placed them under arrest. But they released them the same night. "They just gave us citations, little tickets, and we left," said Ren. And just like that, the tour ended. But the problems had only begun.

Back home, TV host Fab 5 Freddy had a *Yo MTV Raps!* film crew tour Compton with them. "That's how we sold two million," said Bryan Turner. "White kids in the Valley picked it up and they decided to want to live vicariously through this music." The segment came about after Eazy called Ted Demme to say, "Hey, Ted, my name's Eazy-E. I'm calling from California and we got this video we want y'all to play." When he received it Demme felt "Straight Outta Compton" was the best rap clip he'd ever seen. While showing it to his boss, he had said, "Do you believe these guys? They've got crazy Jheri curls, they're wearing gang stuff like bullet-proof vests. This is unbelievable, we gotta meet these guys." His boss let him set up an interview but added that MTV still couldn't air the video. When host Fab 5 Freddy and the film crew arrived on a flatbed truck for the tour, Dre got into his ball cap and street clothes. As the truck passed people on the street, the producers, standing on the back of the truck, saw people wave. Fab 5 Freddy waved back, only to hear Demme warn, "I wouldn't do that, Fred, that was just a gang sign." In response, Demme recalled, "Freddy hit the deck." The segment finally got N.W.A. onto the influential music channel, and soon MTV started airing Ruthless' clean version of "Express Yourself." "First one we saw on TV," said Ren. "If you look at that video we look crazy as hell. Got our little 'fros and shit."

But it continued to be a rough year. Someone blasted at Cube's middle-class home during a drive-by (trying to get at a neighbor). Eazy learned a Compton rapper he signed on a Friday had been killed two days later. Dre learned his girl Michel'le was robbed at gunpoint for her car and money while traveling to a hairdressing appointment. And he kept thinking about Tyree's murder.

Dre soon distracted himself by helping D.O.C. promote his album. The light-skinned, goateed rapper had by now posed for his album cover, donning his black L.A. Kings ball cap and standing in front of a religious-looking statue. He'd also seen his first single—the "Misdemeanor"-sampling "Funky Enough"—become a hit and inspire talk of him being one of the most skillful and literate rappers on the West Coast. Dre also noted with satisfaction that his follow-up, "The D.O.C. & The Doctor," proved just as popular, reaching number twenty-one on the Top Rap Singles chart. Both helped *No One Can*

Do It Better sell 500,000 copies in a month—impressive at the time—and clock in at number eighty-seven on the Top Rhythm & Blues chart.

Dre was already looking forward to recording his friend's second album the weekend D.O.C. filmed videos for "Tha Formula" and "Beautiful but Deadly." During one eighteen-hour day they filmed scenes of doctors piecing together a Frankenstein. D.O.C. was exhausted when filming wrapped, but stayed on the set to have a few drinks with some of the sexy female extras in the "Formula" video. After joking and flirting a little, the inebriated rapper entered his new Honda Prelude. "I was fuckin' up," he said later. "Doin' shit I had no business doin'." He thought he could make it home but dozed at the wheel, waking up just as the car slammed into the center median on a freeway. He burst through the back window, bounced on hard concrete, crashed face first into a tree, and later woke up in a hospital.

Dre rushed to his bedside. D.O.C.'s mom was there, too, crying and saying it'd be all right. Eazy and Michel'le also consoled him. And Dre noticed a new bodyguard, a guy named Suge, show up, too. Everyone was relieved when doctors reported he hadn't broken any bones. But Dre kept facing D.O.C.'s smashed and cut-up face. "Dre told me the only way they recognized me at the hospital was because of my haircut," D.O.C. recalled. A day after filming a video in which doctors worked on someone, D.O.C. underwent reconstructive surgery on his face. "That's some crazy shit for real," he said. During the next three weeks, he'd spend twenty-one hours under the knife. But while his face was repaired, his larynx was crushed, turning his once smooth voice into a harsh rasp. To boost his self-esteem, a high-ranking executive at Elektra, distributing his album with Ruthless, later urged him to record another record. Jerry Heller and Eazy-E also tried to show support. But Dre advised against it. "D.O.C., them motherfuckers call you the greatest ever and I'd go out like that." D.O.C. didn't want to hear this but Dre continued. "You got a really good thing going up here. You're writing all these songs that are worth a lot of money. Keep your ass up in here and keep working until you figure out what the fuck you want to do."

As if this weren't bad enough, the group seemed to be falling apart. Writer Allan S. Gordon remembers Cube's problem with Jerry Heller beginning when Cube's solo album was next on the schedule. Midway through recording a song, said Gordon, Heller arrived and said Ruthless would next release the Above the Law album. (Above the Law was another group signed to Ruthless.) And after this, Cube could write another Eazy-E album, then one for N.W.A. before releasing his own work. At the time, Gordon continued, Cube wasn't under contract, so he sat back and reflected on what he'd earned for his work with N.W.A. ("which was about $75,000 maximum," Gordon added). Since he was closest to Dre—he'd known him before N.W.A.—he told him he was unhappy with his arrangement with the group. Then he told M.C. Ren, "Nigga, we need to get more money." And Ren joined him in asking Eazy, "Why they getting more than us?" Eazy had a quick answer. "'Cause they doing the beats."

"But why Yella?"

He helped Dre.

"But he ain't doing what we doing!"

Eazy said they each handled one job, rapping, while they multi-tasked.

Just as quickly, Eazy alienated Cube by refusing to allow the group to appear on an episode of Jesse Jackson's new talk show, *Voices of America*, that would discuss hip-hop. Cube had already told radio DJs in the Bay Area the next N.W.A. album would include a few more inspiring messages for black listeners and wanted to show the community they were on their side. But Ruthless vetoed the idea since they wouldn't be paid. "There's no way on this planet that N.W.A. shouldn't have been on that show," Cube said later.

Then Cube reflected on how he'd written ten of thirteen songs on *Straight Outta Compton*, including every word on "Dope Man," "8 Ball," and Dre's solo single, "Express Yourself." He had also written lyrics for *Eazy Duz It*. "This significant contribution to over three million records sold has so far earned Ice Cube $32,000," *SPIN* reported. And $23,000 of that came from their tour (which earned $650,000, *SPIN* added, "of which manager Jerry Heller took $130,000").

In his old room at his mom's place, Cube decided he could use a raise. The group's publicist, Pat Charbonet, lent a sympathetic ear and urged him to get a lawyer. "They got mad when I did that," said Cube. "Jerry told me that lawyers were made to cause trouble. But lawyers only cause trouble if there's trouble to cause." When his attorney, Michael Ashburn, approached Ruthless,

Ashburn said, they gave him nothing but a statement showing Cube had been advanced $32,700. "It was like Jerry Heller didn't care whether Ice Cube, someone who unarguably had made a major contribution to the group, left or stayed," Ashburn told *SPIN*. Cube wanted to keep recording with N.W.A.— noting he had no personal problems, "not even with Eazy or anybody in the group"—but they had reached an impasse, his lawyer explained. "He's owed at least another $120,000, plus his publishing royalties, which he hasn't received a cent on so far."

Though jolted by Tyree's murder and D.O.C.'s accident, Dre convened N.W.A. in his new million-dollar home in Calabasas. The touring and interviews were all good, but mostly he was impatient to get back to his music, where the others expected him to be the field general. Usually they hung out, drank, smoked, and watched TV before heading to the studio in Dre's upstairs bedroom. But one day, while Ren, Yella, and Eazy went up, Cube didn't move. Dre said they were gonna start now but Cube said he'd sit this one out and watch TV. "So I was like, 'Aw shit.' I knew something was going on."

Dre soon received a call from Cube. If two albums sold millions, and their tour sold out arenas, he wanted more money, royalties, merchandising, publishing. After noting Dre's achievements, he then asked, "Is your money right for sure?"

"Nah, man, my shit is kinda shaky, too."

They spoke for hours, then Cube said, "I'm about to go to New York, man, to do my motherfucking record. I'm about to leave the group. I just can't handle it."

"You crazy," Dre said. "Don't do that."

"Man, I got to go. . . . Well, let's just have a meeting, man, no Jerry Heller, just us five. Let's try to get this shit straight."

Dre sighed. "Alright, when you wanna have it?"

"Let's have it tomorrow, man, up at the studio." Dre however didn't show— no one else did, either—so Ice Cube left the group. "I was broke before I jumped in that shit, so it wasn't hard to walk away," he explained. "I preferred it that way." Once he left, Yella recalled, "we all talked about him, even Dre."

Cube moved on, signing a solo deal with Priority and working with Public Enemy's Chuck D and producer Hank Shocklee in Manhattan. In the studio, they gave him more freedom, let him include a few political themes, and quickly reached for some Parliament and Steve Arrington samples. But then, Dre saw *SPIN* quote Jerry Heller saying Cube left because of his ego. "He was jealous because not only is Eazy a key member of N.W.A. with a successful solo career, he's also the president of his own record company," the quote read. "Eazy E is a major star and a successful businessman. Ice Cube isn't."

At the same time, Dre saw Frank Owen of *SPIN* claim Heller told him Cube also had publicist Pat Charbonet urging him to go solo. Cube and Charbonet both denied this and what could have been a quiet, amicable split suddenly became a public feud. "Jerry Heller lives in a half-million-dollar house in West Lake, and I'm still living at home with my mother," Cube now told *SPIN*. "Jerry's driving a Corvette and a Mercedes Benz and I've got a Suzuki Sidekick." He claimed Jerry was making all the money when he had "no creative input into the group; he just makes all the fucked-up decisions and gets all the fucking money."

The *SPIN* article went from calling N.W.A. "the new Sex Pistols" to claiming they were "Niggers with Activators" who lost their soul and intelligence when Cube left. "The media myth that U.S. crime is black is peddled daily in newsprint and nightly on the networks," Owen added. "Sadly, it's a myth that N.W.A. do little to dispel."

N.W.A. had just lost its main spokesman, its lyrical center, and the songs he'd written for an album-in-progress. But Dre struggled to save face by claiming his production techniques, and not Cube's talent, made Cube a star. "You could've grabbed anybody off the street that could rhyme and could've been a fuckin' Ice Cube." He claimed Cube sounded good only because he, Dre, kept having him record verses a line at a time. "And when you hear it back? It sounds like they just flowed all the way through. So I could'a just did that shit with anybody."

Dre continued making similar claims even as Cube's debut, *AmeriKKKa's Most Wanted*, arrived in stores May 16, 1990, went gold in ten days, and quickly sold a million copies in two months, without a video or lead single. Then Dre saw the influential rap magazine *The Source* give Cube's debut a rare Five Mic rating, naming it an all-time classic. Privately, Dre understood why Cube had left. "He wanted to do his own thing," he said calmly. "He felt

like he wasn't being treated right—and he wasn't—so he said, 'fuck it.' He
got out." But N.W.A. had an image to protect, especially with music magazines claiming they'd fall off, they'd lost any political relevance they may have
possessed, and might be, as Cube claimed, softies letting themselves be controlled by a white manager. This was the mood when Dre visited Priority one
day, and heard Bryan Turner invite the group into his office. "I want you all
to hear this song."

Titled "Jackin' for Beats," Cube wanted to include it on his upcoming
December 1990 EP, *Kill At Will*. In horror, N.W.A. heard him start the song
by yelling, "Gimme that beat, fool," and jeering them over their unreleased
"Prelude" (which would introduce their next full-length album). The others
bellowed and objected. "Fuck that," Dre said. "He can't use our beat. This
man ain't gonna use our beat and be clowning us. If this nigga uses our beat,
we ain't fuckin' with you." Turner told Cube they wouldn't let him use the
track, and Dre tried to put Cube's departure behind him.

◆ ◆ ◆

As Ruthless' house producer, he was expected to work with the group Above
the Law, musician Jimmy Z., and white female rapper, Tairrie B. Above the
Law member Hutch had already started producing their funk-filled debut,
so between shows on his tour, Dre heard tapes of songs in progress. Ruthless
would credit him as producer, though Ren recalled, "Hutch did a lot of that
before Dre even came and sat down."

Dre also didn't mind the Jimmy Z project since Z was a musician. In the
studio, he programmed a pretty flat drum machine beat, recorded Z's riffs,
then tried to say a few corny raps ("The funky funky flute is just what Jimmy
gave ya"). But he wasn't that enthused about the Tairrie B. project, D.O.C.
recalled.

A curvy blonde, Tairrie was a break-dancer and graffiti enthusiast who'd
met one of Eazy's employees at a N.W.A. concert, then brought her demo,
a cover of Jimi Hendrix's "Foxy Lady," to the studio. She was leaving when
someone asked, "Do you want a record deal?" Originally, Dre was to produce
while Cube wrote lyrics, but with Cube gone, Tairrie wanted to write her

own songs. Another plan called for N.W.A. to produce the album closer, "I Ain't Your Bitch," and spend most of it calling her names before she fired back and said, "I ain't your bitch and here's why, blah blah blah."

Dre was ready to produce this song and others when she thought, "Fuck that." With a Led Zeppelin sample as backdrop, she spent her eight-minute "Ruthless Bitch" rapping that she *was* a bitch, calling N.W.A. out, and saying, "Go back to wearing sequins, 'cause you look like a faggot." Dre apparently didn't like the song or lyric, she said, so he confronted her during the 1990 Grammy Awards. That night, Dick Clark, New Kids on the Block, and Janet Jackson were all on hand to give or receive awards. Tairrie was, too, along with with her female manager and DJ. Her album wouldn't be released for another three months, but Dre got in their faces and started talking shit, she said. She talked some, too, thinking "he wouldn't do anything because we were at the Grammy's but he was drunk and fucked up and hit me right in the mouth. Full on." When she didn't fall, she added, he then socked her in the eye. "The police broke it up," she continued, and within minutes, in a precinct down-town, she told the cops, "You know that band that sings 'Fuck tha Police'? N.W.A.? Well, Dr. Dre just did this to me."

Within twenty-four hours, however, she dropped the charges, saying that someone advised her to do that if she wanted her record to come out. "I was stupid and didn't really have good advice." She returned to the studio to rap about being slugged at the Grammys, she filmed videos for "Murder She Wrote" and "Swingin' Wit T," then left the label.

The others already knew how drinking affected Dre and kept quiet. But this incident was public, and even more embarrassing than Cube telling reporters they posed as tough black men but let a little white man take their money and boss them around.

Morale was low, and Dre was distracted by the birth of his son Marcel (with Michel'le). He was thinking about Cube's departure and his own arrangement with Ruthless. He was also considering the changes he'd seen in Eazy. His friend seemed to be believing his press clippings and forgetting who produced the platinum-selling albums that made Ruthless so big Heller once bragged, "We've got the makings of a company that's going to be to the nineties what Berry Gordy's Motown was to the sixties."

Though Cube helped, too, he saw Eazy claim Cube's departure just meant "we get more money." He also saw Eazy not even comment on Cube's claim of being underpaid. "On to the next subject." Then he saw Heller quoted as saying he had to teach Eazy how to open a checking account at a bank (after they received a six-figure check from Atlantic for the J.J. Fad *Supersonic* album Dre produced). Everything about Ruthless now seemed to be about Eazy and Jerry, he felt. Even so, he kept working with N.W.A., and struggled to find inspiration while creating their stopgap EP, *100 Miles and Runnin'*.

He wound up imitating Public Enemy on the title track by stacking break beats onto each other and adding noises and horns that evoked the blaring clarinet on "Rebel Without a Pause." With Cube gone, they were reduced to borrowing a plot from a stock Tom Selleck thriller, *An Innocent Man*, and writing about running from the FBI. The song found M.C. Ren saying the FBI could kiss his black ass and there'd be no peace since "police and little black niggas don't mix." Dre said he was a confused "nigga with nuthin' to lose" and soon insulted Cube. "Started with five and, yo, one couldn't take it," he said. "So now there's four 'cause the fifth couldn't make it." Soon he told a reporter, "It only deals with what's going on" despite the fact that he now lived far from the ghetto ("I've got a million dollars, house, car," he said during the same period), and the FBI had no interest in them.

During another session, they created "Just Don't Bite It," which found Ren harping about a woman that gave lousy fellatio. For its chorus, Dre had a sample shout, "It's the world's biggest dick," and the others chant, "Don't matter, just don't bite it." They then tried a "Fuck tha Police" sequel, "Sa Prize," that found Dre adding one or two little noises to the original track. "Fuck the motherfucking police!" he shouted. "They don't want peace, they want a nigga deceased." He tried to show the magazine writers N.W.A. hadn't lost anything, and said the cops were like the Klan; black cops were "house niggaz"; the government shipped cocaine to the hood; and armed brothers would fight back. "You got a gat, I got a gat, so whassup with that." But his heart was more into "Real Niggaz," a simpler track with loping piano and more discussion of Cube's departure. Amid attacks on imitators, Ren admitted their self esteem was shaken. "They played out, that's what niggaz were chanting/One nigga left and they said we ain't happening." By song's end, however, Dre said he was glad Cube left. "We started out with too much cargo," he claimed. "So I'm glad we got rid of Benedict Arnold." That Cube actually left the group didn't matter. Dre quickly joined the others in denouncing Cube again on their skit "Benedict Arnold," this time saying, "When we see your ass, we're gonna cut your hair off and fuck you with a broomstick."

Though Dre was growing unhappy with his situation with Ruthless, he still helped N.W.A. promote the new EP with a rare October 1990 interview with Fox Television's *Pump It Up*. He agreed to the interview since he was cool with hostess Sista Dee (whose vocals as part of the duo Body & Soul appeared near his own on the socially conscious single, "We're All in the Same Gang"). But when the segment aired, he was furious. As their interview was winding down, instead of cool final words that would draw fans to their post-Cube work, viewers inexplicably saw footage of Cube on the set of a movie called *Boyz N the Hood*. "And that nigga, outspoken like he was, said 'I got all these suckers a hundred miles and runnin',' " Ren recalled. The cameraman turned his lens on the hostess, who said, "Sista Dee, always in the middle of controversy right here on *Pump It Up*.' " Dre felt she'd orchestrated this to boost ratings. Dee told Eazy it wasn't her fault; a producer did it on his own. But one December night, Dre crossed a crowded nightclub to confront her.

Dre saw Dee at a party for Def Jam artists No-Face and Bitches with Problems in a Santa Monica nightclub. It was an industry party, winding down, and Dee stood against a wall, near a record promoter and MTV host Ed Lover. Dre grabbed her shirtfront. The promoter tried to pry his hands from her shirt; one of Dre's new pals slammed a fist into the guy's jaw, knocking him to the floor. Dre, Dee later said, yanked her hair and ear and smashed her face into a brick wall. According to Dee, he released her and she crawled to the stairway and tried to stand but he grabbed her again and tried to send her down the stairs. She held on as he lost his balance. She tried to kneel, to become harder to lift, but he tried nudging her with his foot "because I think then somebody might have grabbed him," she said.

She darted into the ladies' room. He staggered behind her. A woman up ahead screamed. He burst into the room, grabbed Dee's hair again, and punched her head, she recalled. Then he shoved her to the front of the room. "I just duck down and . . . take my ass whipping, you know what I mean?" Eventually, someone pulled him off and helped him escape.

Soon after the incident, a *Rolling Stone* reporter heard Dre say, "I was in the wrong, but it's not like I broke the bitch's arm." Yet in public, once Dee pressed criminal charges for assault and battery in February 1991 and filed a $22.7 million lawsuit against him, he began to issue a string of vehement denials even as Dee made sure everyone knew, "There's a lot of women that he beat up, a lot that he smacked around. But I'm the one that fucking pressed charges. Nobody else did. Now he's got a record."

Dre even denied it during an interview with *SPIN*, when Eazy said, in front of him, "You lying. You beat the shit out of her."

"I was drunk," he said that night.

When the media reported on the attack, Dre's image took a beating as brutal as the one he gave Barnes. A number of rap groups were already denouncing N.W.A. and other gangsta rap acts, accusing them of being non-skilled posers sullying the genre with primitive lyrics. Now, the goodwill Dre managed to accumulate, by speaking out against whites and the cops and saying things many of his poor black fans couldn't, evaporated. Rappers lined up to denounce him. *The Source*, which usually offered glowing praise, now quoted Bronx rapper Tim Dog (of "Fuck Compton" fame) calling Dre a "pussy" and challenging him to "step to a nigga like 'D.' Tim D-O-G so I can beat up on his ass like that." At the same time however, the attack allowed Dre to step into a menacing new image as a loose cannon and, for a time, caused everyone to finally forget the days when he and Yella wore shoulder-padded blazers, eyeliner, and Jheri-curls, and offered the Cru's female listeners wine, candlelight, and love and affection. With criticism reaching a fever pitch and female rap fans viewing him as nothing less than a brute, Dre was about to enter another shocking phase of his life and career. And it all started because his pal D.O.C., drinking just as heavily, said he and a friend were forming their own record company.

As distant as Dre had been from N.W.A. in 1990, he was even more removed when they start recording their next album during the first months of 1991. Now that *100 Miles and Runnin'* has sold over 500,000 copies, their confidence is back. "We could do this shit," Ren says. "We could keep on rolling." Dre keeps recording *Efil4Zaggin* (*Niggaz4life* backwards) but it's a real drag. Where *Straight Outta Compton* felt like a party, sitting around with brew, rhyme books, and great ideas, *Efil4Zaggin* finds them struggling to prove they can endure without Cube.

At the board, Dre starts moving past drum loops and drum machines, especially since other rappers face multimillion-dollar lawsuits for their own use of old songs. As he gathers musicians to cover grooves from old funk records, the break beats of *Straight Outta Compton* give way to live playing that evokes old Sugarhill, and his mom's record collection. But he's thinking, as always these days, about money. "Some people had money, some didn't," says D.O.C.

Between takes of songs, Dre hears his pal D.O.C. say he's started a new company. After his crash D.O.C.'s friend Marion Knight, nicknamed Suge, kept visiting the hospital. Like Dre, Knight urged D.O.C. to keep writing songs for N.W.A., but also wanted to keep working on their own label, Funky Enough. Once he received a demo from his old friend Mario Johnson, D.O.C. flew him from Texas to his home in Agoura Hills, and passed the tape to Knight, who ran Funky Enough from an impressive Beverly Hills suite. Two months after signing a contract, Johnson, nicknamed Chocolate, and band mate Tee Low delivered a finished album. But everything changed after Vanilla Ice's debut, *To the Extreme*, arrived in stores. With Ice's video for "Ice Ice Baby" on BET, Chocolate told Suge he'd been underpaid for his work on Vanilla Ice's album. Suge and a few friends visited Ice's hotel room but couldn't resolve the issue so Suge huddled with Dick Griffey, an older friend who ran Solar Sound of Los Angeles Records.

Griffey, whose label enjoyed a successful run with groups like The Whispers, Shalamar, and Lakeside during the 1980s, suggested a good attorney in New York. They sued EMI, which was Vanilla Ice's label and the case was eventually settled out of court. Now, Suge wants to make a few changes at the label and alleviate D.O.C.'s own pain over having sold Eazy publishing rights to a few songs for some jewelry. "Don't worry about it," Knight told him. "We'll handle it." Talk of more money interests Dre, so during breaks in recording, D.O.C. adds, "If Eazy's fucking me then he's probably doing it to you, too."

He says this just when Dre sees Eazy speaking with DJ Quik, another Compton producer who plays live music, and Quik's group The Penthouse Players Click. "Dre ain't his main man anymore," a Ruthless employee explains. While it's the same routine Eazy pulled to lure him from the Cru, Dre continues to listen when Suge joins the choir. Before long, Dre says, "Fuck Jerry. Fuck motherfucking Eazy!"

Knight's and D.O.C.'s talk touches on issues near and dear to Dre's heart: creative control, freedom, and of course more money for Dr. Dre. Dre is also eager to use his production process to create new stars and platinum-selling albums for his own company, and the lion's share of profits. He also sees how quickly they move and efficiently run their company. Already they have a suite in Beverly Hills. "While you checkin' the D.O.C.'s shit, check on my shit, too," he tells Knight.

At Solar, Suge informs Griffey other song-writing clients have gone unpaid for big-selling work. The next thing Dre knows, Suge and D.O.C. deliver him to Griffey's doorstep, where he offers his version of events. "At that time I was owed money but they weren't paying it, you know what I'm saying?" Griffey seems like a professional enough person, but Dre's cautious about making any changes. His house, his cars, everything he has comes from Ruthless. "How can we be assured we'll get paid in the future?" he asks.

"Look, Dre," Griffey replies, "if you can make the records the way you make records, I'll show you how to start a company. You won't have to worry about people paying you. You'll have a company you own and control." That's all he needs to hear. He agrees to join D.O.C., Griffey, and Suge as a partner in a new label. Griffey will deal with major labels. D.O.C. will help with lyrics and artists. Suge, quiet, and helpful, will "handle the day to day business, dealing with the artists, dealing with distributors, and record companies, what have you." Dre himself will stay in the studio, pushing buttons and making records. But before this can happen, they have to resolve things with Ruthless. "Why don't you guys go talk to Eazy and see if you can make a deal where Dre continues to produce Eazy for Ruthless, to produce N.W.A. and other acts?" Griffey asks.

Dre stays as quiet as he did while nursing a broken collarbone during his youth. As Suge has skilled attorneys comb through his and Michel'le's contracts, in the studio he shows no sign of feeling estranged. He keeps everything to himself: his anger over Cube claiming Eazy and the group are pawns of Jerry Heller; media reports about his attack on Barnes; and Eazy suddenly wanting to write more songs like "Automobile" and "I Want to Fuck You," so as to more deeply burrow into song-writing monies. While greatly dissatisfied with the economics of the group, Dre keeps working on some of his most challenging music to date. He starts "Prelude" by saying, "The motherfucking saga continues . . ." He rails against cops on "Real Niggaz Don't Die." "Niggaz4Life" explains why he uses shock value lyrics: they pay more in a week than a doctor earns in a year. It's better than crime, which would lead to prison. "And then I get called a nigga anyway/Broke as a motherfucker and locked away."

He works a Cube insult into "Always Into Something," claiming M.C. Ren entered his Benz one morning and said, "Dre, I was speakin' to the bitch O'Shea." But he also unveils a darker side. "To Kill a Hooker" finds him claiming he tied a woman to a bed and killed her, since she didn't have his money. "Findum Fuckum & Flee" claims he'll flirt with a woman in front of her man, and if she backtalks, "I smack the bitch up and shoot the nigga that's with her." "Approach to Danger" is dreary, death-obsessed, and filled with descriptions of murder, poor people, dead bodies, a stroll through a graveyard, and loading guns. He sounds most honest on "The Dayz of Way-back," N.W.A.'s equivalent of the Beatles' era-ending "Something." Over a melancholic funk riff, nonverbal shorthand for how sad Dre feels about greed ruining this crew for good, he raps about how Compton's become too vio-lent. Everyone's killing, stealing, or dealing, and the concept of black unity is dead, he feels. Now, he explains, "Your best friend is your worst friend." The ghetto's a "fuckin' survival test." If listeners want to shoot a gat, "That's 'cause you livin' in the Dayz of Wayback."

By March 1991, the new N.W.A. album's done. It's the most ambitious thing Dre's ever created. Alongside the everyday break beats, he's had a band play some funk. He's created R&B tracks for Eazy to sing over. He's included rock guitar on "Real Niggaz Don't Die." And he's openly described a few regrets and disappointments, and transcended his one-note gangsta image.

◆ ◆ ◆

In Knight, Dre has seemingly found another role model. Dre's always thought of himself as a big guy—especially after seeing his videos and reading descriptions of himself in magazines—but Knight is huge compared to him. He stands over six feet four inches tall, and is a well-muscled three hundred plus pounds. He's a carefree weightlifter with a past in semipro football and security for Uncle Jam's Army parties until someone crosses the line. Originally, he worked at Ruthless as a security guard, Heller recalls. Heller thought him charming and gracious. Eazy, meanwhile, immediately sensed "he was going to be a problem." Dre, however, sees someone cool, someone who won't back down from Ruthless' tough talk and threats. The youngest of three children, raised by two parents in working-class Compton, Knight has just as many ties to the street as Eazy, as many of his friends banged with the famed Treetop Pirus, one of the oldest Blood sets. Knight himself could more than hold his own. In November 1987, while playing ball at the University of Nevada at Las Vegas, he was arrested for grand larceny auto, carrying a concealed weapon, use of a deadly weapon, attempted murder, and battery with a deadly weapon. The charges were all dismissed but according to media reports he was arrested again on December 14, 1990, for battery with a deadly weapon.

In February 1991, Dre's working on *Efil4Zaggin*, setting aside less than perfect songs, when the first salvo in what looks to be a long battle is fired. Suge arrives at Ruthless and tells Eazy and Heller, "You know who I am? I'm Dre's manager." He requests royalty payments for Dre, D.O.C., and Michel'le then keeps dropping by, one executive claims, with gangbangers and "a huge gun sticking out of his ass pocket." Another employee claims Suge is phoning in threats and, in a sworn affidavit, remembers Suge making him write an apology to Michel'le. A third resigns, fearing people might harm his wife and kid.

Ruthless tries the usual intimidation tactics—hiring two armed weightlifters to patrol the office—but, according to an unnamed employee, "Suge makes them get on they hands and knees, walk around like a dog, you know?"

It's something out of the recent Warren Beatty gangster movie, *Bugsy*, but, Dre feels, probably necessary, as it will clear the way for him do what he has to do.

With N.W.A. poised to achieve its greatest success, Dre tells Ren, "Somebody I know wanna holler at us because we ain't getting paid right." Dre figures he and Ren—with D.O.C. writing for him—can continue the string of million-selling albums, keep money rolling in, and also allow Ren to earn more. Ren accompanies Dre to Solar and listens to others explain what they can do for his career, but seems skeptical. "From what I saw, one nigga trying to get niggas to come over with him," says Ren. He had by now received more money. He wants more, of course—who wouldn't?—but immediately thinks, "Fuck this. This is a worse situation." He stays with Eazy and Ruthless.

Dre also tells Yella he's out, and invites him to the new label. Yella says he'll get back to him but never does. Eazy didn't cheat him or anyone, he feels, and Dre shouldn't be complaining. "Put it like this: You living in a million-dollar house; Eazy's living in a two-million-dollar house. How can he be cheating you if you living in a million-dollar house?" Eazy earns more because, as label owner, he has many other acts generating income, Yella feels. "The reason behind the breakup was simple," he believes. "Egos started getting in the way. N.W.A. started making too much money, so everyone wanted more." Dre leaves N.W.A. just as workmen arrive to build stage props for their tour.

His next move, surprisingly, is to meet Ice Cube for lunch. They discuss collaborating on a few cuts for Cube's second album, *Death Certificate*, but then Dre changes his mind. "I found out about that song," he says. It's called "No Vaseline," and calls N.W.A. homos and pawns of Jerry Heller, but it won't be in stores until later that year.

So Dre spends his days in Griffey's modern, well-appointed Solar Records Building in Hollywood, where Griffey is currently in talks with Sony about Dre creating a soundtrack for its grim undercover cop film, *Deep Cover*. Suddenly, Dre's excited about work again. There exists the possibility of earning huge sums of money. Griffey tells Sony that Dre's working on the album can happen now that he won't record for Ruthless anymore. But with Ruthless withholding payments, he adds, Dre's in danger of losing everything, and needs money. Dre is happy beyond belief when Sony offers to pay a cool million for some music publishing rights. But just as quickly, he remembers that, personal feelings aside, he's still under contract to Ruthless.

In April, Eazy claims, Dre calls Ruthless. He's surprised to hear from the recalcitrant producer but agrees to meet him at the Solar Building to discuss their differences. Eazy claims he arrives without security and Dre isn't there. But Knight is, and tells the five-foot-five-inch label head his artists Above the Law, Michel'le, Kokane, The D.O.C., and Dre all want to leave Ruthless. "I knew that they wanted me to sign releases," Eazy says, but other Ruthless execs urged him not to. But as the meeting continues, Eazy claims, Suge says he's holding Jerry hostage in a van. "Then he told me he knew where my mother lived." Eazy adds that two men holding lead pipes entered the room and that when contracts were slid across the table he reached for a pen. "I figured I'd either sign the papers, get my ass kicked, or fight them." Dre is thrilled. His new handlers fax copies of the release to Sony. But within twenty-four hours, he learns Ruthless' lawyers have filed a state court action to invalidate the release. Ruthless also has a few RICO (Racketeer-Influenced Corrupt Organization) attorneys preparing another $248-million lawsuit against him, Knight, and others. His image takes another beating when Eazy tells a reporter, "Dre now works for a bodyguard that used to work for him for, like, seventy-five dollars a night."

Dre couldn't help but feel optimistic when he arrived at the Solar Building to work on the *Deep Cover* project. Around him everyone stayed busy. In one studio, Chocolate recorded with singers Paradise and Lydia Harris (whose imprisoned husband, Michael, had invested $1.5 million into the label). In others, Rhythm D and Unknown laid down tracks. And in the halls even more eager young talents hoped to work with them, including his stepbrother Little Warren, who kept pitching his group 213. "They were handlin' business, getting everything going," Chocolate recalled. "They had the right producer, the right writers, and the talent." With Sony sending $500,000 for some publishing rights, Dre viewed Suge as nothing less than a godsend. He was not only his "fifty-fifty" partner, "we like brothers and shit."

Meanwhile, Eazy's claims were forgotten by most of Dre's fans, so Dre's image remained that of the rap industry's most consistently successful producer. If anything, striking out on his own inspired some reporters to hint he was now a positive symbol of black advancement. But some would begrudge him his success, he felt. Though free to enter a studio and devote all of his energy to creating a worthy followup to *Efil4Zaggin*, he sat at the massive mix board, faced the usual self-doubts and perfectionist thoughts, and considered how some people were even now predicting he'd fail.

Publicly more successful than ever, Dre nevertheless remembered how fans and reporters claimed N.W.A. couldn't survive once Cube moved on. *100 Miles and Running* should have proven them all wrong, but instead gossips moved on to claiming Dre couldn't make it without N.W.A. But once black bass player Colin Wolfe set up his acoustic Clevinger Jr., Dre pushed these thoughts aside and listened to Wolfe improvise. Wolfe had been playing for thirteen years, and after seeing him perform a bass solo onstage at L.A.'s China Club, Dre hired him to tour with Michel'le. Now, in the studio, a jazzy four-note progression caught his ear. "Wait a minute. Keep playin' that."

After sampling Wolfe's melody, he added a beat like the one on Sly & the Family Stone's "Sing a Simple Song," a piercing piano note, and a plaintive sample from The Undisputed Truth's 1975 cover of "(I Know) I'm Losing You" (the phrase "I can feel it"). Listening to it over and over, he liked how it sounded like nothing he'd done before. It had the sort of jazz edge popular on the East Coast but was also tougher.

Before he could get to the lyrics, however, he decided a break was in order. He arranged a bachelor party for his friend L.A. Dre, who had played keyboards on earlier productions.

While setting it up in May 1991 his stepbrother Little Warren asked to attend. Where Dre spent a childhood avoiding gangs, Warren, out in Long Beach, hung with members of the Insane Rolling 20 Crips. But since 1988, he'd been shopping demos of 213, which included rapper Calvin ("Snoop") Broadus and singer Nate Dogg, who usually sang in a church. Though no label would sign them, he kept recording on old equipment, calling himself Warren G, and passing Dre some shitty demos. Even so, Dre told Warren he could come to the party.

Midway through it, the music stopped. No one rushed to put another record on, so Warren slipped a tape into the player. Dre saw people dance and nod along to this song. They started asking who made the tape. He walked over and repeated the question. "Dre, this is me, Snoop, and Nate," Warren replied. "This is what I've been trying to tell you about!"

People invited Dre to have another drink, but he sat and analyzed the tape. "Check this out," he finally said. "Ya'll niggas come to the studio Monday." Grabbing a slip of paper and a pen, he wrote down the telephone number. He was surprised to hear from Warren before their meeting. "Dre, I got Snoop on the phone, man," Warren told him. "He don't believe that you want us to come up there!"

"This Dre," he said, taking the phone. "That shit was dope."

Bright and early Monday morning, Dre sat at a huge desk in a corner office at the Solar Building. The receptionist announced Warren and Snoop were there. Dre noted how nervous Snoop was. Born Calvin Cordazar Broadus on October 20, 1971, Snoop was also from 21st Street in Long Beach. He grew up enjoying old R&B, soul, and funk and was the class clown during junior high. He tried to play football and basketball, and worked an after-school job before drifting into petty drug sales with pals in the Rolling 20s. But his new career choice landed him in jail about four times between 1989 and 1991. Now, he was "a full-time rapper" whose style evoked Slick Rick's manner of "rhymin'-with-a-singing-jingle." He was also someone who frequently considered how, of twenty-eight friends from his football days, twelve were killed, seven were in the pen, and three were on crack.

Dre relaxed him with some small talk, then leaned over the desk and asked to hear a freestyle. Snoop played to Dre's ego—calling him number one, listing titles of hit productions—so Dre smiled. "You all come down to the studio tomorrow morning at eight o'clock," he told Warren. "I got something I'd like to use you on."

Within days, he had Snoop crash at his house (since he lived far away and didn't have a ride). The next morning, Dre had yet to write lyrics. D.O.C. couldn't make it to the studio. The phone kept ringing and people kept saying they needed this song. Ninety minutes before the session Dre told Snoop he was heading to the gym. He gave him a loose concept: Start the lyric with the words, "Tonight's the night I get in some shit. Deep cover on the incognito tip." When he got back, he was pleased to see Snoop had written about his final arrest for drug peddling. Dre made the song a duet, included references to the movie's theme (killing an undercover cop), and signed Snoop to his new label. Then he asked Snoop's 213 singer, Nate Dogg, "You wanna sign?"

Nate said, "What? Is you crazy? Yeah."

. . .

On June 15, 1991, Dre was shocked to hear *Efil4Zaggin* debuted at number two on *Billboard*'s Top Pop Albums chart, but was also relieved since it silenced gossip in local industry circles about the Dee Barnes incident, Eazy's claim of coercion, and the fact that Dre now had some Crips and Bloods hanging around. But when it superseded Paula Abdul's *Spellbound* at number one a week later, June 22, it inspired negative press of another sort. As expected, reviews of the album itself were mixed. *Rolling Stone*, for instance, felt it found N.W.A. "with less to prove but also with less to say." It praised Dre's experimentation ("from an ominous, Public Enemy–style siren to quick-lipped Jamaican patter and R&B howling"), but felt "the rest is so hateful toward women, and in such a pathetic and sleazy manner, that it's simply tiresome."

Dre sensed many of these critics wanted to stop his brand of gangster rap. But when they couldn't, when they saw it reach number one, they went from insulting the music to attacking the audience. *Time* quoted a Tower Records store manager in affluent Woodland Hills as saying, "T.B.W.A.s, that's who's buying N.W.A.'s album. Teenage boys with attitude." And these were "rebels without a clue."

Billboard editor Timothy White felt *Efil* offered white teens "danger at a safe distance." Jon Shector, editor-in-chief of *The Source*, claimed "most of the black community doesn't like them. There's a lot of positive, intelligent rap out there and N.W.A. is negative to the extreme." Yet despite this, Shecter devoted a full page in *The Source* to reporting on *Efil*'s success and also praised Dre's production abilities. "High Powered Productions—Dr. Dre and Yella— is the most consistently exciting production squad in the industry today," he wrote. Dre's "clean, bold sounds," crisp highs, "earth-shaking" lows, live instruments, and "perfect samples," represented how "real rap is supposed to sound. You can't front on it." But others came out of the woodwork to complain about their final work. Even singer Sinead O'Connor got in on the act, calling their attitudes "increasingly dangerous. The way they deal with women in their songs is pathetic."

In the past, Dre might have cared about these reviews. But he was focused on the next glorious phase of his life and career. Negative articles wouldn't change the fact that his production sent *Efil4Zaggin* to the top without radio play or videos. So he focused on *Deep Cover* and on creating his Sony followup, *The Chronic*. "Dre didn't really have no money," Snoop recalled, but he was happy. Griffey owned the studio, so he didn't have to worry about recording costs. He had rappers re-record verses or sing parts until they were flawless. Working in the middle of Hollywood, on some of the same equipment Shalamar, Lakeside, and The Whispers once used for their own hits, Dre relished the fact that he was, at long last, his own boss.

But Eazy wasn't happy about his April meeting, so on August 23, the diminutive label owner sued Sony, Marion Knight, Solar Records, and Dre. "*The Chronic* was going to be a Sony release but not until we sued did they take it off the release schedule," said Ruthless' Michael Klein. " Then [Sony] said, 'This is too deep for us, and we're going to have problems if we go ahead.'"

That quickly, Dre no longer had a deal. Even worse, Suge allegedly edged new mentor Dick Griffey out of the picture. "We didn't know exactly where to go," D.O.C. recalled. "To be totally honest with you, I had to talk Dre into doing his own shit. He was all we had, you know. It was either him or the fucked-up voice, and the fucked-up voice wasn't happening."

Dre, meanwhile, felt Snoop should be the first act. But everyone kept telling him, "Yo, man, you got the name, you coming off the whole N.W.A. thing." They said he'd be the perfect person to draw customers to the label. He told himself he could record an album-length commercial for the label. "I'm figuring, everybody that's on my album is gonna get crazy juice," he explained.

At the same time, money was scarce. The unfinished album had swallowed the $500,000 Sony gave him in April for publishing rights. He had hours of great material on tape but couldn't release anything. "I went to a lot of record companies," he explained, "tried even to get a little production work to pay for rent and shoes, but nobody wanted to take a chance on me because of all that legal shit, all the cease-and-desist letters. Ruthless did anything and everything they could to fuck me up, and I have hate for everybody there."

Dre sat in the studio at the Solar Building, confident he'd make it through this and create a compelling replacement for *Deep Cover,* since Sony held the copyright to this hit. He kept recruiting new acts but shifted gears. The L.A. Posse—a production group that worked with his old pal DJ Pooh—played him their album. While it sounded decent enough, he was really drawn to two songs featuring Lady of Rage, born Robin Allen. Rage wasn't like the other gangsta rappers on the label. "Rakim was my only influence," she said. She also kept up with other female rappers: feeling she can outdo Salt 'N Pepa, enjoying MC Lyte's lyrics, hearing other acts like Antoinette and Nikki D and thinking, "Okay, lemme stop fronting. Lemme give them props."

Dre asked the L.A. Posse how he could contact her. They said call lower Manhattan's Chung King Studios. Suge called first and said Dre wanted to speak with her. When they were both on the line, he told her, "Yeah, this Dr. Dre. We getting a new record label and, um, we're interested in you and would wanna know if you down to come out here."

"So how do I know you're Dr. Dre?"

"There's only one way to find out."

They sent a ticket. And when she mentioned owing her grandmother in Virginia money for a phone bill, Suge sent that, too. Since they told her she'd be the first artist, she excitedly boarded her flight. "Wow, shit is going to happen," she felt.

A day after her arrival, Suge led her into a studio, where Dre was mastering an album. Hearing her freestyle increased his belief that he had another future star on his hands. Rage, meanwhile, was not too thrilled to learn they already had Snoop, singer Jewell, Warren G, and Nate Dogg. "So it was gonna be *us* but that's not what they told me. They were like, 'It's gonna be *you.*'" And the roster continued to grow.

During his twenty-seventh birthday party, Dre saw Snoop lead a skinny kid over. "This nigga harder than a motherfucker," Snoop said. "We need this nigga on the team."

"All right," Dre answered. "But if the nigga's wack, we gonna throw him in the pool and kick his ass out."

Dre handed Kurupt, a rail-thin rapper from Philly, the microphone, then watched him free-style about his birthday. He was offered a deal so now it was him, Snoop, Rage, and Kurupt on Death Row.

Snoop then brought his cousin, Delmar "Daz" Arnaud, around. Daz was back in town from Oklahoma and flopping in Snoop's crowded apartment.

During sessions, Dre and Warren G offered production tips. Snoop then included Daz (and lyrics he supposedly wrote for him) on Dre's song "Deeez Nuuuts," but Dre didn't object. Then Snoop brought still another cousin to the studio. An older, mature, college graduate, Eric Collins worked as a store manager and rapped for fun as RBX (or "Reality-Born-Unknown"). But when Dre heard him recite a political rap between takes of a song, he said, "W'sup. You wanna get down?"

This roster—storytelling Snoop, political RBX, the gangsta-rapping Dogg Pound duo (Snoop urged Daz and Kurupt to team up), balladeer Nate Dogg, Rage, and Dre himself—would have been more than enough to help Death Row compete for an audience, but Dre kept seeking new talent. This was why, when he heard Rage playing a Freestyle Fellowship tape one day, he asked if she knew how to contact them.

She snapped, "How you gonna sign somebody else when you can't even take care of the artists you already got?"

"How you gonna question me on what I can take care of?"

"You can't take care of your own artists!"

"If you don't like it, you can leave."

"Well, gimme my ticket and I'm gone."

"I ain't giving you shit!"

The next morning, Suge smoothed things over during a meeting. "Everyone is under pressure," he gently told Rage. And it was true.

Once this blew over, twenty-seven-year-old Dre was able to turn his attention to trying to land a distribution deal for their new Death Row label. He attended meetings and glad-handed executives but this only added to his frustration, especially when one major label expressed interest in distributing the album then swiftly reversed its position after hearing the lyrics. And when he and Suge played the tape at another company, Dre held his tongue when another executive snapped, "Well, I don't see anybody else knocking on your door."

At every company, Dre saw executives refusing to work with him. And at Death Row, some artists were disenchanted. After four months, Rage said, "I started to feel that they were lying to me because they kept saying that we would be in the studio by a certain time and it'd never happen." Dre pulled her aside and let her know he was having trouble finding a distributor. "Instead of telling us what was going on, they didn't want to discourage us."

Despite, or perhaps because of, what he perceived as ongoing affronts to his image, Dre's work in the last months of 1991 and the first half of 1992 revived the vengeful persona heard on N.W.A.'s best work. With his ego battered by various situations, his vision of a unified gangland gave way to attacks against opponents real and imagined. "It was a period in my life when I had just left Ruthless, and talk on the street was I wasn't going to be able to do it without those guys," he later said. "So I felt I had something to prove."

He still dressed as he had in Niggaz With Attitude—black ball cap, sweatshirts, and baggy jeans—but much had changed. If someone complimented *Straight Outta Compton*, he might say he despised that work. "I threw that thing together in six weeks so we could have something to sell out of the trunk."

In his chair at the mix board, he smoked weed and worked to dissociate himself from his past. Critics later claimed *The Chronic* didn't involve sampling but Dre in fact set crowded milk crates of records near the mix board and reached for many of the overwrought breaks he'd used on earlier productions: James Brown's "Funky Drummer," Bill Withers' "Kissin' My Love," Solomon Burke's "Get Out of My Life, Woman," The Honey Drippers' "Impeach the President," Joe Tex's omnipresent "Papa Was Too," Lou Donaldson's "Pot Belly" and, despite its appearance on two or three N.W.A. works, the Ohio Players' "Funky Worm." Dre also sampled classic East Coast rap hits like MC Shan's "The Bridge," Whodini's "Friends," the same Led Zeppelin loop The Beastie Boys used on *License to Ill* ("When the Levee Breaks") and even the dialogue that started LL's recent "Farmer's Boulevard."

Another song found him leading session players in covering Leon Haywood's backing track for "I Wanna Do Something Freaky to You." And when Warren G arrived one afternoon with a copy of Donny Hathaway's "Little Ghetto Boy," Dre bawled, "Hold on, gimme that." He reflected on an earlier time, when his name didn't frequently appear in crime stories in the *L.A. Times*. "Back in the seventies that's all people were doing," he said, "getting high, wearing Afros, bell-bottoms, and listening to Parliament-Funkadelic."

He had his players Colin Wolfe and Tony Green and guitarist Ricky Rouse re-create some of these grooves, humming what he wanted them to play, or encouraging ad-libs until he heard something he liked. Even if his mix of melodies and stock break beats sounded good, he might still have players drown everything in Moog keyboard, and live playing. His songs were relaxed, emptier, and showcased the best-known parts of funk hits. To make every bit instantly recognizable as his work, like rock bands on concept albums, he kept using the same drum and synthesizer sound.

Creatively, he felt more inspired than ever. But away from the spacious control room, the fabric of his life quickly unraveled. After lengthy, sometimes collaborative sessions, Dre invited many new artists to his huge home in Calabasas. They were broke, subsisting on cheap Popeye's chicken, but they were showing up at the studio each day, so Dre tried to thank them by financing booze and weed parties when he could. "We was livin' at Dre's house and everything," Nate recalled. "We was doing it all, in the 'broke years' as I call them."

Near the pool out back, Snoop sat with both feet against a wall, tapping out a beat and rapping for an hour. Inside, Warren used Dre's home studio and quickly knocked out his own tracks. Suge spoke incessantly of selling millions of albums. But tensions ran high since members of rival gangs were meeting up in Dre's million-dollar home.

On the streets, the very first truce between the Crips and Bloods (which had begun after the 1992 riots and inspired peaceful gatherings in Compton parks) ended after two short months. The murders resumed, and the Crips and Bloods from various artists' entourages were quarreling in Dre's home. During one pool party, two men went from a shouting match to preparing for a fight. Other guests dutifully rearranged Dre's costly furniture to form a makeshift boxing ring. A short fighter knocked Suge's taller friend around until others charged and knocked him out.

During another afternoon, Dre saw his bodyguard B.J.'s kid brother bicker with Warren G. B.J. jumped in, and people moved furniture to create the usual ring. With members of rival gangs insulting each other, Suge slapped one of the two and had them make up. There were other incidents involving issues as trivial as the color of one's clothing. A reporter at the Solar Building arrived in a red T-shirt. It was a mistake since red was the official color of the Blood's gang. Daz asked, "Why you coming up in here wearing that color?" Dre calmed him down but rumors tied Dre to some heavy people; and executives began to fear him when he most needed a deal. "I was broke," he later claimed. He didn't receive one quarter that year, he added, since Ruthless hoped starvation would lead him home. But he stood firm, submerged his anger with parties or studio sessions, and vowed he would move back in with his mom before he worked for them again.

He also continued to hold court in his backyard right until the day he lost his home. The incident began with him grilling food during a backyard barbecue. Without warning, a neighbor ran over. "The side of your house is on fire!" Dre and friends ran to extinguish the blaze, but it reappeared on his roof, he claimed. Dre, laughing and visibly intoxicated, was soon standing in front of his burning home as fire engines, sirens blaring, arrived. Two firefighters were hurt while trying to douse the flames. Some people speculated that Dre may have set the fire himself for insurance purposes but he dismissed such talk by saying a firefighter cited electrical problems with his air conditioning as the cause of the blaze. Whatever the case, Dr. Dre salvaged what he could, rented a new apartment on Venice Boulevard, and claimed he'd have the home repaired within a year, since it was insured and the damage was about $250,000.

As *Deep Cover* entered the *Billboard* chart, Dre was involved in other personal trouble. On May 5, he traveled to an apartment complex in Woodland Hills to visit a woman. While leaving her place, he said producer Damon Thomas was pulling up in his car. Dre said he was entering his own vehicle when the woman ran up to Thomas. "She hit the motherfucker. She hit this kid." Thomas sustained broken ribs and a shattered jaw. "Next thing I know, this kid's saying I hit him, broke his jaw and all this kinda shit."

Later that month, Dre and his entourage arrived at the Black Radio Exclusive convention in New Orleans, a peaceful industry gathering. Dre claimed he and a friend were standing in a lobby when a group of men ("I guess they was from New Orleans") stopped walking a few feet away. "Matter of fact, we were kind of drunk," he explained, and were imitating a scene in Eddie Murphy's period piece *Harlem Nights*, in which a broad-shouldered boxer stops by a gambler's table in an eatery, grins, and stutters, "Come Friday night, I'm knockin' somebody the fuck out."

The local guys heard this, Dre said, and one came over to tell his friend, "Yo, I bet you can't knock my homeboy out right here." Dre claimed his friend said, "Go on wit that shit, get outta here," but the local guy walked up on him. His friend pushed him away, Dre added, so when the local approached yet again, "My friend hit him. Bam! And all this shit broke out. They start comin' at us—BOOM! We got in a little tussle and I start headin' for the front door." After police grabbed him and led him to a vehicle, he asked, "Yo, what y'all grabbing me for?" Media reports included Dre's name near a description of a riot in which four police officers were injured and a fifteen-year-old fan was stabbed, and the New Orleans district attorney wanted to charge him with criminal damage, resisting arrest, battery of officers, and inciting a riot. "Yo, man, I didn't do jack," he claimed.

He was back home by June 2, and pled guilty in a Van Nuys courtroom to one count of misdemeanor assault for hitting Damon Thomas. The judge ordered him to pay a $10,000 fine and wear an electronic tracking device during ninety days of house arrest. After denying involvement in the New Orleans brawl, Dre was ultimately convicted of hitting a police officer. That same month, he was evicted from his new apartment, presumably for partying too much. With seven platinum albums to his name—including chart-topping *Efil4Zaggin*—he moved back in with his mom and wondered why he couldn't land a distribution deal. "I mean, I had talent; talent that had already been proven with huge record sales from N.W.A. So you had to wonder what the fuck the problem was."

During the course of a day, fifty people might stop by the studio. Many were starving or avoiding landlords due to unpaid rent. "They was begging for weed," recalled one insider. "They were just running in the studio rappin', havin' fun." Around Dre, they argued while playing dominoes; danced in front of each other, waved their gang signs, and made one of his sessions resemble some uncontrollable party. But the embattled producer could feel something taking shape, the groundbreaking music he'd spent months talking about.

Soon these people were trying to influence the process. Rage would hear one track and say, "I don't like that beat." Another night, she heard something else and cried, "I like that." Everyone had stopped drinking and drugging long enough to rap about their partying during an impromptu jam session. It was the sort of thing the Juice Crew—Masta Ace, Craig G., Big Daddy Kane, and Kool G Rap—did on "The Symphony," and that A Tribe Called Quest and Leaders of the New School had recorded for "Scenario." It was also a bit sloppy and casual compared to the rest of the album, but Dre would later release it as a B-side, "Puffin' on Blunts and Drankin' Tanqueray."

He was at the board one day when D.O.C. heard an unfinished drum track and said, "That sounds like a load of shit." It was still pretty empty, but Dre planned to add lots of funk and tough talk. "Okay," he said tensely. "We'll wait 'till tomorrow." Once the music was down and D.O.C. called it great, Dre heard Snoop recite a lyric attacking Luther Campbell, the DJ whose Miami-based label, Luke Records, released popular albums by the 2 Live Crew. Dre wondered why until Snoop noted one of Luke's acts had denounced Dre for hitting Dee Barnes on a new song. Dre, image-conscious as ever, joined Snoop on "Fuck Wit Dre Day" in which he pretended to hunt Eazy. "Mister Busta, where the fuck ya at?" he began, feeling tougher than ever with so many Crips and Bloods around. He said Eazy shortchanged his "dawgs" so he wanted to slap his face and make him bow before Death Row. "Fuckin' me?" he asked. "Now I'm fuckin' you, little hoe." The chorus was even more belligerent, with Dre claiming he and his new crew had Ruthless surrounded. Snoop then challenged Dre's critic Tim Dog to fight before they both belittled Luke, with Dre threatening to rob him in Compton and blast him in Miami. The number ended with Snoop singing that Eazy-E, Tim Dog, and Luke could all "eat a fat dick." Everyone felt it had the makings of a big hit but Dre's heart wasn't into attacking others. "Man," Snoop told himself, "if Dre ain't trippin' what the fuck am I trippin' for?"

Like a director casting a film, Dre would ask whoever was closest, "Why don't you go in the recording booth and record a vocal?" D.O.C. kept coaching the untried newcomers and tried to help "make the white man understand what they were talking about." If a rap about gangbanging and smoking pot wasn't good enough, Dre tried another rapper. The goal was "all hits and no bullshit," D.O.C. recalled, and many seemed interchangeable. But before long, Snoop was on every song. "I guess I just wanted it a little more than everyone else," he said later. And D.O.C. attached himself to his side like a boxing manager. "For now I'm behind Snoop Dogg, making sure he don't go through none of the bullshit I went through, 'cause it's his time," he said. "I'm takin' my time, lookin' and learnin'. Then when I come back, ain't nobody in the motherfuckin' world gonna be able to touch me." Dre felt the very same way about his own career.

No matter how crazy things got in the real world, he could escape his increasingly troubled personal life in the studio. But some nights he couldn't even do that. One night in July, at about eight p.m., he saw George and Lynwood Stanley (two brothers he'd known for years, Eazy noted) among the artists crowded in the room; then Lynwood left. Within minutes, they all heard Suge arguing with him, then George left to see what was happening.

The session continued until a gunshot rang out. The brothers barged in. One of them had angered Suge by using a red phone. Suge told him to get off of it so he went to a pay phone. But Suge had gone downstairs to his car to get a gun.

Dre was stunned. "Suge was hitting them," D.O.C. said.

Before Dre, Snoop, and Kurupt could react to the sight of the beaten duo, Suge arrived and said, "Get out. Close the door. Go upstairs." Dre had to leave the mixing board and a work in progress while Suge did who knew what to his guests. Upstairs, the younger artists smoked weed. But two or three minutes later, everyone started drifting back downstairs, where the studio was empty save for one of Suge's pals mopping blood from the floor.

All the same, they turned the track back on and kept working until the phone rang, and someone yelled the FBI was coming. "The cops!" Everyone freaked out and started screaming. "FBI in the elevator on the way up!" They rushed to hide weapons. Some even locked themselves in empty offices.

The FBI didn't arrive, but uniformed cops did, with Dre's guests in tow. They were claiming Suge beat one with the gun, ordered both onto their knees, threatened to kill them, fired a shot, and demanded they remove their pants. One of the siblings pointed Suge out. Suge scoffed at the accusations even as a cop in another room found a bullet in the wall and led him away. He continued to deny the Stanley brothers' claims until 1995, when he pled no contest and received a suspended sentence of nine years and five years' probation.

As if this weren't bad enough, in mid-July 1992, Dre joined some of his armed friends for a party in South Central and, *Rolling Stone* reported, got shot four times in the leg. "Jerry Heller said he believed the shooting occurred in South Central Los Angeles," *Rolling Stone* wrote, but Dre denied it happened. "Shot at," he claimed. "I got shot at a whole bunch of times. They never reported it before, though." According to him, he and his new friends were outside of a hotel, calling one guy's date ugly. "So we came downstairs to talk about her, right? Shots rung out. We ran back into the hotel. I don't even know where they came from."

Back at his mother's house, Dre couldn't get over how all of these problems were happening at the same time. Even worse, the phone kept ringing and reporters from *SPIN*, *Rolling Stone*, and *Rap Masters* kept asking about the shooting. "I ain't got nothing to say to y'all," he told each, then slammed the phone down. "He had the Dee Barnes thing, breaking that kid's jaw, driving his car off the cliff, getting shot, New Orleans," Eazy said. "None of that ever happened when he was down with us."

But suddenly there was a ray of hope. In October, Suge Knight was negotiating with Jimmy Iovine at three-year-old Interscope Records. Raised by a Brooklyn longshoreman, Iovine was a former engineer turned rock producer who liked wearing ball caps and casual wear to the office. After working with John Lennon (on his experimental *Mind Games*), Patti Smith, and the group U2, and a stint at A&M Records, he teamed with businessman Ted Field in 1991 to create the $30-million startup Interscope.

When black executive John McClain passed him Dre's album and publicity materials (including a label logo) Iovine hesitated playing it. An accomplished producer himself, he felt many rap albums sounded cheap and hollow. But once the thirty-seven-year-old played the tape on his stereo, he was blown away. Dre's stuff sounded more polished than most rock albums. "I didn't know hip-hop," he said, "but I knew my speakers, and this was fantastic."

Dre hadn't set out to write songs that would create a larger narrative but recent setbacks led to a series of semi-autobiographical tunes that started with revenge ("Chronic Intro") then reflected on violent neighborhoods ("Let Me Ride"), the recent riots ("The Day the Niggaz Took Over"), and black on black crime ("Lil' Ghetto Boy"). His character defied a hostile white society ("A Nigga Witta Gun"), threatened rivals ("Rat A Tat Tat"), and experienced life's disappointments and the burn of disillusionment ("Bitches Ain't Shit"). Song after song described driving through the hood with a gun; lashing out against enemies real or perceived; the newfound unity between Compton and Long Beach ("Nuthin' but a 'G' Thang"); and participating in various beatings, robberies, and shootings. And through it all, he threw in the label's name and tried on various new personas: "Lil' Ghetto Boy's" drug-dealing gangster shot six times after trying to rob a younger gang member; "A Nigga Witta Gun's" trigger-happy "Dre Eastwood"; "Rat-a-Tat-Tat's" survivor laughing at women who rejected him "when I didn't have my sixty-fo' and a lot of dough"; and "High Powered's" band leader saying, "Yo man, gimme some of that old gangsta-ass shit, you know what I'm saying?"

After all of the scripted party and hangout scenes, "Bitches Ain't Shit" then offered final words about Ruthless. "I used to know a bitch named Eric Wright," Dre rapped. "We used to roll around and fuck the hoes at night." He described how, after they scored number one songs, Eric let a "white bitch" ruin everything. He ended the song by saying Eric was so soft now, he was taking Dre to court instead of fighting him.

When they met, Dre and Jimmy hit it off. Dre thought, "He is, like, the smartest motherfucker in the business." Best of all, he didn't have to worry that tales of his indulgences, eccentricities, and violent outbursts would ruin the deal. Jimmy was aware of the stories. "But I just know they had great music and that they were a bunch of guys who wanted to make it out of the ghetto," Jimmy said. "That's something I can understand." He loved the music, the artwork, and the video concepts Dre described. And Jimmy's partner, Ted Field (heir to a department store fortune) was just as enthusiastic. "He's a musical genius," he said.

The negotiations were going smoothly but in October 1992, Eazy-E filed his federal lawsuit, claiming Dre sent thugs to intimidate him into releasing him, D.O.C., and Michel'le from their contracts. His lawsuit was an industry first, since he made the charges under the Racketeer Influenced and Corrupt Organizations (RICO) Act. And now, he claimed five men (not two) held bats and pipes and told him, "I know where your mother stays." In response, Dre wrote a statement that claimed he and Eazy started

Ruthless in 1985 as a joint venture, and had a verbal agreement to split all profits. "I could have gone after half of Ruthless 'cause me and Eazy was equal partners from the jump street," Dre told a reporter, but Ruthless swiftly denied this ever happened.

Dre's ego was battered enough but he then saw Cube's second album, *Death Certificate*, arrive in stores October 29, 1991, including the track "No Vaseline." With a million people buying Cube's album by December 12, Dre was more embarrassed than ever. Cube hadn't liked hearing Dre claim, on "Benedict Arnold," that he'd shove a broomstick up his ass. So, over funk band Brick's breakbeat "Dazz" and a few of N.W.A.'s insults from "Message to B.A." and "Prelude," he said he was happy N.W.A. started it—which they did—then said they were now "just wet and soft." He said they went from threatening to shoot people with A.K.s to appearing in an R&B video for Michel'le, "Lookin' like straight bozos. I saw it coming," he added. "That's why I went solo."

Cube then said they all moved from Compton to white neighborhoods, and had a "white man just rulin'." He called them phonies. He told Dre to stick to producing, said Eazy was screwing him, and claimed Dre was jealous when Cube formed his own company. "Tryin' to sound like Amerikkka's Most," he jibed. "You could yell all day but you don't come close." After claiming Eazy was also sodomizing Ren, Cube yelled that a broomstick would fit Dre's "ass so perfect." This was bad enough but Cube further embarrassed him by discussing their working relationship with manager Jerry Heller. "It's a case of divide-and-conquer," he yelled. "Cuz you let a Jew break up my crew." Before the song ended, he urged them to shoot Heller in the head. "Cuz you can't be the Niggaz 4 Life crew," he concluded. "with a white Jew tellin' you what to do." Dre was at his wit's end but publicly claimed none of this would stop him. He claimed Cube needed to include his name to draw fans to his album. He also tried, unconvincingly, to blame the media for his problems. "People are gonna keep pumping that 'controversy' shit up all they want to try to stop me," he said. "But it ain't. I'm'a keep on doing what I'm doing, making my music, and it ain't gonna have no effect on me." But it already had. He was bitter now, viewing the world as a battlefield where he worked hard to earn money and enemies worked just as hard to take it away. Still, just as he had during high school chess games, he knew how to out-think them. He'd party at home, not in public. He'd surround himself with positive people, and avoid fights that led to bad headlines and nuisance lawsuits. He'd only go to the studio then right back home. And when he finished the album, he'd stop rapping. He'd dabble in real estate. "Music'll be like a hobby, not a job."

With Eazy's lawsuit hanging over him, he decided to meet the press. During a controversial interview with *The Source* he denied hitting Damon Thomas, Dee Barnes, or anyone at the BRE convention; burning down his own home; totaling his car; and taking four bullets in a leg. He also denied Eazy's claim that men with pipes forced him to sign his release papers and claimed Eazy shortchanged him. But Eazy quickly denied it. "Nobody was ever robbing him." The problem, he said, was yes-men filling Dre's head with lies. "He's got people who don't know shit about the music business, telling him he could be this and that, get 'this and that.' Fuck that."

Dre then went to the lot behind the Solar Building and posed for the November 1992 *Source* cover. After a few shots behind the wheel of a light-blue 1964 Cadillac convertible—with Snoop riding shotgun and D.O.C. in the backseat—he saw an associate furtively arrive with a huge .44 Smith & Wesson. Within minutes, Dre stood in front of photographer Shawn Mortensen and pointed the huge gun in his right hand at his own temple. "That's how I felt at the time," he said later. "It was perfect, too, you know? The whole ninety-two was talking about Dre. I just kept my head above water until my album came out."

With Eazy refusing to free Dre from his contract—Eazy claimed he was still owed four albums—Jimmy Iovine offered to pay Eazy, and Death Row, for the right to release *The Chronic*. Finalized December 3, the deal recognized Dre's contracts with Ruthless. It also gave Ruthless a percentage of royalties from anything Dre produced. Ruthless in turn gave Interscope rights to Dre as an exclusive producer and artist. "If Dre leaves Interscope," Ruthless attorney Michael Borbeau reported, "all rights to him as a producer and artist revert back to Ruthless." Eazy couldn't disclose what he earned from each Dre production but said, "I probably make more off Dre's albums than he does. He should have stayed with me and done his solo stuff. He'd be a lot better off." Interscope benefited, too: "All of a sudden we were known as this heavy rock and rap label," said Tony Ferguson. Dre himself stopped caring about the failures of the last few years. With a new sound, and deal, he also saw a new beginning come into view. He focused on proving critics wrong and reclaiming his spot as one of rap's top producers. "Ninety-two just wasn't my year," he told MTV. "Ninety three will be, though. You can believe that."

D r. Dre moved into an awesome French colonial in a restricted gated
community in the Valley. Somewhere along the line, he got used to
living among doctors and lawyers and having a swimming pool and items
like the $11,000 ring with sixty-eight diamonds and the Rolex on his left
wrist with "so many diamonds I've lost count." Where he once had to ask DJ
Pooh to drive him to studio sessions for Eazy-E singles, he now had a BMW
convertible, a white Chevy Blazer, a Nissan Pathfinder, two 1964 Chevy
Impalas, and his beloved 1987 Ferrari.

He was still seeing Michel'le in 1993, and telling her he wanted to do her
album next. He also tried proposing marriage but she turned him down. "She
says she won't marry me until I stop being Dr. Dre." He was still on house
arrest, but throwing wild parties at home. And before each, Sam Sneed
recalled, "he used to tell me to call the women up."

Another change was their office. They were out of the Solar Building and
in a suite two floors above Interscope in a building on Wilshire and Westwood. Suge was hiring staff but along with experienced promoters, a male
receptionist, and an office manager, he hired his wife, Sharitha, to manage
Death Row acts and filled the small office with hardened street guys like

Heron, Buntry, Jake The Violator, and Hen Dogg (who designed the grue-some logo, a hooded prisoner in an electric chair)—all of whom would later be shot and killed in separate incidents. They were all friendly enough when Dre showed up, but he tried to keep his distance. "He got burned out on that shit 'cause he did all that shit when he was with N.W.A.," Snoop explained.

Another change was having to listen when Interscope said it wanted "Mr. Officer" off *The Chronic*. On this song, Dre gathered a few artists to chant, "Mister Officer, Mister Officer, I wanna see you laying in a coffin, sir." It was a throwback to the N.W.A. stuff but Interscope's parent company, Time Warner, was already facing heat for Ice-T's metal number with Body Count, "Cop Killer," so the company said, "No more." Dre had tackled serious issues like race and police brutality with N.W.A. but now aspired to a show busi-ness career. At heart, he enjoyed business and making money as much as he did recording songs. He pulled the chorus from the album and, reporter Chuck Philips recalled, "For a while you didn't hear anything on a Dr. Dre record about shooting cops."

During this same period, Dre translated his love of film into his video for "Dre Day." He wore a heavy Carhartt jacket, some black jeans, and a black baseball cap and filmed himself driving low riders, standing near Snoop, waving a gun, and rapping from his place in a crowd of Gs. As director, he had the crew set up shop in an empty warehouse. Snoop stood behind him as Dre held his coat open to reveal his new Funkadelic T-shirt. The drinking had him a bit heavier than usual, but what could he do? He also filmed a story for the video: A short, bushy-haired Eazy clone sits in a label office lis-tening to a Heller clone give him his marching orders. The Eazy clone then travels through Compton hoods, trying to convince Warren G to dance along with him while the Geto Boys' Bushwick Bill looks on. Then the clone gets some of Snoop's pals to dance, then an old man in a beige suit. But when he enters a shack where gangsters at a table play dominoes, they chase him out with rifles and pistols and he cravenly leaps into the rear of a white van with the words "Useless Records" on its side.

Midway through the video, Dre appears in the office with a huge gun like the Terminator with a red targeting beam aimed at the lens. Then he cuts to the warehouse again and Snoop's trashing of Tim "M-U-T." Meanwhile Dre flashes a gun at the camera while, behind him, Jheri-curled Cube half-walks and dances in the crowd. After adding a few scenes of the roadside Eazy impersonator holding a sign that reads he'll rap for food, Dre moved on to "Nuthin' but a 'G' Thang."

Eager to show inner-city blacks he was tough as ever, he filmed rundown homes in the hood, bouncing low riders, and an all black house party and outdoor barbecue. Then, to emphasize his new image as reformed gangster, he zoomed in on a guy carrying a rack of ribs toward a grill until it was impossible to ignore the gun tucked in the rear of his waistline. Since every video needed a plot, he showed a sexy young black woman not getting along with his fellow gangsters. She gets her bikini top yanked off during a volleyball game, but arrives in a sexy black mini skirt at the house party that night. She walks slowly through the crowd, scowling at everyone until two or three Gs run up and spray her with liquor from their giant beer bottles. During post production he proudly added the credit "Directed by Andre Young."

Though magazines later claimed Suge brought hardcore gangster rap to the masses, Interscope actually side-stepped resistance from radio by buying one-minute ads with music from *The Chronic*, and airing these on fifty stations. Then label executives worked the phones to persuade MTV to air Dre's videos.

Reviews of *The Chronic* were unanimous in their praise. *Rolling Stone* called *The Chronic* "A hip-hop masterwork." *Entertainment Weekly* crowned Dre king of rap producers. *The Source* said the album "must not be missed." *The Chronic* soared to number three on the *Billboard* 200, "Nuthin' but a 'G' Thang," was a national hit, and MTV kept airing "Dre Day" (but for some reason blurred his directing credit).

◆ ◆ ◆

The artists were beginning to believe their press clippings, and that they were tougher than they really were. "Shit, we were all in churches as kids," said D.O.C. "Hell, Snoop used to sing in the church choir." At Death Row, new publicist George Pryce told some artists, "Don't start acting out that stuff with me. That's a role you're playing but the cameras are off for today. Calm down and be who you are." Yet, Pryce soon found himself dealing with real gangsters. One day, while he was on the phone, he heard Suge's female cousin say he had to leave right now. He wanted to finish his call, but she grabbed the phone and yanked him from his seat. While leaving, he remembered, "There were some guys coming in. I think they were armed and they were people that had been disgruntled by something that Death Row was doing, from some gang."

The artists probably would have been faced with these sorts of situations—maybe even worse—if they didn't have deals and were merely Crips and Bloods on the streets. But Snoop's cousin RBX couldn't help but feel their violent lyrics provoked people to want to challenge them. When he urged his cousins Snoop and Daz to tone down references to gangbanging, since they weren't really out there doing it, and they ignored him, he yelled, "You motherfuckers are retarded! Talking 'bout what you did when you were sixteen? You fuckin' retarded. Y'all retards."

Snoop's high-top fade gave way to long hair he tied in pigtails or styled in enormous curls. His yes-men (hustlers from the hood who loved being in on the action and spending his money) were always around.

Suge was also acting up. Where he'd been a humble, helpful guy, he now stopped wearing work boots and jeans and included more red in his wardrobe. He also started implying he might be down with the little-known Blood set Mob Piru.

When they went out, "Dre always had his group of security motherfuckers," said D.O.C., while people around Snoop and Suge scowled at each other, argued, or sometimes had fights. The mood became so tense, Daz—described as a "pussycat" by his cousin RBX—told a reporter, about the office, "Motherfuckers could run up in here right now and start blastin'."

And Snoop was now being stalked by a resentful gang member in his new neighborhood in the Palms district, he claimed. The guy had already aimed a .380 at him. Then, at a gas station, the guy had aimed it again, this time at his head.

Dre meanwhile was still under house arrest, allowed to leave his estate only for work. In the studio, he filled his workspace with his Akai MPC-60 drum machine sampler, his Yamaha SY-77 keyboard, and the eleven-year-old, used Mini Moog he'd bought for $300. While playing drum loops, he typically had musicians ad-lib about fifty bass lines, then decided one would do. But during one session, he liked a note and asked, "Yo, what was that?" The guy didn't know, so Dre reacted by taping everything they did. Now, if something leaped out, he quickly rewound the tape. "One note sometimes, we'll get a whole song, you know."

He surrounded himself with collaborators like the D.O.C., Sam "Sneed" Anderson, and old friend Chris "The Glove" Taylor to begin work on Snoop's debut album, *Doggystyle*. He soon heard Sneed suggest that a scene from the movie *Superfly* could make for a good skit. Dre had Snoop and Warren record the bathtub scene over music from the movie. They then had Sam pretend to argue with Snoop over a woman on another Mayfield number (the skit "U Betta Recognize"). He had people feign smoking pot ("Chronic Break") and filled other inserts with commercials for "DJ EZ Dick's show" on radio station "W-Balls" (his take on the mellow soliloquys often found on P-Funk songs).

Where *The Chronic* was a nonstop tribute to P-Funk, Dre filled the first single, "Gin and Juice," with Slave's emotive "Watching You." He also had Snoop cover Slick Rick & Doug E. Fresh's classic, "La Di Da Di." And when Snoop tackled social issues on "Doggy Dogg World," Dre used drum sounds as warm as Marvin Gaye's *What's Going On*, and coaxed a brilliant performance out of slow-jam legends The Dramatics. Yet despite these experiments, he inevitably filled most songs with keyboards as heavy as those on *The Chronic*. He wound up creating another track with bass, a one-note Moog riff, and a sampled Beastie Boy lyric ("Let me clear my throat"), but while everyone loved it, he set it aside.

Michel'le sometimes brought their three-year-old son, Marcel, by, and he'd leap into his father's swivel chair, roll it to the board, and imitate him by twisting knobs, pulling levers, and nodding. During another visit, he had her join Snoop and his longtime hero, George Clinton, on the title track (but wound up leaving it off the album). Another time, Suge showed up and wound up discouraging a few artists. They were recording Nate's "Ain't No Fun," when Suge reacted to some vocals by griping, "Man, every time I come in here, y'all talking that Crip shit." To placate him, Warren changed a lyric about a blue 1964 Chevy to say "6-4 Chevy, *red* to be exact." But just as quickly, RBX was angered by another song. "Murder Was the Case (Death After Visualizing Eternity)" found Snoop playing a few characters. But RBX angrily refused to play the devil. They were "entering some shit," he said before storming off. Snoop ignored him and quickly cast Daz for the role. Dre finished up the long day's work then went home for some rest. "That was all it was with Dre, the studio to the crib," said Sneed.

With *The Chronic* a hit, Snoop kept his huge Elvis-sized entourage around: Hugg, singer Nate (gladly handing out songs he wrote for his debut in an effort to keep his name before an audience), Kurupt (who wanted a solo album), Daz (whose array of innovative styles on *The Chronic* were replaced by less-inspired gangster lyrics), The D.O.C. (who felt Snoop wasn't as hungry anymore), his bodyguard Malik (silent and armed), and Warren G (who felt Death Row poached his bandmates but still wanted a deal). While Dre worked, they drank, smoked, joked, yelled, played dominoes, battled with pot-induced rhymes, or acted so rowdy, nine studios kicked them out.

◆ ◆ ◆

By August, *The Chronic* had sold two million copies and was still in *Billboard*'s Top Ten. Dre was working with Snoop's cousin, Ricky Harris, and Harris' wife, Dee Barnes, was willing to settle her civil lawsuit. Eazy's federal lawsuit, meanwhile, was dismissed on August 9. Dre had also introduced Snoop to Cube and discussed collaborating with them on something. And he was planning to tour with his one-time favorites, Run-DMC.

He was busy enough trying to finish *Doggystyle*, but Interscope wanted another Dre video. So he got back into his black Ben Davis shirt, ball cap, and jeans, and filmed "Let Me Ride" in the relatively safe Leimert Park area. When he couldn't shake everyone's hand or chat them up, a few people gossiped that he let fame go to his head. There was nothing he could do. As with earlier clips, this one featured the usual shots of people exhaling smoke, freeways, and Dre driving around (this time in a black '64 Impala rolling on two wheels). He also concocted another self-mythologizing plot. This time, he drove past a sexy woman licking a big ice cream bar. He got her in the car, frowned at the lens, then drove her to a car wash, where he saw even sexier black ladies working in shorts. He invited one over, jerked his thumb at the first—to say beat it—then invited the other woman in. While her man cursed and fretted, Dre drove away with a hearty laugh. Between takes, he looked over and saw Jimmy Iovine wave from the sidelines, trying to get his attention. He ignored it, and took his place in the crowd. He rapped to a camera in a helicopter but someone stopped the music. His assistant director held a bullhorn and told the extras surrounding Dre, "MTV won't play anything with gang signs. And if y'all want to throw them, you'll have to go home."

With Interscope asking for the Snoop album, he was anxious to return to the studio. Already, magazines were predicting *Doggystyle* would be the first rap debut to enter the charts at number one, and he had his own high standard to meet. It not only had to redefine funk music, it had to also be the first perfect rap album. As he saw it, *The Chronic*, Public Enemy's *Nation of Millions*, Eric B & Rakim's *Paid in Full*, and Boogie Down Productions' *Criminal Minded* all came close, but *Doggystyle* would outdo them all. He already had about eleven songs on thirty-seven reels but felt nowhere near achieving his goal.

But he soon had to join Snoop for a few videos. He chose Fab 5 Freddy— who'd recorded that "Change the Beat" record Dre used to always scratch, and had toured Compton with N.W.A. and MTV—to direct "What's My Name." Freddy wanted to film Snoop standing on the roof of his old hangout, V.I.P. Record Store in Long Beach. Dre arrived on the set at eight in the morning and saw Snoop start rapping on the roof. But by eight-thirty, a crowd of one thousand had formed and not everyone was happy to see him. One crew member felt it was a mistake to film here when word on the street painted Death Row as a harbor for Bloods. Some gangsters in the crowd chugged forty-ounce beers and jeered Snoop's every move. "And tensions were really high," said crew member Johnny Simmons.

By noon, some of the Crips were drunk and one kept shouting, "We gonna get your ass!" Dre was very concerned, especially when others marched through the crowd shouting, "Fuck you!" Finally, the crew loaded equipment into trucks and moved to the next location, a park four blocks away, to film a family picnic. By the time they arrived a crowd of at least one hundred people had already gathered.

Snoop left his minivan and saw an entourage member yell at the crowd. Then one guy confronted Snoop and they argued. Other brawls erupted and a few people hurled items at police officers. The cops moved in with barking dogs, plastic shields, and helicopters. "It was a mess, man," remembered one witness. Before anyone could get near Dre and Snoop, however, Suge rolled up in his Mercedes, got them into the car, and took off. Meanwhile the film crew had to pack and leave.

Dre was disturbed by the melee but returned to the park another day. Fab 5 wanted to film a woman stroking a Doberman's head. Using special effects, he'd have the image morph into her braiding Snoop's hair. Dre assured him Snoop would be there that day. But after the camera set-up was ready, Freddy asked, "Dre, what's going on?"

"I'll talk to you in a minute."

Freddy filmed a few more shots then came over while crew members were changing the lighting. "Dre, what is going on? What time is Snoop gonna get here?"

"Yeah, we gotta little problem."

"Well, what is it, a one-eight-seven?"

Dre said yeah.

"What do you mean? Snoop?"

"Yeah, some guy had been following him around, putting up his gang signs, and they bumped heads, got into it, shots were exchanged, he's dead." Obviously, Dre had been misinformed.

It was August 25, and Snoop was in his new pad with bodyguard McKinley Lee when he heard their pal Sean Abrams argue with someone out front. He ran outside and saw the guy with the .380, twenty-year-old Philip Wolde-mariam, run to an idling car. Later, stories claimed that Abrams had flashed a gang sign at the passing car and that Woldemariam leaped out to challenge him. Either way, Snoop (already on bail for a concealed weapons charge) ran to his Jeep. With his friends nearby, he followed the car for a few blocks then turned onto a side street.

Within minutes, Snoop drove into Woodbine Park. He jumped out as

Woldemariam and two friends sat with Mexican take-out food. According to Snoop, Woldemariam then reached for his .380, so his bodyguard fired from the Jeep, killing him in self-defense. But a coroner said Woldemariam, who was armed, was shot in the back, and L.A. deputy district attorney Ed Nison said Snoop can't claim self-defense if he'd pursued him.

Snoop never made it to the set of the video that day. He resurfaced two days later at the MTV Music Video Awards. "He went, gave out an award, and turned himself in," said Freddy. Death Row's attorney got him released on $1 million bail just as Snoop's face appeared on the covers of *Rolling Stone*, *VIBE*, and *The Source*.

Despite his legal woes, Dre saw Snoop prepare to join them on his *Chronic* tour and become more famous than ever, in spite of, or perhaps even because of, the murder charges. On September 7 Dre performed with Run-DMC, female gangsta rapper Boss, and the group Onyx on the bill, and amazed fans with a huge skull prop that appeared and yelled at the crowd. Then he and Snoop drove a convertible on stage. Snoop lit a joint or two while the others joined them for their hits. The entourage, as usual, had a few fights backstage but Dre stayed out of it. He didn't really like traveling, especially with an unpredictably violent entourage, but kept getting on stage and running through his hits. And the album kept selling, along with T-shirts, and hats.

The artists kept promoting a unified family image even though a few issues threatened to divide them, one being the issue of credit. When reporters came around to discuss the album, Dre rarely corrected any that credited him alone for ideas. In *Rolling Stone*, when asked how he came up with the Leon Haywood bass line, he claimed, "I sit around by myself in the studio at home, push buttons, and see what happens." Yet, just as quickly, he might tell a book author visiting the studio about musicians jamming over his drum machine. On the sidelines, Warren G—who'd reportedly brought him the Haywood record—knew he, Daz, and Chris "The Glove" Taylor helped with the album ("all of us producers together as one") but remained silent. Kurupt and Rage were a bit frustrated, too, as both wanted solo albums, and RBX was unhappy with other people at Death Row automatically receiving lucrative publishing rights for songs that included a few of his lyrics. Royalties and advances were fine and dandy, but publishing was where someone really earned money. The owner of a song's publishing rights was entitled to a payment whenever the work was played or performed publicly. At the same time, a rights holder could keep earning money by repackaging the song and re-releasing it. But it wasn't until they were backstage for a show at Chicago's Regal Theater that things finally came to a head.

RBX had played football alongside Suge at UNLV, and he remembers frequently hearing Suge bring up gang-related battles their relatives had decades ago. The latest, and final, incident started when RBX left the stage after a show and saw eight cartons of take-out chicken waiting backstage. Since there were eight performers he grabbed some food and began to eat. The others did, too. But Suge walked in and exploded, RBX claimed. "Who eatin'—? Aw, you motherfuckers eatin' my chicken?" He had bought them for his entourage, not his artists. RBX was disgusted that someone would fight for food. "Man, why you beefin' over fuckin' chicken?" he asked before storming out for good.

Dre was taken aback, but said nothing. By September 25, he was on the way home. The tour was over. Death Row claimed a promoter hadn't "live[d] up to its obligations." While the label promised they'd all be back on the road before you knew it, Dre decided he wasn't touring anymore. He was sick of traveling, sick of hearing about fights, and already sick of some of Suge's antics.

When reporters asked about RBX's departure, Dre claimed it wasn't like his leaving Ruthless. "My business was fucked up. I'm not fucking over my people." He added: "I'm just watching everybody's back." RBX was going to get the publishing deal he wanted, an insider said, but he left before Dre could step in and get the ball rolling.

◆ ◆ ◆

Despite his personal and financial woes—he was said to be selling weed to close friends to make ends meet—Snoop continued to record lightsome raps over Dre's music. During some sessions, he'd smoke a joint, enter the booth without a lyric, and improvise things like "Gin and Juice" and "The Shiznit."

Dre meanwhile saw his dream of the perfect album crushed by Interscope's desire to release *Doggystyle* by Thanksgiving. At the same time, Snoop had first-degree murder charges hanging over his head. At some point—the chronology's unclear—Dre bowed to pressure and rush recorded the entire second half of the album. "We went through about nine fifths of Hennessy," he said. "We was up for, like, two days. I was under house arrest at the time and I couldn't leave the studio anyway."

Meticulous planning gave way to crowded posse cuts like "Serial Killa," using the Ohio Players' "Funky Worm" again, and co-producing with Daz. Then he and Daz filled the skit "House Party" with jive talk about an unnamed rival suffering from AIDS. Snoop included Lil Bow Wow on "You Betta Ask Somebody." Snoop had seen the six-year-old (whose real name was Shad Moss) get on stage and rap during a break in one of their last concerts. After inviting him backstage, he flew him to Los Angeles the next day, gave him his stage name, and hoped to sign him to Death Row. Snoop then filled "Gz and Hustlers" with more pot-induced free-styles. Dre tried a duet with him called "The Next Episode," but set it aside. Then, when Snoop recorded "Gz Up, Hoes Down," Dre used the same Isaac Hayes sample ("The Look of Love") Ren had on his solo work "The Alley." Finally, Dre closed the album with "Pump Pump," yet another crowded work, before dreaming up "Who Am I (What's My Name)," a single with melodies from old P-Funk records and Tom Brown's bass-heavy "Funkin' for Jamaica."

He submitted the album, which *Time* now called "the most anticipated release in the brief history of rap," and saw anticipation for it spill over to the release party the label arranged on a yacht at scenic Marina Del Rey. Once guests reached the parking lot an employee handed them a free Snoop poster. They stood on line as security guards let people onto a walkway one at a time. Couples were separated, so people grew tense. Then balloons popped, and everyone flinched, assuming it was gunfire. To make matters worse, the captain of the boat saw the crowd waiting and said, "Okay, nobody else on the boat." "And that was some of the wrong people to be talkin' shit to, you know?" said one attendee. "And they was ready to throw his ass into the water."

The vessel began its cruise. But a police helicopter flew right over it so people couldn't hear Snoop's album or each other. Then a huge fight broke out. One artists' Crip entourage was singing along and waving their gang sign around when some of Suge's Blood pals attacked. By the time the boat returned to the dock after a very short cruise, there were three helicopters over it—one from the police, shining a bright searchlight on guests, the others from local media—and twenty police cars waiting. The party ended quickly and news reports described it as a "rap riot" even though one guest said, "It wasn't really a problem until the police came and ruined the party."

◆ ◆ ◆

Back in October, Dre was still mixing *Doggystyle* when "Who Am I (What's My Name)" landed at number eight on the *Billboard* Hot 100. It wasn't the most exciting thing on the album, but was similar enough to "Nuthin' but a 'G' Thang" to draw *Chronic* fans.

During this same period, he learned Eazy-E released *It's On (Dr. Dre) 187um Killa*, an entire EP devoted to insulting him, and Yella was among those who produced its music. Eazy started the EP by thanking his bitch Dre for making him some money with *The Chronic*. Then "Real Muthaphukkin' G's" called him and Snoop "studio gangsters" who could suck his "doggy dick." He claimed Dre wore eyeliner with the Cru and said he went "from wearing lipstick to smoking on chronic at picnics." After calling Dre a "bitch-ass nigga" again, he ended the song with gunshots killing a Dre impersonator. "It's On," meanwhile parodied Snoop's simple style, noted Compton was on Eazy's side, and reminded everyone of how Dre beat women. Then he mimicked Snoop's singing on "Nuthin' but a 'G' Thang": "Talk a gang of shit but it don't phase me. That punk nigga Dre still pays me." But he wasn't done yet. His album cover included a 1986 photo of Dre in the Cru, wearing a tight sequined shirt and eyeliner, standing in profile, smiling, and waving at the viewer.

The EP, however, didn't match sales of *The Chronic* so more people believed Dre was the street guy he claimed to be (even as he lived in a huge mansion and had little actual contact with the Compton streets he rapped about). As a result, fans rushed to buy Snoop's second single, "Gin and Juice," which also reached number eight on the Hot 100 in November.

But two weeks before its scheduled release, Dre was still working to finish the album. Where he once tried new things, he now seemed to be afraid to fail in public. Art took a backseat to what would be a good career move. Then he feared someone might get a tape to bootleggers in Compton, so he told Interscope if anyone wanted to hear the music they could stop by; he wouldn't let anyone hear more than two songs away from the studio. People felt he was being excessive, but he refused to turn the album in until nothing else could be done to improve it. And on November 23, 1993, he saw his hard work pay off.

That night demand for *Doggystyle* was so high, record shops stayed open long after midnight and fans waited on long lines outside to buy copies. *Doggystyle*, as predicted, entered the *Billboard* chart at number one and sold 803,000 copies in a week. Then it stayed at number one for two more weeks. And despite its profanity and street themes, white fans couldn't get enough of it. "Little white kids were walking around with their asses out and rapping," George Pryce recalled. "I think that's where it really became a problem, not for us, but maybe for certain factions in America."

Though some of the album was rushed, and more than a few ideas were questionable (such as having a child curse during a skit) critics rushed to praise the album. *Rolling Stone* gave it four stars. *Entertainment Weekly* called it the smoothest gangsta album to date. *VIBE* wrote that Dre stole the show (after Snoop did it on *The Chronic*). And *Musician* called Snoop "the gangsta Marvin Gaye of Dr. Dre's Motown."

But not everyone was happy about the album's success. Away from Death Row, a backlash was forming. In Manhattan, Reverend Calvin Butts held a huge rally denouncing gangsta rap. While Snoop lashed out in *Time*, the Reverend Jesse Jackson also denounced the music. West Coast magazine *Rap Sheet* announced it wouldn't run ads in which rappers held guns, and a group called The National Political Congress of Black Women was creating a national petition to convince major labels to stop releasing these sorts of albums.

9

The feelings of panic first gripped him the moment he heard Suge wanted a soundtrack for some urban in-the-hood movie, *Above the Rim*, to be the next album. It was Autumn 1993, and Dre was thinking about following *Doggystyle* with albums by Michel'le and Lady of Rage. Until now, Rage had willingly done guest-raps, but she was tiring of them. And Dre couldn't blame her. They had told her she'd put an album out after *The Chronic*. "Then they said Snoop's, but after Snoop's, mine," she added. But as fifty-fifty partner, Suge wanted a say in the creative direction. He also wanted to attract bigger stars. He'd already reached out to a few artists signed to New York–based label Uptown, including popular R&B quartet Jodeci and singer Mary J. Blige. Then he hammered out a deal for Death Row to release the soundtrack to the film *Above the Rim*.

In a way, it was good business. The market for R&B was as big as that for Death Row's gun-happy gangster rap. But image conscious Dre worried rap magazines would claim he was selling out; that he'd get bored recording the music (which he enjoyed hearing at home); or that the idea might slow whatever momentum back-to-back hits *The Chronic* and *Doggystyle* created. Even so, Suge said *Above the Rim* was next and tried to woo another artist to the label.

His name was Tupac Shakur, and he was already on Interscope, and having a rough year of his own. At first, he'd been a mild-mannered eighth grader in Baltimore, wearing a shirt with iron-on letters identifying him as MC New York. But in northern Cali, after a stint as a backup dancer for Tommy Boy Records' act Digital Underground, he inked a solo deal with Interscope.

He starred in the urban drama *Juice* and moved to Los Angeles in 1992, where gangs saw lots of red on the cover of *Strictly 4 My N.I.G.G.A.Z.*, and assumed he was a Blood. Like Dre, he stayed neutral, but threw his new friends' war stories into his lyrics. Then he bought a gun, frequented firing ranges, tattooed his stomach with gang-like slogans, and started lifting weights. Brash, confrontational, but also insecure during private moments, he returned to Marin City on August 22 to attend a celebration, and argued with former neighbors. Guns were fired, and a six-year-old boy was killed, shot in the head. Then on September 22, Vice President Dan Quayle said his album *2Pacalypse Now* had "no place in our society."

Tupac rebounded with a role in John Singleton's 1993 film *Poetic Justice*, but kept promoting gang-like attitudes with his Interscope/Time Warner side project, the group Thug Life. Then he made headlines again, for supposedly shooting two off-duty cops in Atlanta, and just as quickly for sexually abusing a nineteen-year-old woman in his midtown Manhattan hotel room. Dre felt the Snoop case involved the label in enough controversy but Suge told Pac, "Yo, give me a song, dog." Pac submitted "Pour Out a Little Liquor," one of seven songs churned out in a three-day period and originally intended for Thug Life, then *Poetic Justice*. Suge paid "damn near an album budget," about $200,000, and more money for other songs, before inviting him onto Death Row. Dre opposed the move but Suge still met with Pac, Jimmy Iovine, and Pac's manager and according to Suge, heard Iovine say it'd be better if Pac went to Death Row to work with Dr. Dre. Sell millions. Get rich. Be on a label that supported his music.

Dre meanwhile also sought new acts. At Gladstone's restaurant in Malibu, he ran into CPO, an old friend from the N.W.A. days, now between deals. "I got the soundtrack coming up on *Above the Rim*," he told him. "You wanna get on it, come to the studio tomorrow, we'll hook up." By now the divide between him and Suge had widened to the point where he hardly stopped by the office. He only saw Suge if Suge stopped by to see how the music was going. He was beginning to feel everything was going to hell. "None of those guys knew what they were doing," The D.O.C. said. They didn't know how to handle or spend money. "Suge's wife was Snoop's manager." And Snoop, now the star, kept saying, "Man, fuck this shit. I'm not havin' this shit." He was tired of being controlled.

Suge's handpicked employees, meanwhile, were trying to run the company by the same rules as in their gang; though there was "no loyalty among street niggas," said D.O.C. Suge himself was dividing and conquering, he added, telling one person, "Yeah, that motherfucker ain't shit," then another, "Yeah that motherfucker ain't shit," then both the same when they were together.

Then Dre saw another controversy erupt during the creation of the soundtrack.

After Dre and Snoop did *Deep Cover*, Warren helped with *The Chronic* "and then motherfuckers blew up!" Warren felt left out of the excitement and media coverage but rapped on the *Doggystyle* number, "Ain't No Fun." But when he inquired about a deal of his own, Dre told him, "You need to go on and be your own man." With the label still not offering a deal, Warren thought, "Fuck it. I'll do my own motherfuckin' thang!" He filled a demo with songs like "Regulate," "This DJ," and "Indo Smoke" and let director John Singleton include the latter on the soundtrack for his film *Poetic Justice*. "And it took off, it was hot!" Since then Warren signed to Def Jam and wanted to include "Regulate," which featured Nate Dogg, on his debut. After Death Row told him it'd have to be on *Above the Rim*, he complained about this to *The Source* magazine. "I thought that was quite fucked up 'cause I made Death Row, if you ask me," he was quoted as saying. "And I'll tell 'em straight up, 'Nigga, I made y'all.'"

Once he calmed down, he asked the magazine to delete the comment. Instead, it appeared as an enormous pull quote. After that, one person claimed, Warren was allegedly carrying two 9-millimeter handguns. "'Cause of that interview with *The Source*. When they got a hold of him saying that he made Death Row, motherfuckers didn't like that." A few guys from the office supposedly broke into his home one night "and woke his ass up with guns in his motherfucking face and kinda put it on him a little bit." One of them, this person continued, said, "Nigga, don't you ever come out your face saying some shit you know ain't true," and Warren allegedly explained, "I never even said that shit." According to this person, they smacked him a few times. If this indeed happened, this was not what Dre had signed on for.

◆ ◆ ◆

Dre had little to do with the creation of the *Above the Rim* album. After deciding to include "Regulate," Suge filled the album with R&B songs by outside producers. Second-tier stars like DJ Quik, Aaron Hall of Guy, Al B. Sure!, and SWV appeared on a few songs, but most of the album featured unknowns like B-Rezell, Sweet Sable, DJ Rogers, Thug Life, Rhythm & Knowledge, and Paradise. What rap there was included tired funk, obvious samples, or themes already done to death on *The Chronic* and *Doggystyle*. Then Suge included lesser-known Death Row talents like Jewell, Operation from the Bottom, and CPO. Daz meanwhile produced two Dogg Pound songs that also mimicked Dre's trademark sound ("Big Pimpin" and "Dogg Pound 4 Life") and teamed with Dre to produce a single for Rage. Titled "Afro Puffs," it used the same Johnny "Guitar" Watson sample ("Superman Lover") as had a popular song by New Jersey's Redman.

Though he and Suge were growing further apart with each passing day, Dre's public image remained intact. But then he got into trouble again. This time he was driving in his 1987 Ferrari on January 10, 1994, heading home, when a cop car entered his rear view. Instead of stopping, he stomped on the gas. He went ninety miles per hour but they were still there, so he sped into Westwood. Ultimately the chase ended with cops learning he was driving drunk. A blood test determined he failed a sobriety test with a reading that was 0.16 percent, twice the state's legal limit. He was arrested at a point when everything had been looking up. But not many people knew this happened, so his image was unharmed when the 9,000 members of the National Academy of Recording Arts and Sciences nominated his song "Let Me Ride" for a Grammy.

During the Thirty-Sixth Annual Grammy Awards, in March, Dre was up for two categories. While sitting in the audience, he couldn't help but notice what little hardcore rap was actually included. Then he heard host Gary Shandling joke, "I'm a big Snoop fan. His album *Doggystyle* is a very romantic album to play with your bitch. I swear." The audience broke out in derisive laughter. Then the rap awards were handed out off screen. In the first category, "Best Rap Performance by a Duo or Group" he saw Digable Planets' jazz-flavored "Rebirth of Slick (Cool Like Dat)" beat "Nuthin' but a 'G' Thang," Arrested Development's "Revolution," Cypress Hill's "Insane in the Brain," and Naughty by Nature's radio hit, "Hip Hop Hooray." When "Best Rap Solo Performance" rolled around, he figured LL Cool J's "Stand By Your Man," MC Lyte's chant-heavy "Ruffneck," Paperboy's "Ditty," or Sir Mix-A-Lot's "Just Da Pimpin' In Me" would beat "Let Me Ride." Instead, he won. Before he knew it, Madonna—one of the world's largest pop stars—wanted to work with him. But he told *Newsweek*, "I have no interest in working with Madonna." He wanted to work with malleable newcomers, which allowed him to keep telling reporters his production process, not their individual contributions, was responsible for everyone's success.

Despite the dearth of fresh sounds or memorable lyrics, *Above the Rim* sold 2.1 million copies after its release on March 22, 1994. The album also landed at number two on *Billboard*'s Hot 200, topped the R&B/Hip-Hop chart, and yielded two successful singles: "Part Time Lover," and Warren's "Regulate." But the latest success made many people at the label start adopting even bigger star attitudes. "After *Above the Rim*, they were tripping," one employee recalled. And now even Dre seemed to believe his press clippings.

One day that spring, he sat in Monty's Steakhouse, a trendy eatery in Westwood, and over fried lobster tail and his usual tall Hennessey and coke, watched a car on the freeway trail smoke from a tailpipe. "That car needs to be Midas-ized," he joked.

His female publicist said, "You should know. You have the Midas touch."

"It ain't the Midas touch," he replied. "Midas only turned things into gold. I turn them into platinum." Shortly after this conversation, he saw this quoted in print, in a *Newsweek* story that called him "the Phil Spector of rap."

He wasn't the only one succumbing to ego. At Larrabee Studios, with Snoop's fifteen-deep entourage, Dre told Kurupt, "Kick me some rhymes." While Kurupt delivered another tepid battle rap, "The Things Niggas Do," he lifted his Orlando Magic jersey, pulled a black gun, and cocked it into the mike. Then he kept waving it around until he finished his verse.

Before Dre knew it, Suge announced that a project called *Murder Was the Case* would be next. Dre went with it. It was another soundtrack—for an extended-length video—but it was also a project that would let him leap further into film making. The script called for Snoop to play a gangster killed in a drive-by. After selling his soul to the devil, he returns to Earth and makes it as a rap star. But by the third act, the devil's already hatching plans to send him to prison for a murder. Dre figured that along with directing the seventeen-minute video, he could use its soundtrack to reunite with Cube.

Cube had sold about six million records, married, fathered children, started his own record company, and recorded his fourth solo LP: *Lethal Injection*. Magazines sometimes reported on scrapes he had with other artists, one person said. "But basically he's selling an image at this point and doing a hell of a good job doing it." Once Dre left Ruthless, Cube was willing to meet with him. During their talk, he felt "he was back to the old Dre." After some initial nervousness, testing the water, they met again in Dre's home. "We weren't trying to bullshit each other," Cube explained. "He was the same motherfucker I had met, and I was the same motherfucker he had met. We just clicked, started laughing about old shit."

Before Cube knew it, Dre said, "We ought to do a record together."

"Shit, that's the bomb." Each had projects to finish but Dre wanted *Helter Skelter* out by mid-1994, and to include Ren and Snoop. Since he was bored with gangster rap, he wanted a concept album about "the end of the world kind of theory," D.O.C. recalled. That summer they kept hanging out and discussing the project. When reporters asked what they were up to, they joked, NWE: Niggaz Without Eazy. They were actually working on a song Dre originally started with Sam Sneed.

After directing some of the seventeen-minute "Murder Was the Case" video Dre had returned home one day and heard his guest Sam Sneed play a few works in progress. Liking what he heard, and extremely busy, he asked, "Whatchu gonna do with them?"

"Whatever you wanna do."

"Man, we need to put that on the soundtrack."

Sam was amenable to the idea so Dre joined him for a duet, "Natural Born Killaz," and included Cube on the chorus. But the label was excited about Cube and Dre reuniting and asked Dre to remove Sneed and have Cube say a few raps. Sam was displeased even as Dre reminded him he already had the song "Recognize" on the album. Sam said he didn't like that song, but Dre predicted it would do well.

"Natural Born Killaz" found Dre grimmer than ever. He rapped that his verse was a journey through the mind of a maniac and that he was "doomed to be a killer since I came out the nut sack." He was in a murderous mind-state, he added, "with a heart full of terror" and saw the devil in his mirror. Then he borrowed an old Cube lyric about shooting people with a sawed off. During a tag team chorus he and Cube said they'd shoot someone's heart out of their chest. Dre's next verse was even more dismal. He said he was trigger happy with his Tec-9; he'd aim at your head like the Terminator and send someone to the funeral home. "I'm hot like lava; you got a problem?" he asked. "I got a problem solver and his name is Revolver."

Cube's verse was just as fictitious. He claimed opponents lined up to kiss his ring; his raps sent people to their graves; he'd punch rivals in the nose; and he hadn't seen the sun in sixty-six days. Then for shock value, "I never, ever, ever made a ho stay/but I'm down with Dre like AC is down with OJ." He ended his verse by saying he'd snatch "Charlie Manson" from a truck, crown him with a brick, then start dancing.

It was his hardest song in years, and Dre felt energized by the reunion. He wanted *Helter Skelter*, with Cube, in stores by fall but instead Suge said they should release albums by singers Nate Dogg and Jewell.

Since he had to direct the movie, and cope with his own problems, Dre wasn't able to produce the entire album. But he did handle its centerpiece, "Murder Was the Case (Remix)." He tried to invite other Death Row artists into Sneed's video for the song, but Sam recalled, "Didn't nobody show up." By now, many of them were gossiping about how Dre did little on the album but seemed to be receiving the lion's share of credit. But instead of addressing this complaint to Suge—who was responsible for this development—the other artists continued to jockey for position and talk behind Dre's back.

For all their talk of independence and talent, however, the rest of the album offered many poor imitations of the keyboard sound Dre was beginning to tire of. And none of the material was as memorable as *The Chronic*. The one-note Dogg Pound tried to dis Eazy on "What Would You Do." Snoop offered weak free-styles on his guest-crammed "21 Jumpstreet," and "Who Got the Gangsta." Nate Dogg did a great job with his downhearted "One More Day," but Jodeci's "Come Up to My Room" was no different than anything else on the market. DJ Quik raised a few eyebrows by insulting Crip-affiliated MC Eiht on "Dollars Make Sense" but most of the raps were grim, death-obsessed, and downright depressing (including CPO and Slip Capone's "The Eulogy"). In the past, Dre might have stayed in a studio, obsessively reworking songs until they met his standard of excellence, but the material held little to interest him. And he had to handle another more pressing situation.

In September, Dre had to head to court for the drunk driving incident. He pled no contest to the charges and heard L.A. Municipal Judge Paula Adela Mabrey rule that he violated the probation he'd received for breaking Damon Thomas' jaw. But when she sentenced him to eight months in jail, he was shocked. Then Judge Mabrey ordered him to pay a $1,053 fine and attend an alcohol education program.

Death Row's lawyer David Kenner begged the judge to sentence Dre to mandatory appearances in public service announcements against drinking, but she wanted him behind bars. Dre didn't know what to say, especially when his own mother said this was a blessing in disguise. But then the judge offered a choice as to where he'd serve time. Hearing one option was L.A. County Jail, Suge told Kenner, "Them motherfuckers will kill him. He ain't from the streets." They arranged for Dre to serve his sentence in a halfway house in Pasadena where, Suge said, he could "check in, look at TV, and check out." Until he had to report to the prison in February Dre tried to distract himself with work.

On October 18, 1994, he was happy to see *Murder Was the Case* released to generally positive reviews. Critics singled out his duet with Cube and Sneed's East-Coast–styled "Recognize" for praise but Dre didn't think much of the album overall. About the only good thing one could say about it was that it featured less R&B than *Above the Rim*. Other than that, the album was just further proof that the label was running in place, and, artists soon learned, it had become another source of controversy in gang-infested local hoods, where Crips heard Quik insult Eiht and decided Death Row was a haven for Bloods.

Dre was itching to keep his name out there and to try something new, so he teamed with Sam Sneed again for "Keep Their Heads Ringin'" a throw-back to the days of early Sugarhill singles that he and Sneed both enjoyed. "Yeah, whattup, this is Dr. Dre," he said over a smooth track. "The party's goin' on. Thank God it's Friday." Along with another KRS-One vocal sample, he had a choir of women sing, "Ring ding dong," and spent much of the lyrics bragging about his skills or urging listeners to dance. He also threw in the latest East Coast slang, "Keep it real," rapped a few punchlines that weren't very funny, and tried to woo the female audience by saying, "I'm six-one, two-twenty-five of pure chocolate." The end result was pretty dull, and made Dre sound even more out of step with current tastes and trends, but all of his yes-men said they loved it, so he let Ice Cube include it on his *Friday* soundtrack.

Then he started working on *Helter Skelter* in earnest. He had his hero George Clinton join him and Cube on a song called "You Can't See Me," then told his other house guest The D.O.C. a few things he hoped to accomplish with this concept album. By now D.O.C. was drinking more than ever and even more dissatisfied with his career. But he stuck around, he said, because Dre was living good; Dre was the shit. "He was bringing all the shit to the table so he's getting all the pussy, he's getting all the money, and he's getting the Five Mics." By Dre's side, D.O.C. kept "eating the greatest meals every day," and if he needed money, he'd say, "I need five grand, now go see your people." But the partying was doing something to him. Even though Dre was financially supporting him and letting him crash, D.O.C. felt no one was considering his feelings. "What about me, motherfucker?" he'd ask artists. "I wanna rap, too." Even if they included him on their songs, he'd complain, "They relegated me to comic relief." He told Dre he wanted to rap again. Dre said he didn't think he'd make a good record with that voice, D.O.C. recalled, but he insisted studio techniques or overdubs could fix that.

"You're Dr. Dre, goddammit! There's nothing you can't do in a studio." Dre, he felt, could've found a way.

After he let D.O.C. hear a few ideas for *Helter Skelter*, Dre then heard D.O.C. recite a few lyrics for a new song based on the concepts. He did not know D.O.C. wanted *Helter Skelter* to be his own comeback vehicle when he told D.O.C., "Hey, you need to let me get that song up out ya." D.O.C. concealed his anger and waited until Dre wasn't home one day to pack his stuff and move to Atlanta. But Dre eventually found out a few reels with beats were missing, and that D.O.C. was rush-recording his own version of Dre's concept album (calling it *Heltah Skeltah*) for another label, to beat him and Cube to the punch. When reporters asked about this situation, Dre said they'd fallen out. And in response, D.O.C. told another reporter Dre was a "bitch-ass nigga."

Cube, meanwhile, wondered if the project was still on. "Only track we ever got out of it was 'Natural Born Killaz.'" When no one called him back, he figured Dre had abandoned it. But he hadn't. D.O.C. could keep the idea. Dre was already thinking of something bigger and better.

Unknown to the media, he and Eazy were speaking again, and Cube also buried the hatchet. "They were gonna resolve things," said one Ruthless employee. Away from the media, Dre joined Cube in telling Eazy they'd return to N.W.A. if the reunion didn't involve Jerry Heller. Eazy was elated. "They were gonna reunite. Eazy was obviously getting rid of Jerry. That was one of the stipulations: Cube said 'You get rid of that motherfucker, we'll get back together.'" By December, the secret N.W.A. reunion grew to include M.C. Ren.

But then Eazy got angry at Dre again. By now, he had heard Tha Dogg Pound's lame song on the *Murder Was the Case* soundtrack and was preparing a reply with the same title, "What Would U Do." In the studio, he called them played-out studio gangsters and said he'd kill Suge, slap Dre, blast Daz, and sodomize and beat Kurupt. He also called Snoop a crack-head and described catching him in a crack house and shooting him in the head. He said the only fights Dre ever had were against smaller women. He reminded everyone of how Snoop had worn a corny high-top fade. He said Tha Dogg Pound were punks with a lousy contract and ended the latest attack with a skit in which he burst into a Death Row party and finally killed them all in a barrage of sampled gunshots and screams. He didn't put the record out—he wanted to finish his entire album—but he did call Dre a liar during an interview he gave in February 1995. He discussed how everyone believed Dre's claim that Ruthless underpaid him. He said all that happened back then was that Dre breached his contract with "Deep Cover." "Dre went out running his mouth off, and nothing he said was true," he said. "Everything was false."

Dre wanted the N.W.A. reunion to happen but had to report to prison to begin serving his five-month sentence on February 10, 1995. Eazy was hospitalized for three days after experiencing trouble breathing. He was released February 19 but resting at his home in Topanga Canyon, where he was wheezing and sounding short of breath. Then, Friday, February 24, he was back in the hospital, where doctors gave him antibiotics for a lung infection before diagnosing him with AIDS on March 1.

Thirteen days later, Eazy married his girlfriend, Tomika, and hoped to undergo surgery the next morning; doctors planned to drain excess fluid from his lungs. But at dawn, they instead placed him on life support in the intensive care unit. He was too weak for surgery. With a respirator tube in his mouth, the heavily sedated thirty-one-year-old remained in critical condition. "I didn't know at the time that they had paralyzed him from the neck down with medicine so he wouldn't move," said Yella. "When he first got on the machine, he didn't like it so he was moving around."

Dre stopped by on the afternoon of March 16. Though Eazy had recently made a few disparaging comments, Dre didn't hold it against him. He faced his weakened friend in bed and felt horrible. "I didn't believe it until I went to the hospital. He looked normal. That's what makes the shit so fuckin' scary, man. But he was unconscious so he didn't even know I was there."

Still, his decision to visit touched Ren. Dre "made his peace with that nigga." He didn't let the industry divide them anymore. In the end, all this bullshit had been over records. "This rap game broke up a lot of friendship." Everyone now remembered they'd been friends before music. They accepted that you can't beef forever. People get older. Eazy died of AIDS-related pneumonia on March 26, 1995.

◆　◆　◆

Dre continued to serve his time. The public chalked his absence up to him being in the studio. "I had nothing to do in there but think about how much I was screwing up," he said. But as July approached, he decided to change his entire life. "Before then, I just reacted, you know?" He'd change his musical direction; start his own label, and do something new. "Basically, it was just time for me to move on to the next level." He'd also work in film. It was a good plan. "And one thing about me: I don't just come up with a plan and then tell everybody about it. I execute my ideas." Stupid people talked while smart people acted, he felt. It didn't matter if you failed, so long as you tried.

One day, during work release hours, he stopped by the studio and learned of Suge's latest decision. At first, the plan had been for Rage to follow up her critically acclaimed single "Afro Puffs" with a full-length album. Dre felt she'd been patient enough and a good sport about having to do guest raps. "Okay. They'll get to hear me and then I can build up some hype and then come out," she remembered thinking. But with the media focusing on Snoop, *Doggystyle* had come next. She could have come out after that but Suge decided to do these soundtracks. But without warning, critics praised "Afro Puffs" and Dre felt they should strike while the iron was hot. "It didn't happen," she said, and she didn't know why. "Then I started thinking, 'Maybe it's something personal; maybe it's a female thing; maybe I'm too good; maybe—shit! I don't know.'"

Dre serving time didn't help her cause any—especially since he was the one who had signed her. But Rage didn't let this stop her. She entered a studio alone and spent a month trying to create songs. And for a month, she thought, "Damn. If I'm the next artist, why am I in here by myself trying to produce my own tracks?"

Unknown to Rage and Dre, Tha Dogg Pound were recording demos in Daz's home studio. "Me and Kurupt was getting hot, but Dre wasn't producing for us, so I had to do it myself," Daz claimed. When Rage emerged from the studio, Suge felt her songs were unfit for release. Dre was there the day Tha Dogg Pound finally stepped up and said, "We got a record." Snoop and Suge were also present when the hungry duo played DATs of their songs. When they ended, Dre said, "Nah, we not going to Dogg Pound right now." The songs were a little weak.

But Suge contradicted him. "Man, we rollin' with Tha Dogg Pound. This is what we gonna do."

Though the duo kept talking up Daz's production, D.O.C. said Dre contributed immensely to their album. "You could hear it in the music. Their song ideas needed work." But by now, Dre was tired of being surrounded by "fifty thousand gangbangers in the studio," D.O.C. continued. As a result, the music he made was softer, more melodic. "He started having pretty singin' in every piece of the shit. Even though niggaz was talkin' about murderin' motherfuckers, the music sort of made you wanna go to sleep."

Even with calmer music, though, Dre still saw or heard about violent incidents in the studio. One night, an executive slapped a producer in the face a few times. The producer would have fought back if eight or nine of the executive's friends weren't surrounding him. Armed guards now frisked everyone coming in, even reporters. Certain Blood rappers sat around, got drunk, and started beating or threatening to beat people up. And Suge kept wearing red, showing up with his friends in the Bloods and throwing his weight around. Dre kept working up in the studio, but "started leaving the streets even more then," D.O.C. explained. For Dre it wasn't fun anymore. And the studio continued to teem with strangers. "And me, I don't like working in a room full of people I don't know," he noted. "It makes me uncomfortable."

Dre then learned about an incident at a recent after party at the El Rey Theater. That night, out front, a Crip argued with Bloods in another artist's entourage. The Crip, a member of the large Rolling 60s gang, humiliated the tough-talking rapper but got jumped and stomped on by his pals. The incident ended and the artist entered the club for the after party. But inside, his entourage started drinking and saw the Crip from outside, one attendee recalled. "They just beat and stomped and kicked that poor dude to death." The attack was so brutal, bystanders screamed and ran for exits. The artist slammed a chair into the Crip's head while his many friends punched and stomped him, eventually breaking the young man's spine. That they murdered him infuriated other Rolling 60s members. Though Death Row had nothing to do with this killing—the Blood-related artist had simply appeared on soundtracks—Crips felt the Bloods hanging at Death Row were to blame. A few weeks later, Snoop saw a hundred of the Rolling 60s jeer the very sight of him at another rapper's party. From the balcony, they yelled, "Sixties! W'sup, cuz!" Everything had gone so horribly wrong with this label, and in so short a time.

Upon his release from prison July 10, Dre returned to Death Row with a new attitude. Now, the rivalries and intrigues seemed petty. People were believing their press clippings and taking themselves too seriously. Suge's decisions and the roster's reliance on the same themes were also ruining things. Where once he'd let it all get to him, he now viewed the world with new eyes. While serving his time, he'd finally grown up. He'd been wrapped in the "Dr. Dre image," but incarceration actually turned Dr. Dre into Andre Young. Though they were eager to usurp his position as the label's top act, Dre nevertheless kept trying to help Tha Dogg Pound. On the set of their video for "Let's Play House (Runnin' Fo' the Fence)," yet another forgettable freestyle, he waited until they'd filmed scenes in a rented modern $4-million home then invited them into a van to hear some new beats on a tape deck. He would have gladly handed them over if the group liked them but they continued to understate his involvement with their album.

Within weeks, things went even further south. On August 3, 1995, Dre accompanied Suge and the artists to New York for the *Source* Awards. He won an award that night but during the ceremony, saw Suge and new signee Danny Boy get on stage. By this point, Suge had seen Bad Boy's CEO, Sean "Puffy" Combs, score hits with singles by Craig Mack and The Notorious B.I.G.'s album *Ready to Die*, a *Chronic*-inspired work teeming with witty lyrics, smooth R&B samples, and well-produced tracks. Suge had also tried to lure the R&B group Jodeci and singer Mary J. Blige—both of whom started with Combs—to Death Row and his management firm. Clad in a red golf shirt and chain, Suge grabbed a mic and said, "If you don't want the owner of your label on your album or in your video or on your tour, come sign with Death Row."

In his seat, Dre kept a neutral expression as around him, the Death Row entourage leapt to their feet, and the audience booed. This was the last thing he'd expected. He kept his face just as blank when Puffy took the stage and said he was the guy Suge had insulted but that he had no malice toward him or anyone. And by night's end, Puffy presented an award to Snoop, and embraced him, then left. But during his own performance, Snoop held a walking stick and paced the stage, berating the crowd for supposedly ignoring Death Row's contributions to rap. In his seat, Dre thought a coastal rivalry was inane. "There's definitely no reason for it," he said later. "That's the biggest case of black-on-black crime I've seen in my life."

After the show, Dre tried to smooth things over by hitting the press room to give out tidbits about future projects: Tha Dogg Pound's *Dogg Food*, Snoop's new album, *The Doggfather*, The Lady of Rage's *Eargasms*, and a few film projects. With the mood uneasy, he quickly mentioned East Coast rappers he'd love to work with, including Rakim.

Dre then heard Tha Dogg Pound's new song "New York." It was inspired, Snoop claimed, by Kurupt's victory over three hundred MCs outside of a nightclub. So, back home, he rapped about the incident and Snoop—fresh from their recent trip to the Big Apple—chanted "New York, New York, big city of dreams." With the song coming so soon after Suge's comments at the *Source* Awards, Dre knew fans and peers might view it as Death Row insulting the East Coast again, but Snoop insisted it didn't insult any people, boroughs, or record labels. "It was just a song," he claimed, and a tribute to Grandmaster Flash, whose group the Furious 5 originally recorded the chorus. But upon its release, New York rappers and fans did indeed view it as another example of Death Row saying, "Fuck New York." They took it wrong, Snoop claimed. "But that's when the east-west thing started."

People were already gossiping about potential problems between the labels when Suge and a few friends attended a party in Atlanta. That night, September 24, Puffy, Biggie, and members of Biggie's side project Junior M.A.F.I.A. were there. Suge supposedly had a problem in the club and the evening ended with people shouting and fleeing from the venue. According to Puffy, he left his limo and approached Suge to ask, "What's up, you all right?" then shots rang out. They both turned, Puffy recalled, and saw someone right behind them falling to the ground—Suge's good friend Jake "The Violator" Robles. "I think you had something to do with this," Puffy remembered Suge saying, to which he replied, "What are you talking about? I was standing right here with you!" But after Robles died in a hospital a week later Suge remained angry with Puffy.

At the same time, Dre saw the label come under fire from C. Delores Tucker. To prevent the release of *Dogg Food* she asked Time Warner to drop Interscope. Then during a Time Warner shareholder meeting, she addressed 2,500 people for seventeen minutes. "I asked the [CEO] of Time Warner, 'Do you know what you're doing to our black boys?'" she recalled. Meeting his stare, she told him, "You are destroying not just a generation but a race of people. That's what your music is doing." She remembered him not saying a word, and predicted, rightly it turned out, that Time Warner would sever ties with Interscope, and by extension Death Row.

Death Row acts, however, ignored her, and even joked that she was helping sales, even as Time Warner canned label head Doug Morris and asked Suge to delay the release of *Dogg Food*. Morris' replacement, Michael Fuchs, then flew to Los Angeles to meet with Suge and Tucker at Dionne Warwick's Beverly Hills home but waited for Suge in vain for five hours, then left. Before Dre knew it, Time Warner split amicably with Interscope but not, Iovine claimed, because of records or lyrics. They were trying to get a cable bill going through Congress and didn't need the adverse publicity (presidential candidate Bob Dole was by now speaking out against the genre). An executive at Time Warner told him, "Look, it's got nothing to do with how I feel about this. It's got to do with something that we're working on in a much bigger field." After the split, Interscope negotiated with Doug Morris, who landed at MCA. But *Dogg Food* would be distributed by Priority.

10

J ust when it seemed things couldn't get any worse, Dre saw Suge and
Interscope post a $1.4-million bond for Tupac, who walked out of
prison on October 12, 1995, and into a waiting limo. Dre was already disgruntled, but Suge signing Tupac to Death Row, RBX explained, "was the
straw that broke the camel's back." Like everyone else in hip-hop, Dre had
followed Tupac's exploits in various rap magazines. Tupac was known for
inspiring message raps like "Brenda's Got a Baby," "When My Homies Call,"
and "Trapped" but he was nowhere near as famous as he became once he
started attacking his former friend The Notorious B.I.G. and claiming
Biggie, as he was called, stole his style.

Since then, various shootings, setbacks, and public outbursts had clue-
less reporters acclaiming Tupac as one of the genre's most notable, instead
of noisy and dissentious, figures. But the turning point arrived in 1994.
One night, he told *VIBE*, he needed money and told a promoter he'd
appear on a song for $7,000. But when he arrived at the studio, he said,
the promoter had two armed robbers meet him in a lobby. He claimed
that he pressed the elevator button, turned, and saw both aiming identical
9 mms.

"Don't nobody move," he quoted one saying. "Everybody on the floor. You know what time it is. Run your shit."

Everyone obeyed but "I just froze up," he claimed. "They started grabbing at me to see if I was strapped. They said, 'Take off your jewels,' and I wouldn't."

As he told it, a light-skinned guy jumped on him. Another man aimed at one of Pac's friends and said, "Shoot that motherfucker. Fuck it."

He said they shot him five times, once in the testicle, and that when he made it upstairs to the recording studio, he saw Puffy and Biggie among the forty people present. He also said he noticed everyone had jewels on and that the promoter who had invited him looked surprised. Other people meanwhile said the two men did try to rob him, but that he went for a gun while high on weed, and accidentally shot himself in the groin. Either way, since taking five bullets (including one in the skull), Tupac had been suffering headaches. He'd wake up sweaty and screaming. "All I see is niggas pulling guns, and I hear the dude saying, 'Shoot that motherfucker.'" The psychiatrist at Bellevue hospital—a Manhattan medical center and hospital for the mentally ill—called it post-traumatic stress.

The shooting already had him in the headlines but Tupac inspired even more controversy when he arrived at a courthouse for a hearing on the sexual abuse case the next morning in a wheelchair, with a huge bandage wrapped around his head. He left quickly for an area hospital, and was watching coverage of his trial on television when lawyers came in to say he'd been found guilty.

While serving time in Clinton Correctional Facility in Dannemora, New York, for sexually abusing a nineteen-year-old woman, he granted interviews to *VIBE*. In one he claimed to have turned over a new leaf; he'd be leaving the street attitude behind. But just as quickly, he gave another interview and accused Puffy and Biggie of orchestrating his shooting when he knew they'd done nothing of the sort. Then he told his new wife, "I want you to set up a meeting with me and Suge."

After Interscope gave her the number to Death Row, and she got them on the phone, Tupac told Suge, "Yo, I want to be with the Row." He played to Suge's own massive ego by saying, "I want you to manage me because I'm in jail—and no one is handling my business while I'm in jail, nobody's putting it down like I want to put it down." Suge fell for it, and Tupac no longer had to worry about whether he even had a record deal anymore now that Interscope had left Time Warner.

His last album, *Me Against the World*, was still on the pop album chart after twenty weeks (at number 108) when Suge flew to New York on a private plane to visit him. Dre didn't want Tupac on the label but Suge had his lawyer look into Pac's cases then made his offer. In jail, Pac wept openly, hugging a male visitor and saying, "I know I'm selling my soul to the devil."

Interscope granted a verbal release and Suge's attorney David Kenner drafted a three-page contract. Tupac signed it. On October 12, Suge and Kenner chartered a private jet, flew to upstate New York, and picked Pac up in a white limo. Pac was visibly grateful. "When I got out of jail, he had a private plane for me, a limo, five police officers for security. I said, I need a house for my moms." Suge got him one.

That same day, Suge led him into the studio two hours after his flight landed. "I'm paranoid, I just got out of jail," Pac explained. "I've been shot, cheated, lied [to], and framed and I just don't know how to deal with so many people giving me that much affection." But he got right to work.

Tupac was knee deep into his own smear campaign against Biggie and Bad Boy and filled his songs with threats, insults, and much cheerleading for the beleaguered label. "But he wanted to get off, though," said Nate Dogg. To meet his contractual obligation for a set number of works, he added, "he pushed out at least two to three songs a day."

Suge interrupted the first session to give him a chain with a Death Row logo pendant. While accepting, Pac made a big show of gratitude. Then he kept working. By this point Daz was relishing the fact that, with Dre not coming around as much, he had become the label's top producer. He played Pac a piano-based track similar to one Dre had just used on the R&B group Blackstreet's "No Diggity." Pac wrote "I Ain't Mad At Cha," then young singer Danny Boy recorded the saccharine hook. While Daz added final touches, Pac had a few drinks and said, "Man, this is it!" But as usual, he got plastered and belligerent. He was soon yelling at engineers because he felt they were moving too slowly. "Come on, man, what the fuck?" he roared. "This ain't too goddamn hard. All you have to do is press fuckin' Record. Press fuckin' Record. Now!"

By this point, Suge's ego was just as colossal. He was trying to promote Death Row as a sort of gang instead of a collection of small-time criminals and entertainers who rapped over keyboard-driven R&B. "Whether the odds are in your favor or appear to be stacked against you, the Death Row family sticks with you," he told a reporter a day after Pac's release. After that, he kept popping up in the media alongside Pac.

With so many people looking to kick his ass, Pac was eager to have such a big friend standing near him. He even vowed to make Death Row bigger than ever. "Not stepping on Snoop's toes, he did a lot of work," Pac said. "Him, Dogg Pound, Nate Dogg, Dre, all of them. They made Death Row what it is today. I'm gonna take it to the next level."

In the studio one day, Sam Sneed was working on music for his upcoming album when Pac walked over and said, "Hook me up with some of them beats." Sneed, still trying to be part of the Death Row family even though no one showed up for two videos he'd filmed, replied, "Man, that ain't no problem." Before long, Suge told all of the other acts, "When it's time to work on a project, everybody needs to give everything to whoever's project it is."

When Dre didn't show up to submit tracks, Suge located the tape for his *Helter Skelter* number "You Can't See Me," erased Dre and Cube's vocals, and had Tupac rap near George Clinton's chorus. Although Pac included Michel'le on his song "Run tha Streetz," Dre still wanted nothing to do with this album. "That's it," he told engineer Tommy D. "I'm done with Death Row now that Tupac is here."

This was when Pac turned "Got My Mind Made Up" into an excuse to feud with Dre. Daz claimed he originally recorded the song for *Dogg Food* and invited guests Redman, Method Man, and Inspectah Deck of Wu-Tang Clan onto it. They got it done in about four hours and Kurupt said, "Man, this is the one. We need to drop this, we need to put this on *Dogg Food*." Daz agreed and prepared to mix it. "I had transferred it at Dr. Dre's house and had left it out there," he claimed. But he didn't feel like mixing it, so it didn't make the album. Now, according to Daz, Tupac was bragging in the studio. "I got a beat with Method Man, Redman. Dre made it."

Daz walked over. "That's my beat. I did that."

"That's your stuff?"

He claimed it was and this began Pac's feud with Dre, he explained. "Dr. Dre was taking credit and wasn't doing nothing, wasn't coming around."

Daz didn't mention, however, that studio sessions were now filled with belligerent gangbangers and other strangers (including the Stanley Brothers, now signed to a deal, and the daughter of a law enforcement official involved with his probation). "It got to the point in the studio where brothers were sticking their hand out like 'Yo, what's up, I just signed to the label,' and I was like, 'I don't even know you.'" While Dre worked, they surrounded his chair, boozing, puffing weed, and yelling. Some of them even started waving gang signs and yelling lyrics. Then he saw people attack others and no one step in to break it up. An artist once attacked an engineer because a machine took too long rewinding a tape.

Publicly, Pac kept promoting the label, as promised. But behind the scenes, he started picking on Rage. He called her the weak link since she wouldn't insult Puff and Big at Bad Boy, but she didn't fall for it. "I don't think that makes me the weak link," she told him. "I think it makes me the strong link. I'm an individual."

"You not my homegirl?" he asked.

"Yeah, I'm your homegirl."

"You not gonna dis someone? They tried to kill me."

She asked, "Why don't you see 'em face to face?"

"I'm not tryin' to kill the motherfucker. I'm tryin' to kill his career."

Before long, Pac's album seemed to take precedence over everything else. Can-Am Studios was filled with his massive guest list, rowdy gangbangers and security guards with sidearms. And with so many reporters interested in interviewing Pac—portraying him as a tough guy when he was the victim of the tough guy who shot him—Suge was able to stand near him and appear in just as many magazine features and television interviews. During these, Suge chose to present himself as a sort of red-clad kingpin of crime, as opposed to a show business guy with friends who rolled with real street gangs.

Signing Pac was bad enough. But then Dre heard Suge had signed MC Hammer. As a performer there was nothing wrong with him. Born Stanley Burrell, he had recorded the big hit "Can't Touch This," a rousing but commercial number set to Rick James' "Superfreak." But in the years since that hit, he'd blown his fortune on Lear jets, salaries for old buddies from the Oakland projects, jewelry, cars, and a home on a hill. Hammer was thrilled to be working with Suge, who reportedly helped with security during Hammer's successful 1989 tour. "He wasn't just the 'muscle' side," Hammer said later. "He had a lot of movie things and a lot of soundtrack things going on. He was in the midst of diversifying his company." Meanwhile, other artists, like Snoop, claimed Hammer's arrival was a blessing. "Hammer sells a million records," he said. Hammer's past in pop-rap didn't bother him. "That's what he do. And he do it to perfection. Can't nobody do it better than him."

But no matter how they tried to spin it, Hammer was an odd choice for the label. Still, Suge figured they could reinvent him: Replace the sequin outfit, glasses, and high-top fade with a wool cap, an O.G. tank top, some Locs, and heavy Carhartt jeans and work coats. Hammer, in financial doldrums, was eager to help. "I've worked around the real Gs," he now told a reporter. "I ain't talking about none of that fantasy stuff. I'm talking about looking at the bodies drop." From afar, Dre realized Suge had derailed whatever vision for the label he once had.

At home, he worked on a solo album, he said, "and 'California Love' was the first song." For this one, he set a rollicking Joe Cocker piano, first heard on a single by New York's Ultramagnetic MCs, near party lyrics and a Zapp-like Vocoder chorus. He was finishing it, considering whether to use it for a new company, when Suge somehow heard the song and felt it'd be a hit. Before he knew it, Suge arrived at the house. "Suge was like, 'Fuck it, we're putting Tupac on that shit, and this is going to be the single off the record,'" said Tommy D. Instead of standing up to Suge, Dre told himself this would benefit his career. It would take him at least six months to form another company and get a single in stores, so this would keep his name in front of paying customers. He returned to the studio and replaced his second verse with one by Pac. He also let him ad-lib at the end, and even joined him in a *Mad Max*–like video featuring futuristic shoulder-padded warriors riding dirt bikes in the desert.

But before he knew it, Dre heard Pac was badmouthing him. This time, the beef was over Snoop's trial (for the murder of Philip Woldemariam). On February 6, 1996, the prosecution offered closing arguments in Los Angeles Superior Court. As they had each day, Suge, MC Hammer, Devante Swing of Jodeci, and Tupac sat in the audience. Dre, however, didn't show up during this phase of the long-running trial. Fifteen days later, after deliberating six days, the jury finally acquitted Snoop and Death Row supporters cried, "Thank you, Jesus," then headed to Monty's Steakhouse to celebrate. But Dre didn't show for this, either.

But by February 1996, Suge didn't really feel he needed Dre anymore. Not with *VIBE* giving Tupac more pages in which to insult Puffy and Bad Boy Entertainment and to claim he had slept with Biggie's wife, Faith. And not with his double CD, *All Eyez on Me*, debuting at number one and selling 566,000 copies—earning Death Row $10 million—in seven days.

When Dre read the *VIBE* feature, he was appalled. The writer described showing up at Suge's office and seeing a "big, light-brown German shepherd rolling on the floor." One of Suge's friends said, "That's Damu," another word for "blood." "He won't bother you," the guy added. "He's only trained to kill on command." Then, while the reporter asked questions, Suge kept the dog near his side, baring its fangs and salivating; not exactly the best image for the company. Neither was Tupac bragging, "Muthafuckas is scared shitless of Suge."

11

Thirty-one-year-old Grammy-winner Dre saw Death Row earn $125 million in four years. But he also saw his plans for the company turn to shit because of short-term thinking and baseborn characters. "I was trying to take it places no other record company had ever been. Not just limiting myself to R&B and hip-hop. I wanted to branch off into jazz, reggae, and black rock 'n' roll." He reflects on the days when he did *The Chronic* and Snoop's debut to get things rolling, when "it was just a big family thing." He liked Suge back then, since Suge involved him in the business side, and was enthusiastic about Dre's plan for the label. He felt confident letting Suge handle the business side while he created records. But Suge started getting a big head, wanting to be as big a star as the kids on the records. He started wearing red and filling the office with ex-cons and strange faces. Not all the hangers-on were professional so the mood at Can-Am studio became oppressive. Then, along with unruly gang members, he began to see armed security guards, many of them off-duty cops wearing sidearms. Then Dre heard Suge supposedly threatened reporters.

And now, Suge is riding on Tupac's coattails, popping up on the cover of the *New York Times Magazine* with a red suit and big cigar and telling another reporter, "The folks who really did the production and wrote stuff on *The Chronic* and Snoop's first album started complaining about credit." He is trying to credit Daz with producing over half of *Doggystyle* and says he let Dre take full credit but had to stop since "niggas was mad. Things wasn't right by them. I can't have that." Suge also harps about wanting more credit for his own contributions to the label. He concedes that Dre is a great producer—he has to since *The Chronic* earned $50 million, *Doggystyle* earned $63 million, and Dre can say that since N.W.A., his music helped various companies earn a staggering $250 million—but he adds that "Dre didn't become Dre on his own. I went out and got the *Above the Rim* soundtracks for the company. We needed something," he claims. "Dre didn't do nothing on it. He did one song on *Murder Was the Case*." This isn't true. Dre did more than that. And as for needing something before he got *Above the Rim*? Dre had wanted to work on Michel'le, Rage's album, and *Helter Skelter*. But despite these self-serving comments, Suge still wants Dre to produce music for Hammer. And to his chagrin, "The nigga just kinda hid, stopped callin'."

Now, Death Row talks about Dre's obvious absence at label events and Can-Am Studios. Stories also claim Suge is supposedly seeing Michel'le, mother of Dre's son, Marcel. Then R&B singer Danny Boy tells a security guard, "That punk-ass motherfucker Dr. Dre." Then a second later: "Man, you ain't heard? Gay-ass Dre . . ." He says this when other stories claim he and Suge are very close.

Dre has been around these people for years and knows how they operate. He isn't surprised to hear they've graduated to branding him a traitor during meetings. They keep harping about his non-appearance at Snoop's trial or the post-acquittal fete at Monty's. Then someone, probably Suge, tells everyone including gullible Pac that during the trial, a witness claimed Dre was in the Jeep when Woldemariam was killed. If Dre had taken the stand to tell the jury this was a lie—which it was—it would have helped Snoop's case. But Dre didn't show. "I don't like the fuckin' courtroom," he later explains. "That's my reason for not going. I don't like going up there and I never did. And I never will. I talked to the lawyers all the time and I knew he was going to get off. And if Snoop wanted to chill he came by the house and we kicked it."

But someone keeps spreading rumors, quoting Dre as dismissively saying he's too busy to show up. "That's how they told me," Pac recalls, so instead of confronting Dre, like a man, to discuss this, he keeps badmouthing him at every turn, and in print says, "There are secrets that everybody's gonna find out about . . ."

But he does so when many artists and employees at the label still respect Dre. So word reaches Dre that Pac keeps trashing his good name. At one point, Pac tells a bodyguard, "Fuck Dre. Dre didn't support his homeboy and he's supposed to be part of Death Row and he's not even down." Another night, at Suge's home in Vegas, he claims he'll fuck Dre up if he ever sees him. Then at a Death Row party he yells, "Fuck Dre."

At home with his new girlfriend Nicole and her son Tyler, Dre's confusion slowly turns to anger. "Fuck that. I ain't do nothing but help Tupac."

Dre can't relate to these puérile attitudes anymore. "I'm a grown up now," he says. "I'm ready to handle my business." In March 1996, he calls Jimmy Iovine at Interscope. "I'm ready to bounce," he says. "Make me a deal and I'll make you some hit records.'"

Jimmy's supportive, and took a chance on Death Row when no one else would. "They put up the money, bought me out of Ruthless, and they've been looking out ever since." Interscope might also hold exclusive rights to him as a producer—obtained through the earlier deal with Ruthless—but then again, it might not. Dre doesn't say. What is clear is that Jimmy understands Dre feels stifled at the label and his music makes money, so that quickly, Dre's off Death Row. "Very simple," Dre says. "I ain't got nothing to say to nobody. I'm just out. Period. I don't like it no more."

It will mean distributing two labels with top executives not getting along, but he accepts Dre's proposal for a joint venture and tells a writer, "Suge and Dre are both enormously talented people. They both understand what it takes to make a great record, and they would never settle for anything less. I don't have any question on how successful either person will be."

Dre, meanwhile, feels he's learned from past mistakes. He accepts that he fled Ruthless for Death Row only to make even worse mistakes. But from here on, "I'ma be able to do whatever I wanna do," he says happily. "If it works, it's on me. If it fails, it's on me. But I'm an innovator. I like trying things."

He grants a *VIBE* interview and proudly says he's the sole owner of his new company, even though Interscope actually owns part of it, too. "Suge does not get a cut of anything that I do. Nobody gets a cut of anything Dre does—except Interscope."

Once he leaves Death Row, he quickly sells his car collection. He only drives one car at a time, and doesn't need to showboat with thirty of them. At a car dealership, he buys a white Mercedes with tan interior he's had his eye on. But soon, he finds out Suge has told a reporter Dre sold the cars at the urging of his new accountant, since he's broke. "Actually, I have more money than I had with Death Row," Dre says. "And my business is being handled a lot better."

He also moves into a new $3.25 million home in Chatsworth, a 10,000-square-foot number on seven and a half acres, complete with five bedrooms, a game room, a six-car garage, a swimming pool, and a tennis court.

He calls his new company Aftermath Entertainment and begins hiring a staff of black women to oversee the label's day-to-day office operations. As he puts it, they'll be "Dre's Angels," while he's "like Charlie: unseen, just heard."

He also meets with former Death Row artist RBX, who insulted him on his year-old solo album, *The RBX-Files*, for smaller Pre-Meditated Records. After accepting his apology, Dre vents about his departure from Death Row. He says he's tired of Suge's unpredictability and recording songs about gang-banging. "I'm sick and tired of drive-bys and all that shit." The conversation ends with Dre offering a demo deal for RBX's song "Blunt Time."

Dre also meets with former N.W.A. members. With Eazy's final album *Str8 Off the Streetz of Muthaphukkin' Compton* in stores and Yella's solo album, *One Mo' Nigga to Go*, coming soon, Dre revives plans for a group reunion. "It won't be the same without Eazy," Ren says, "but it's not like he's still alive and we're trying to do this without him."

Dre being off of Death Row makes it easier since Yella—who can bring unreleased vocals by Eazy—won't do it for that label. And Dre and Cube won't record for Ruthless. Yella proposes a neutral label and that they allocate one-fifth of profits to the late Eazy's children and Dre tells a reporter, "I'm totally into that shit. The ultimate goal is to do an N.W.A. movie about the life of N.W.A. and do a soundtrack for that. There's a bunch of shit people ain't even knowing yet." He also regrets not doing *Helter Skelter*. Even though D.O.C. released his sleazy knock-off, which tanked, Dre glumly says "If Cube is still into it, I definitely wanna do that record. I don't give a fuck if it's ten years from now, and we're, like, walking on canes with gray hair. That record will be amazing."

Dre also looks forward to repairing fractured relations with the East Coast. But he learns that on March 29, 1996, Tupac and Biggie ran into each other outside of the Soul Train Awards in Los Angeles. Thanks to Tupac's falsifications, Biggie took the stage to accept an award, mentioned his hometown of Brooklyn, and heard the audience jeer and boo. Then Tupac, Suge, and all their friends arrived in fancy vehicles. Tupac, in camouflage gear, hung out of a window, trying as always to get attention by yelling, "West Side, outlaws!" They saw Biggie and Junior M.A.F.I.A. and rushed to confront them. By now, Death Row had released Tupac's repugnant "Hit Em Up," which mimicked Junior M.A.F.I.A.'s "Players' Anthem" and found him repeating his claim of having bedded Biggie's lovely wife, Faith. They hadn't seen each other since the Times Square shooting but when Biggie took one look at Tupac's face he reportedly thought, "Yo, this nigga is really buggin' the fuck out." As Tupac blocked his path, Suge and his Death Row bodyguards stood nearby "and they was like, 'We gonna settle this right now,'" Biggie recalled. But Biggie's intoxicated friend Lil' Cease had enough of Pac's useless prattle. "Fuck you!" he yelled. "Fuck you, nigga! East Coast, motherfucker!"

"We on the West Side now," Tupac railed. "We gonna handle this shit!"

Their entourages were getting ready to scrap but once again Tupac didn't really want to fight. After this latest rubbish, Dre reaches for a telephone and calls Puffy to say he had nothing to do with Suge and Tupac's smear campaign. "I have love and respect for what he's doing," Dre explains.

When Dre officially announces his departure from Death Row in late March it seems more like an afterthought. He's already looking forward to a brighter future. He doesn't take any of the acts with him but that doesn't mean he isn't thinking of them. He asks mutual acquaintances how Snoop's new album sounds. He also asks about Rage and hears, thanks to the producers at the label, the music sounds like garbage. "I hear she's got Luke-type beats on it," he tells someone. He feels this is the worst thing about leaving the label, not being able to work with Snoop, Nate, Rage, and even Kurupt and Daz. "I hope God will bless them and they will become successful," he says with a sigh, "and that their business will be handled the way it's supposed to be."

But his departure leaves many artists at the label stunned. "I didn't know he was leaving until he was gone," says Rage. Then Dre receives shocking news from Sam Sneed during a telephone call. Before leaving the label, he'd invited Sam to his new company, Sam recalls. Now, Sam says Death Row called his home and said, "Sam, come in. We're having an artist meeting." When he arrived at the office, he learned the meeting was really about Dre's departure. In the conference room, artists nitpicked about the lack of local talents in Sneed's video. He replied that he'd invited them all to the set but another artist, probably Tupac, bitched about Sam not yelling "Death Row" enough on his songs. Sam felt nervous. Then the artists all attacked him. They beat and punched and kicked him until Suge called them off like dogs and Sam left. He considered heading right over to Dre's house, but Suge invited him to a party for Snoop. He went because he was from out of town, had few friends in L.A., and they knew where he lived. And at the party, he recalled, Suge told him, "'You don't need to be with Dre. He be taking people's credit.'" Once Sam relayed the entire story, Dre was floored. "He was upset. But there wasn't nothing he could do. That's the bottom line." Within a week, Sam boarded an airplane and left the West Coast.

Death Row now turns their attention to Dre. They're struggling to save face by claiming he didn't leave, but rather, got the boot. Tupac includes the false-hood in yet another windy *VIBE* interview. He also contends Dre allegedly took production credit for beats by other artists. "And I got tired of that." Then he gripes about Dre "takin' three years to do one song. I couldn't have that." Yet, amid much bluster, he admits, "But it was not my decision. Suge was comin' to me." Dre ignores their bitchy comments and rumors. He's away from them, at his own company, gathering talent for its first release. Everyone from Rakim to Melle Mel (creator of the "message rap style" that birthed the gangsta genre) is calling the office and before he knows it, he receives a page from a strange number, and calls back. "Who this?" he asks.

CPO.

"W'sup?" Dre invites him to dinner.

In the past, CPO had been slimmer, and had taught some N.W.A. members karate in their Compton hood. Ren also produced his debut for Capitol. At the table in a restaurant, Dre, CPO's brother, a woman named Kim, and Dre's bodyguard Bruce joke about CPO's weight. "Lemme tell you like this," Dre says. "Do you realize how much records you would sell if you was a little smaller?"

"Dog, that ain't gonna matter," he replies, citing Biggie.

Dre agrees.

The portly rapper mentions a demo but adds Dre already heard it. "The motherfuckers is now damn near a year and a half old."

"Don't matter. Lemme hear 'em anyway."

He would prefer to create new material but Dre insists on hearing this tape. Then seconds later, he says, "Matter of fact, lemme tell you something. You don't need no fucking demo. Just, when you get off the Death Row contracts, sign."

CPO excitedly writes a song promoting the new label and sends his tape to Dre. But Dre's bodyguard Bruce tells him, when he calls, "Yeah, uh, Dre didn't really like that song." He asks which and Bruce says, "Uh. Neither one of them." After much debate and a few curses, CPO demands to speak with Dre. But Dre doesn't come to the phone and when CPO keeps calling the studio people keep asking, "Can we take a message?" Dre's busy with a few other things, so the rapper finally stops calling. "Next thing I know I found out he ain't wanna hook up with gangsta rap," he says.

◆ ◆ ◆

"Motherfuckin' Dre!" Nas cries.

Dre sounds embarrassed. "Uh."

"Whassup, my nigga?"

"Sup, Nas?"

"Chillin', God."

They're on a microphone in the studio, working on this respected New York rapper's second album, *It Is Written*. Dre met Nas on the set of *Murder Was the Case* one night and agreed to produce this song, "Nas Is Coming."

Dre figures, in addition to positioning him as someone with no animosity toward the East Coast, it will improve Aftermath's chances of signing Nas's side group, The Firm.

As the song continues, they pretend to smoke weed together, then logroll. "Niggaz is stealin' your whole techniques and shit," says Nas.

A second later, Dre says, "Just like niggaz can't do what you do." He has a choir of ladies sing, "Nas is coming," and introduces a tame beat. Then he returns at the end to say, "Let's get paid, sit back, and watch all these moth-erfuckin' clowns out here riffin' and beefin' about this bullshit."

Dre prides himself on having a company where "tape talks," artists have talent, and positive people all love the company as if it's their own. No one's getting beat up. People aren't drinking beer or showing up in blue and red outfits. Everyone rallies around him as he tries to create bomb videos with unusual concepts and new sounds for his marketing people to peddle to the media. Everyone passing him in the halls has a purpose. Most can throw tracks together, which is great since Interscope wants this compilation in stores pretty quickly.

As Dre sees it, it'll be like *The Chronic*, introducing the talent and sounds they'll try at Aftermath. He'll also try other new things, relinquishing a bit of the control, having faith in the people around him. He'll oversee every album, but won't take over if something sounds complete. "I trust my artists." And where he once claimed he was like Midas, he hears other producers have hot ideas, too, and accepts some of his stuff isn't always good. Like anyone else, he has bad days, too.

Away from the office, he's in a new relationship. Her name's Nicole Threatt and she was once married to a famous ball player named Sedale. That she's white inspires whispers that Dre is trying to sell out and fit in, but he doesn't care. Nicole provides the stable, peaceful home environment he's always wanted, dinner's on the table on time, and she supports his move into softer R&B now that labels are getting dropped, labels and fans on both coasts are feuding, and the federal government's looking into whether imprisoned drug lord Michael Harris financed Death Row by handing Suge $1.5 million. With Nicole and her son Tyler around, Dre finally stops trying to make nice with Michel'le. "She's like my sister," he says. "We don't get along. She's doing her thing and I'm doing mine. We only gotta communicate about our son."

He never tells anyone why he and Michel'le broke up.

He spends the month of April signing eighteen acts to demo deals. He has various producers, including a group called The Soul Kitchen, churning out smooth R&B in various studios. He's mixing songs, choosing a label logo (a big "A"), hiring people like DJ Mike Lynn, meeting with artists and managers, and wondering if he should team with a stuntman for a violent action movie script.

And instead of going to clubs—where he'll run into the Death Row retinue—he gathers co-workers (including his bodyguard Bruce and producer Chris "The Glove" Taylor) to "go out to eat." Dining's his new hobby and it's beginning to show but he jokes about it, saying he's blowing up. "I'm a lot more humble, a lot more laid back."

People around him are confused by some of the changes but only because they know the image he created. He plays hip-hop during his commute from the studio but turns it off before entering the house. Around Nicole and her son, he really gets into smooth love songs by Toni Braxton. It's a great life, but some nights he feels antsy so he'll get into his car and drive while listening to some hardcore Too $hort.

In the studio, he tries to experiment with orchestras and violins. He's showing an interest in learning the tango. He soon tells a reporter, "I'm the innovator of hip-hop soul. I practically invented the shit with Michel'le: R&B over hip-hop tracks."

Dre takes a much needed break in May, to marry Nicole and honeymoon in Hawaii, then returns, more energetic than ever, to work on his N.W.A. script, "Please Listen to My Demo," his TV pilot, *Half-Way*, about troubled youth, and the label, which he sees as a fresh start for Dre—he refers to himself in the third person—and "for the man who created him: Andre Young."

Though he recently considered an N.W.A. reunion, he's embarrassed by some of the things they said and did back then. In the studio, he struggles to step into a new identity. He doesn't want gloomy keyboards. Instead he experiments with bongos and his usual samples from hip-hop records. He's recording a song called "Been There, Done That," which tells critics (and Pac types), I been there, done that/You got guns? Yo, I got straps/A million motherfuckers on the planet Earth talk that hard bullshit 'cause that's all they're worth."

He follows this catchy, mature hook with lyrics about rap being a business. "No question, it's all about the d-o-e/So if money is the root I want the whole damn tree." He tries some East Coast paranoia (mentioning a secret society called the "Illuminati" that supposedly want to destroy all black people), discusses his net worth (he has enough to buy an island) and offers a job description: "Since way back, I've been collectin' my fee/With the 48 tracks and the m-i-c." He tells listeners he got a bargain on his new home (in the Hills, overlooking the sea and worth $8 million, "but I only paid five-point-three") then describes how he listens to demos in a stretch limo. He also throws in some Biggie-styled verses about partying on exotic islands.

The second segues from a self-description as a "young, black Rockefeller" to saying, "Ladies, get your paper, too. Don't expect for no man to support you: keep it true." He says guys don't want a moocher. "My woman's independent, makin dough by the caseloads." He's rich but keeps working hard so as to grow old with his millions. "That's where it's at," he continues. "You got drama, I got the gat/But we both black, so I don't wanna lay you flat." He stumbles on the last line (about watering his lawn with Moet) but comes back after a chorus to urge fellow millionaires to " throw a stack in the air." If they do, he predicts niggers will plot, bitches will stare, and broke gangsters will "make the fo-'five flame with no shame." In the end, he's ambivalent about money. Ignorant and greedy people kill for it, it's "the root of all evil and sins," but "Luciano in all amounts, that's all that counts."

Dre will also include a second single on the album, so he invites Nas, RBX, and a few other people to his home studio one night to watch them "smoking a pound of weed and just vibing to this track." Dre likes it, too, and starts chanting "East Coast [pause], West Coast." Before he knows it, the others are helping him write a chorus, shouting "Killer!" They know he isn't a killer at all—that he's stressed by Suge and Death Row—but they also want to see him succeed, since his turning over a new leaf might inspire the many young black people who look up to him. Within minutes, Dre is rolling tape and RBX records a freestyle. In the hallway, Nas sits on the floor and constructs another intricate Rakim-style verse. "Oh shit," Dre thinks, "we might have something here." The next day he plays the tape and tries to figure out who'd sound good on its empty bars. He decides to include B-Real, whose group Cypress Hill has an enormous following on the East Coast. In the studio, B-Real raps that people attack coasts when they "can't survive on both sides/so they try and break off, eliminate ties." Dre still has a few bars to fill so he reaches out to raspy-voiced Method Man, of the critically acclaimed New York group Wu-Tang Clan. But Meth can't make it, so he thinks, "Well, damn, who else is fly? Who else is the shit? Bam. KRS-One."

After years of sampling KRS-One's voice, Dre now hears the self-described "Blast Master" rap, "Yo, why do they make me wanna ruin they career? Before I bust your shit let's get one thing clear." KRS soon works his way around to another attack on the tough-talking style favored by Dre and his ilk. "I check one-two's and who's in the house," he rapped. "Like shit, your lyrics ooze out ya mouth."

Pleased with the results, Dre moves on to the obligatory interview with *The Source*. In another cover story, he explains why he left Death Row. He knows Tupac's out there badmouthing him and generally tries to avoid getting into it with him. He's not trying to be a gangster anymore. He's not starting anything, but he's also no punching bag. He just wants to live his life. But midway through the interview, he loses his cool for a second. "And what's he talkin' about, 'Dre jumped ship'?" he asks of Tupac. "Dre built the ship he's on right now. All that is bullshit." That said, he gets back to building his company. He's done with Death Row but Suge keeps calling for master tapes he plans to throw onto a *Death Row Greatest Hits* album. Then, according to Dre, someone rings his bell one day in June 1996. He doesn't answer the intercom but the person who does let him know it's Jimmy Iovine. "Jimmy Iovine? Let him in."

Dre pads to the door with four-year-old stepson Tyler. He opens it and sees Suge with eight or nine of his Blood friends. "Yo, w'sup, fellas? Come on in," he says.

Suge says, "We trying to get the tapes."

"Okay. All the tapes are being copied right now. 'Cause I want a copy of all the work that I did."

"Okay. Can I talk to you for a minute?"

"Let's go in here in my family room."

They sit.

Suge's smoking "a big-ass cigar" and asks for an ashtray.

"No. You can use this motherfucking coaster."

"He started talking about, 'Yo, man, there's no reason for us to be beefin', we need to be making millions, getting together, this-and-that,'" Dre recalls.

Okay, that sounds good to me, he thinks. But out of the blue, Suge adds, "Well, um, you should put the Death Row logo on your upcoming record."

"Huh?" This won't happen. It'd insult him and everyone at his new company. But he says sure. Tell him what he wants to hear. Avoid problems in the house.

Suge leaves happy but Dre feels violated, disrespected. Suge could have come over alone, he feels. Like a man. He'd be more than welcome. He didn't need to bring eight or nine motherfuckers. If he had some shit that was his, Dre would return it. "But when he came over with all his guys, automatically I thought he's coming to bring the noise. But I ain't tripping," he adds, "'cause I ain't that kinda nigga."

Within days they meet at Gladstone's restaurant in Malibu to work things out. Dre won't discuss specifics. "Let's just say I'm very, very, very financially stable and I don't have to push any more buttons if I don't want to." Though he held the title of president at Death Row, he takes nothing when he leaves. But he doesn't need it. "We'll just see who's on top in the next five years."

He thinks that's that, but sees Suge pop up on the cover of *The Source* a week after their meeting at Gladstone's. In one photo, Suge wears a red suit and stands near a Rolls Royce. In another, he's seen with MC Hammer and Tupac, with Tupac flashing a "W," for West Coast, on three fingers. The text finds Suge describing his version of his recent visit in such a way that readers will think Dre's a coward. Suge claims he sent a messenger to get the tapes, heard him say they won't let him in, then told this guy he's on the way; that when he got there Dre hid while an off-duty cop came out, nervously holding a gun; that Suge still went inside, casually shot some pool, then saw twenty cop cars arrive. But he still left with the tapes. "I ain't no playa hater but don't be no bitch about it," Suge says. "Be a man, motherfucker. Dre know he like to go places and do thangs but now he up in the house. 'You put yourself under house arrest, what kind'a shit is that?' I told him he should just been a man about it instead of hiding out at home."

The comments are upsetting but Dre stays cool. He's seen Suge and Pac launch similar campaigns against Puffy and Biggie. "The mentality there is, you have to be mad at somebody in order for yourself to feel good, even to be able to make a record." They hope to spur sales with a feud "instead of just laying back, getting off everybody's dick, making some strong music, and going on with your life."

But now everyone's gossiping. Stories claim former label mates attacked Dre. One guy even says he missed a photo shoot for *People*; that he sat in a car outside a supermarket with a battered, bruised face while someone shopped for him. Another claims he's been shot in the left arm. "It's a million fuckin' rumors floating around," he says during an interview. "I've gotten shot. I've gotten beat up and all this ol' shit. Ain't nothing happened to me and ain't nothing gonna happen to me." But his bodyguard Bruce is nervous. Bruce, strapped, already has friends asking why he'd work for Dre when he can get killed. He says Dre's not like other stars. He made it to the top but always extends a helping hand. If Dre's foes come blasting, he'll go out defending him. But again, "I don't wanna die over this. No one does."

Dre doesn't let Death Row stop his forward motion. He shoots a video for "East Coast West Coast," rents a small office in North Hollywood, and starts editing this video and a second clip, "Been There Done That." "East Coast West Coast Killas" shows his guests rapping for a crowd of punk-rock extras and gang members in a dreary prison yard. While editing the video on a computer he sees an image of RBX strapped to a burning crucifix. "MTV might not go for all that fire," he quips. KRS' face appears on a large monitor overlooking the crowd. "KRS is the shit, but what's with all the green lighting? I feel like I'm watching a Sprite commercial." Nas shows up in black leather and a doo-rag and Dre nods along, but when someone mentions Interscope wants more footage of Dre during the chorus, he frowns. The second video, "Been There Done That," is more sedate, and unveils his conservative new image. In a tasteful Italian suit, he grins and watches the sun set from the balcony of a corporate tower.

When *VIBE*'s reporter shows up, Dre says, "I just want to be positive, helping people help themselves." The real Andre Young. "I want nothing that has to do with Dr. Dre. I wanna even take the 'Dr.' off my name and just be Dre. Just being Andre, true to myself." He hangs with the writer one August night at upscale eatery Georgia on Melrose, where entertainment mogul Russell Simmons stops by to say hello. Then Motown's president and CEO, Andre Harrell—who reportedly had his own situations with Suge—calls him over for a thirty-minute chat. Then basketball star and part-time rapper Shaquille O' Neal waves from across the room. "All right, Shaq, baby."

He tells *VIBE* everyone says, "Yo, man, that was the smartest move you coulda made." He can't help but think, "Damn. Was the situation I was in that fucked up?" But even as Patti LaBelle, Luther Vandross, and Magic Johnson keep reaching out, he knows Death Row is spreading rumors.

He knows Tupac told a high-ranking *VIBE* executive Dre's a closet homosexual and that the voluble rapper made similar claims on his songs "Toss It Up" ("check your sexuality, it's fruity as this Alize") and "To Live And Die In L.A." ("'California Love' Part motherfucking Two without gay-ass Dre"). As with singer Danny Boy, Pac says this even as people claim he was the one who got raped in jail. At any rate, Dre tells the *VIBE* writer—the same guy who wrote that image-shaping *Source* cover story in 1992—that his fans will hear records insulting him. "So from here on out, Death Row records don't even exist to Dre." And about being gay? "Now that's gotta be the funniest shit I've ever heard in my life," he says. "I can't even respond to that dumb shit. All I gotta say to that is, I love my wife and that's the only person I love. That's it. That's the only person I go to bed with every night."

Dre makes good on his word. He doesn't address Death Row anymore. Instead, he focuses on getting the compilation ready. He's happy to see it coming together quickly. And while "my producers Bud'da and Stu-B-Doo" create most of its R&B, he does inject a few ideas into various works.

He fills "Aftermath (The Intro)" with a sample of some howling wind, a little wildlife, and a beeping countdown to an explosion. It worked with N.W.A. and Death Row, so why not use it again. As the beeping quickens, he says, "This is dedicated to the niggaz that was down from day one." Then, after the explosion, "Welcome to the Aftermath." New rapper Sid McCoy then includes themes near and dear to his heart: Aftermath's sound has national appeal; the company will dominate R&B and rap with new sounds; Aftermath is for the East and West Coasts. "And we don't set trip, we set trends." Dre is even more pleased when McCoy adds they are all very professional people that view keeping it real as "moving the cash markets," generating income, and leaving something for their children.

He then hears newcomer Kim Summerson sing "Choices," Maurice Wilcher perform "Please," RC sing "Sexy Dance" and "Fame," and Jheryl Lockhart croon "Do 4 Love." The audience never heard of any of them but Dre sees unlimited potential. He's just as proud of new rappers Miscellaneous, Whoz Who, Sharief, and Nowl (who record melodic non-gangsta works "As The World Keeps Turnin'," "No Second Chance," "L.A.W. (Lyrical Assault Weapon)," and "Nationowl"). Then he has RBX rap about weed and good times, and sing a chorus to the tune of "Summer in the City," over "Blunt Time"'s stodgy drum track.

With the song done, he returns to recruiting acts for his roster, including King Tee, who has just left MCA. "It was about the time that all the labels were shutting down," Tee recalls. After buying MCA Seagram's is consolidating divisions, so Tee can use a deal. Dre meanwhile wants to work with Tee. He has a name, he can deliver gangster themes, but he can also throw in the sort of punch lines the East Coast likes. Dre produces "Str8 Gone" and likes the results so much he has the humorous, good natured rapper join lesser-known singer RC on a glossy cover of Bowie's "Fame." He figures fans might enjoy Tee's brand of self-deprecating humor. In the studio, Tee more than delivers, calling himself "the chubby alcoholic rhymer" and adding that his bald head isn't swollen with ego.

With only a few more songs to go Dre hears thirty seconds of a demo tape by Melvin ("Mel-Man") Bradford. Mel's "Shittin' on the World" starts with the well-known vocal style from Audio Two's old hit, "Top Billin." "M-E-L: Man, niggas call me most," he raps. "I be rockin on the East and the West Coast." Dre signs Mel, includes his novelty on the album, and lets him co-produce a few other tracks. Then he signs another East-friendly group, Nas' The Firm, and tells a reporter, "The album is gonna be on my label. And it's gonna be hot."

But in the end, he knows his audience, and Interscope, view him as the biggest draw, so he has to get on a few songs and let everyone know a new act like Hands-On (his version of En Vogue) is Dre-approved. During "Got Me Open," he calls for more edgy lyrics, then delivers the gentler rap weary genre fans might now enjoy. He includes the civil rights catchphrase "eyes on the prize," admits he studies "every song that dies," and says he's been selling large amounts of records since N.W.A. and has "family and fans from New York to L.A." "Welcome to the Aftermath," he concludes. "Ayo, Crystal, what you got to say?" This woman sings that, when her man touched her spot, she never wanted him to stop. "I swear you got me open," she wails.

When recording wraps, Dre is happy about the album featuring assorted styles, new twists on workaday R&B themes (a guy telling a woman *she* has to beg to come back), references to the East Coast, slang phrases popular among younger listeners, and long-winded rappers alluding to socioeconomic realities. It isn't a Dre record—in fact most of it sounds nothing like him—but he claims he's happy about this. Some of it is deficient but he needs to show the industry he isn't a one-trick pony who only does gun-happy party rap. He would have loved to create more songs, but his new wife likes it, the media prefers this softer image, and he was busy getting the label and his new house in order. At the same time, Interscope wanted the album on time. He turns it in and tells himself he'll do another Dre album soon, and take his time with that since it'll have to be "as good or better than *The Chronic*. It has to be."

12

With two tires blown and the windshield smashed, Suge floored the BMW and made a U-turn against oncoming traffic.

Vehicles scattered.

Two policemen at the Maxim Hotel saw the caravan make U-turns.

They leaped into their car and chased Suge's BMW.

It was the night of September 7, 1996, and a few hours earlier Pac had slugged a reputed member of Compton's Southside Crips in the lobby of the MGM Grand Hotel, where he, Suge, and their ever-growing entourage had enjoyed the Mike Tyson–Bruce Seldon boxing match. Suge was driving Pac to his nightclub, Club 662, in a rented black BMW 750 and had stopped for a light when a late-model Cadillac with California plates pulled up to Tupac's window and someone opened fire. "I could see Tupac trying to jump into the backseat," someone in another car explained. "That's how his chest got exposed so much." Two bullets tore into his chest. Another went through his hand, severing his middle finger; a third in his leg. Bullet fragments grazed Suge's head. After thirteen shots, the Cadillac peeled off to the right and left the scene.

Now, Suge Knight stopped the black BMW. Cops arrived. Tupac lay stretched out on the backseat, bleeding heavily. Ambulance lights flashed.

"There was blood everywhere," a witness recalled. Suge exited the car, his face covered with blood. He told a cop he'd been shot in the head. The cop raised a shotgun. "If you don't get down on your knees right now, buddy, you're going to get shot in the fucking head again." Suge repeated he'd been hit. The officer kept his shotgun aimed. "Get down."

"I gotta get my boy to the hospital."

"Shut up. Get down."

Suge did as told.

Tupac Shakur died six days later in a Vegas hospital, and fans worldwide mourned the loss. He was brash, outspoken, and downright rude sometimes but he also had a very large audience. The media reported on the killing, and implied he lived by the sword and died by it. Other critics used it as an opportunity to denounce the genre as violent. When attacks on the music didn't kill it, they again graduated to criticizing the audience.

At Aftermath, Dre was suddenly asked to comment on the murder. He didn't want to get wrapped up in this. "It's nothing personal against you," his general manager told the *VIBE* reporter still in town. Dre also didn't want anyone from Aftermath saying anything, either, but RBX granted an interview in which he remembered urging Suge to be more professional, only to see him sign Tupac. And Tupac, he added, didn't know what he was talking about: "Death Row" and "Death Row's the shit!"

"I would've been the first person to tell him to shut the fuck up 'cause Death Row is what Dre, Snoop, and I made," he continued. As he saw it, the murder wasn't surprising. You couldn't "keep poppin' off, talking trash." And about Pac having been some sort of "leader," as newspapers now claimed? "Tupac was noisy. Nothing of substance. You know," imitating his loud voice: "'*Aw, fuck you and your mama.*'"

Reporters kept asking his opinion so, despite Pac calling him a fag, Dre said, "It's hard for me to believe that Tupac is no longer with us. It's a real tragedy." He was showing *Los Angeles Times* reporter Chuck Philips a new video in a Sherman Oaks studio when he said it. "He was a real talented individual," he continued, "and I feel very bad that it all had to end like this."

Dre felt the same way about the compilation album. *Dr. Dre Presents The Aftermath* sold a million copies when it arrived in November but Dre heard many people call it wack and imply that Aftermath was over with. Whether his attempt to create a new identity stemmed from his reading of the marketplace or a desire to disassociate himself from the past was unclear, but he was deflated when most reviewers and fans brushed the album off without much of a thought. The *Los Angeles Times'* Neil Strauss claimed some of its artists were among "the top ten acts of 1997" and called RBX's "Blunt Time" a great song but his endorsement didn't change public perception of the album. Neither did co-producer Mel-Man's spirited defense: "It went platinum and shit."

With the record sitting in stores, King Tee opined, "Dre just left Death Row and I think they wanted to see him come back with some Snoop or gangsta shit." New songwriter Shari Watson said, "I think it wasn't Dre. It wasn't him at all. Dre wasn't happy about the compilation. I think he just got married. He's a little too happy."

Dre himself now disliked it, and regretted changing direction. So when Snoop (whose Dre-less *Doggfather* managed to debut at number one) stopped by to pitch an album-length reunion, *Break Up to Make Up*, Dre was willing to listen. "We were doing fine by ourselves," Snoop claimed, "but the fans want to hear us together." Dre figured they could work out which label would release it then ship it to stores by January 1997, but then he abandoned the idea for The Firm's debut.

◆ ◆ ◆

In early 1997, Dre was working on this album when he learned Suge had been sent to prison. The night Tupac beat the Crip in the MGM Grand, a security camera filmed Suge kicking the guy, violating the parole he had received for beating up the Stanley brothers. Now people relaxed and felt the acrimony between coasts was over. But a week after Suge was sentenced, March 9, during their last night in town, Puffy and his top draw, Biggie, attended a peaceful industry party thrown by *VIBE* magazine at the Petersen Automotive Museum. After the party, the rapper sat in a vehicle, nursing a leg he'd recently broken in a car accident in New York. When his vehicle stopped for a light, a black Impala pulled up outside of his window. The driver aimed a gun in his right hand, emptied it, then took off. Within minutes doctors at Cedars-Sinai Medical Center pronounced Biggie dead.

At Aftermath, Dre was stunned. He enjoyed Biggie's work and had stayed on good terms with Puffy and Bad Boy. When reporters called to ask his opinion of the killing, he refused to grant interviews. In April, he continued to struggle to regain his footing. Named best producer by supportive mainstream critics, he felt everyone was envious of his achievements and untroubled life, and was delighted to see him fail. In addition, Nicole was either pregnant or had given birth to their first child together, a boy named Truth (Dre has never discussed this in public), and he was trying to adopt her son Trevor, at which he eventually succeeded.

He decided he needed the right artist, and embarked on another maniclike signing spree, though about eighteen acts already had demo deals. When someone gave him The Last Emperor's demo, he figured he'd be one of twelve groups Dre wanted to enlist. During a call to Emp's home in West Philadelphia, Dre invited him to Cali, where he offered a contract and outlined the direction of his album. "It was fly as hell," Emp said. "I was like, I'm rocking over one of Dre's tracks."

Dr. Dre also signed a newcomer named Eve. During a Saturday afternoon meeting with artist managers, he watched them play a tape so she could stand and start rapping. He stopped her after a few bars and said he'd bring her to California. "I had been through a lot of auditions," Eve explained, "so I thought, 'If he calls, he calls; if he don't, he don't.'" He called the very next day, Sunday, and told her to be out there by Friday. Then he immediately started working on her three-song demo.

Next, he signed Dawn Robinson, who provided many lead vocals for En Vogue's Grammy-nominated hit "Don't Let Go" before leaving that group. And in May, he decided to work with songwriter Shari Watson. She'd been half of a singing duo (Suge & Dap) and released a single and video, "Just Another Man," before Giant Records folded. Dre liked her photo and tape and tried to include her in the group Hands-On, since one member left. She wore lounge gear and carried a bottle of white Zinfandel to her audition. "Let's get it started," she said. "I'm here to write, I'm here to make my paper, gotta take care of my baby. Now what?"

He liked her energy but felt she was too good to waste on back-up vocals for a remix of Hands-On's "Got Me Open." "I'm not using you for the group," he told her, "but continue writing and stay on board." He had her write for Dawn Robinson. Then, in July, he leaped back into his New York–friendly Firm project.

On paper, it was a great idea: four well-known younger rappers plugged into the new East Coast trend of rapping about money and power over well-known R&B hits from the past. Dre was excited, and eager to help this group create a well-defined image. One way to do this, he felt, was to have them include their band name in titles of songs they worked on. During "Firm Family," rapper Nature, a huge fan, said working with Dre would help them sell a million copies "in less than a day." Dre agreed to rap a verse filled with trendy references to old-time gangsters, Bentley cars, Cristal champagne, jet-set vacation spots, good-looking women, a Jacuzzi, shopping sprees, and the positive example he was setting for people on both coasts. "That's how we do it," he said. "Aftermath Incorporated."

"Phone Tap" was a slow-moving track about paranoid drug dealers telling each other the feds were trying to lock them up. During the chorus, Dre chanted, "We got your phone tapped, what you gon' do? Cause sooner or later, we'll have your whole crew."

But the momentum slowed a bit when group members began fighting amongst themselves. At the board, Dre sat and waited for them to get it together. Then they wasted more time on songs they couldn't use. One of them, "Fist Full of Dollars" had a spaghetti western guitar and Dre rapping over mossgrown drums but, Firm member Nature recalled, "Columbia didn't wanna pay Interscope set money for it."

Still, by August 1997, Dre and his co-producers finished the album and his contributions were among the most commercial or image-shaping ("Firm Fiasco," "Phone Tap," "Firm Family," "Untouchable," and "Five Minutes to Flush"). Their lead-off single, "Firm Biz"—with Dawn Robinson—garnered a respectable amount of radio play, but in horror Dre saw fans not take to this work, either.

Even as he put the band through its paces and kept reworking songs until they were flawless, the trend of MCs posing as mobsters had peaked. Then there were too many guests (Foxy's brother Pretty Boy, Wizard, Canibus, Noreaga, and Half-A-Mil). And the music had too many chefs in the kitchen. Where Dre usually controlled every aspect of an artist's album, and created all of the music, he now had to share supervising producer credit with The Trackmasters group (who worked on a few singles by Biggie). Then he had to consider ideas his collaborator—longtime friend Chris "The Glove" Taylor—brought to five of six tracks he did. Even worse, Dre's fogyish beats, flamenco guitars, and R&B rhythms didn't mesh well with The Trackmasters' seven melodies.

Even worse, he had better music to include but couldn't use it, his pal Ben Baller recalled, once "some of the producers had problems." After *Dr. Dre Presents The Aftermath*, the production unit The Soul Kitchen slowly became dissatisfied with Dre and the company, Baller explained, "and it just didn't work out."

The Firm: The Album managed to sell a million copies but at home, image-conscious Dre obsessed over how, until now, he could boast that he took the sound with him when he left a label. Now, on his own, the "sound" (or right co-producer) wasn't there. Though he had more than enough platinum hits to his name, he literally couldn't sleep. He wished people in the industry and at magazines would understand having a bad year didn't mean he was all washed up. "After *The Firm* project people were saying that I fell off. Everybody was expecting a classic record, but it's difficult to make a classic every year."

As Dre saw it, he had two flops to his name and needed to work even harder. And now, his joint venture partner Jimmy Iovine wanted to help turn things around.

In Jimmy's garage one Saturday night in October, Dre played him everything he worked on that day. He knew Jimmy believed, "The first one, you're lucky. The second one, maybe you're onto something." And so far, Dre's second label wasn't too hot. Once the tape ended, Jimmy told him, "I want you to check this out. What do you think about this kid?" He brought out a cassette he received from an intern at the company, who taped young Detroit rapper Eminem's freestyle on local radio. The rapper was in town for a contest and Jimmy, after living with the tape for a few days, still liked what he heard.

Dre listened to Em's "Bonnie and Clyde" and "Murder Murder" and wanted
to work with him. And when Jimmy mentioned the rapper was white, "Then
my wheels started turning." A white kid would be a change of pace, and Dre,
who was married to a white woman, felt a Caucasian could say things he
couldn't. "If a black guy said that stuff, people would turn the radio off. That's
reality." Monday morning, he let Em into his huge, well-furnished home.
Born Marshall Mathers, he was chubby, in dire financial straits, and wearing
a bright yellow jogging suit. "I thought he was Tweety-Pie." Dre meant
Tweetie Bird. "I even called him a banana," he added.

◆ ◆ ◆

Em was raised in hardscrabble Detroit, and enjoyed rap since hearing Ice-T's
"Reckless" from the soundtrack to *Breakin'*. He enjoyed The Fat Boys, and LL
Cool J's hardcore classic *Radio* ("the most incredible shit I'd ever heard"), but
was inspired to rap after hearing the white group Beastie Boys' *Licensed to Ill*.
He made the transition from fan to performer but claimed early shows in
Detroit were for scowling black audiences. Meanwhile at home he and his girl
struggled to support their daughter; a ravenous crackhead kept breaking in;
and Mathers finally yelled, "Yo, fuck this. It's not worth it. I'm outta here." He
wanted to move to the suburbs. "Can't you see they don't want us here?" For
six months, he stopped writing but went to clubs and (he claimed) withstood
abuse. But inspired by Nas' tangled classic *Illmatic* he returned to music with
his self-released, little-known *Infinite*.

A day after joking about his yellow tracksuit—a freebie from a Detroit
clothier—Dre had the awestruck kid in his home studio. Dre sat near the
Solid State Logic 4000E/G console, playing a dopey horn-laden track based
on Labi Siffre's "I Got The." Em created a hook ("Hi, my name is Slim
Shady") and lyric that described him and Dre as a team.

Dre played another instrumental and Em had something for that, too,
about smoking weed, taking pills, and dropping out of school. He finished it
up, then Mel-Man, also present, suggested a line for the chorus, "Don't you
wanna grow up to be just like me?" They called it "Role Model." Dre waited
until Em finished a jeremiad against white Detroit group the Insane Clown

Posse ("When Hell Freezes Over") then played another track. "Are you diggin' this?" he asked.

"Yeah, I got a rhyme to spit to it."

But "Ghost Stories" was another noncommercial thing without a chorus, a series of verses about being trapped in a haunted house with bleeding walls ("like some *Poltergeist*-type shit," Em recalled). It wasn't too promising, but the speed at which he worked impressed Dre. "We came up with four joints that night and three made it onto his first album," Dre reported. He also enjoyed Em's animated voice and polysyllabic putdowns. "I felt that."

At Aftermath, Dre auditioned the songs for black employees. Some said, "Yo, that shit is dope," he claimed. He thought so, too, until most asked, "What are you doing?"

"Yo, Dre is fuckin' buggin' out," said another employee.

Even the general manager questioned his judgment. "Look, this guy is blond with blue eyes. What the fuck? What are you doing?" He had to make a choice. Going with Eminem would open him up to attacks from fans, peers, and segments of the media. But this was a business. If he didn't sign him, someone would. He felt Eminem had talent. He was the sort of apolitical jokester pop radio would love. And white skin practically ensured his success with reporters and critics most comfortable when praising someone whose story, or pigmentation, resembled their own. With most rap fans being white, an Eminem album could result in an unprecedentedly high sales figure. And the mere fact that he, Dr. Dre, was working with him would give Em credibility. Best of all, the actual music would be good. He told his general manager, "Yo, this is gonna be one of our biggest artists right here."

Despite a growing chorus of complaints from black artists who wanted Aftermath to release their own music, Dre kept working with his new white rapper. During one session he saw Eminem record a skit called "Ken Kaniff," in which a gay man called him on the phone to proposition him. Kaniff kept calling him "cock boy," and saying they should have sexual relations in a hotel room. Dre didn't know what any of this was about, but watched Eminem respond that the guy was a bitch, then hang up on him. This was controversial enough, but when Dre saw Eminem keep including the word "faggot" in lyrics, he finally warned, "You better get ready. Some shit is about to happen."

With each song, Em went from not knowing how to work a drum machine to learning more about hooks ("This is easy") to absorbing how Dre did things. Finally, during a session, he programmed a drum beat, and sang, "I never meant to give you mushrooms, girl." From here, Em insisted on creating his own drums and melody for a song called, "Still Don't Give a Fuck." As he hummed a tune to Dre's players, Dre told him, "You don't even realize it, but you're producing."

They kept creating songs and Em's story raps consumed two days at a time. Then he'd shift gears and record darker, less accessible rhymes. This was well and good but Dre had a lot riding on this, so he started suggesting song concepts. One day, in the gym, he pitched "Night 'n' Day," a duet in which he'd say one thing then Em would contradict it. It evoked his tag-team "Deep Cover" with Snoop. The next day, he heard Em recite the completed work. Inspired by a scene in the white frat-house comedy *National Lampoon's Animal House*—in which a character about to rape a woman saw a devil on one shoulder say do it and an angel on the other say no—Em had written three cinematic scenarios: a liquor store, a rape, and a jealous husband, and cast himself as the demon.

Dre quickly booked the time and did the beat—drums and a sample from Ronald Stein's "Pigs Go Home" (from a 1970 Elliot Gould film)—then and there. After an announcer from a talent agency recited dialogue over empty bars Dre added sound effects and Em's reference vocal. For a week, he sat with the lyric, going over it again and again, trying to master an intriguing new conversational style. Once he had it down, he recorded it then watched Em, near song's end, suddenly rap about Dre's forgotten attack on Dee Barnes. Instead of being angry, Dre laughed so hard he almost fell from his chair. They made a very good team, he decided.

Snoop meanwhile felt the same about him and Dre. He had finally left Death Row and signed to Master P's No Limit label, which was in the process of churning out about twenty-eight albums in 1998 alone. Though Dre was busy as always, he agreed to produce some of Snoop's No Limit debut, and was also pleased to see how well Snoop had adapted to changes in the genre. During *The Chronic* days, all he wanted to do was rap, make a video, and have fun. Now, he realized "there is a big business here," Dre explained, "and there's a lot of money to be made with it if you handle your business correctly." It was true; that year rap fans were buying a historic eighty-one million albums, helping the genre finally outsell country, which sold seventy-two million.

Snoop's melodic lullaby raps were engaging enough but Dre felt he needed to return to core values. So he filled "Just Dippin'" with an intricately arranged version of the old *Chronic* sound. And while he had long outgrown the image of unemployed car owner—and certainly didn't pal around with gangbangers anymore—he trotted out the old image one more time. "Dippin' down Compton Boulevard," he claimed. "I only rides with my dogs."

"Say what?" Snoop asked.

"I don't give a fuck about none of y'all."

"Fuck y'all," Snoop added.

"I'm ridin 'til the wheels fall off." During his verse, he said he paid his dues and deserved his luxury car; he felt wary driving through the hood without a gun; he'd get a rapper in Fubu clothing; "where there's a hoe there's a hater"; and he had sexy women hanging around since he was living like a pimp. Then Jewell sang another old-time chorus: "Hey, oh yeah, oh yeah. Better watch out, 'cause here we come."

Snoop was very happy with the song, but when recording another, "Bitch Please," Dre felt compelled to tell King Tee's pal, Xzibit, "Look, man, I need you to do this song with my man Snoop." Xzibit got this song, another attempt to recapture *The Chronic's* best-selling spirit of friendship, done in fifteen minutes, and Dre saw it become Snoop's biggest hit in years. So when Xzibit stopped by and asked if Dre would produce a few songs for his own third CD, Dre replied, "Why don't you let me just produce the album?" He knew a good thing when he saw it, and was pleased to hear Xzibit immediately say, "Bet." Then, once he gave him a few beats on tape, he saw Xzibit brag in print, "I got that new Dr. Dre."

During this same period, Dre included Snoop on "Zoom," his contribution to the soundtrack for the Warren Beatty movie *Bulworth*. It was based on a chorus from an old Wreckx-N-Effect dance hit and Snoop did what he could with the subject matter—telling girls he wanted to party, dance, and screw them—but Dre removed his voice and instead had LL Cool J rap. For years, Dre had tried LL's mix of come-ons for the ladies and cocky boasts and insults, and "Zoom" found both in top form. "I got my mind made up, come on, get in, get into it," Dre sang. "Let it ride, tonight's the night, yeah." Then LL included one of Dre's favorite themes in his verse. "Before the album went platinum, ya hardly speak." Then, over snazzy jazz-like piano, Dre coaxed him into some *Deep Cover*–like banter. "All I wanna do is Zoom-a-Zoom Zoom Zoom," he said.

"Mmm, whatchu whatchu wanna do?" LL asked.

"Uhh, whatchu wanna do?" Dre rejoindered.

Then Dre claimed everyone called his cell phone; this was his triumphant return; he still had his performance abilities; and his new song was "the most anticipated since Tyson's return." He also quoted Run-DMC's "Here We Go," a record he loved during the old Cru era. "So come on everybody let's all get down/Cause what we have, is a brand-new sound." LL meanwhile spent his verse telling younger artists they were blind and he was a legend. "I'm like a narcotic, niggaz is microscopic," he insisted. "Dr. Dre and Cool J, is the topic." He added that so-called young talents were "cosmetic/If shorty wanna step up? I'll twist his neck up/You can't get no money battling me; that's like ripping your check up." They teamed for a video in which Dre was able to try on a nice Puffy-like image but the single went largely ignored by even his longtime fans.

Back at Aftermath, artists talked until they were blue in the face, demanding to know when their albums would come out. Many employees were just as confused by Dre's sudden enthusiasm for a white rapper, but in the month of April he signed another black talent, Brian "Hittman" Bailey, to the label. Mel-Man had heard him first and arranged an audition, and that day, the gifted rapper rhymed for Mel, Eve, producer Lord Finesse (Mel's friend), Last Emperor, and others. Though they tried to trip him up by playing unorthodox beats he kept doing well so Mel finally reached for the phone and called Dre. "You got to fuck with this nigga tomorrow." Dre was recording Eve when Hitt arrived and after only a few words, he stopped him in mid-sentence. "That's all I got to hear."

By this point, Dre was working on his next album. To make Aftermath work, he realized, he had to come back with the right material. Fans didn't

want an R&B Dre. And even his wife, Nicole, agreed. She never stopped
playing *The Chronic* in her car's CD player and asked, "Yo, what are you
doing?" Dre explained, as a married man with daughters, he wanted to
respect women. She told him go back to hardcore raps about bitches and
hoes. "That's the real Dre," she added. Dre was relieved. He could finally
abandon this role he'd been playing for a few years now. "Let me get back to
being me," he thought. He didn't care that he was returning to the same
gangsta themes he'd spent most of 1996—and "Been There, Done That"—
renouncing.

Some days, he'd have fun throwing together old-school sounds on the SP
1200, a reminder of how he started. But he put these things aside. The audience expected the usual: funk-flavored music, lyrics about driving through
Compton with a gun, a few boasts, and a circus of guests. And he had to
make this new one better than *The Chronic*.

He had about one hundred tracks. "Some had hooks, some had singin'
on it," Hitt remembered. "Some had a whole song." Hitt—still unsigned at
the time—stopped by each day. He praised Dre's "Xxplosive," the beat formerly on King Tee's "The Future," as nothing less than a masterpiece, and
kept practicing rhymes over beats Dre created. Liking what he heard, Dre
kept inviting him onto his songs. Soon, Hitt was on "Big Egos." For this
work, Dre offered insight into the person behind the impenetrable image
of rap's most successful producer. He said he had more class than other
people; forgave a few traitors; shot at others; and still had to be careful in
dangerous California, since "niggaz die every day over some shit they say."
He was disconnected from the streets, he said now, but also packed a gun
in case he ran into "niggaz that been hatin' me lately." He said he made
stars of Eazy-E, D.O.C., and even Tha Dogg Pound; he owned acres of
land now and bought floor seats to Lakers games; he liked to grab his dick
while posing for pictures; and everyone should play his new song in their
luxury vehicles. From here, Dre then invited Hitt onto "Bitch Niggaz,"
another rant about fair-weather friends. This time, he claimed D.O.C.'s pal
Six-Two told him, "These niggaz after yo' paper, Dr. D.R.E." Then, he
scratched in one record that said, "Attention all personnel" and another,
Audio Two, saying, "Stop scheming and looking hard." Hitt later said both

were "basically my demo songs." And by July 8, 1998, Dre officially signed
him to Aftermath.

◆ ◆ ◆

As 1998 continued, Dre followed his work on Eminem's debut with sessions
in which he recorded R&B and songs for compilation holdovers RC and
Hands-On. He also had Shari Watson write for Dawn Robinson and felt her
reference vocals sounded better than the acts she was writing for. "And I was
like, 'I'm feelin' her.' She was kind of crazy," he said. But he stopped working
with Watson when he ended the Dawn Robinson project after three or four
songs. The results of their sessions were fantastic—Dawn had flavor, and the
musical direction was hot—but Shari Watson felt it might have been a personality thing. Dre had to feel someone worked as hard as he did and would
do whatever it took to make a hit. If someone didn't possess these qualities,
she added, "it's not gonna work with him."

At Aftermath's office Dre learned other artists were growing impatient.
When Eve said she wanted an album out quickly he told her, "Shit, let me talk
to Jimmy and see what I can do, 'cause I'm really trying to concentrate on my
album." He placed her song "Eve of Destruction" (from the three-song demo)
onto April 1998's *Bulworth* soundtrack but before he could work on her
album, her one-year contract expired and she left for upstart New York label
Ruff Ryders Records.

Last Emp also wanted music in stores. Dre was excited about him until
other people questioned a white pop audience's interest in someone named
after a Bertolucci art house film with dreadlocks and army fatigues, rapping
about "animalistics," imitating various animals, and getting heavy and political. Emp himself felt Dre was under pressure; that the compilation flopping
made Dre too cautious. "So we had a lot of disagreements with my image."
Soon, Emp hinted he wanted to leave, and Dre said he understood.

Then King Tee wanted out. Dre had worked on his album in progress, and
liked what he heard. Tee still represented Compton, and the hood, but also
positioned himself as a deep-voiced, Biggie-like "baller" and million-selling
rapper. He also included the sort of financial themes kids wanted to hear at

the time, saying in one rap he was "straight 'bout it / buildin' ideas with self-made millionaires to get the dance floors crowded." And he knew how to promote the label. Midway through "Da Kron," he said, "Aftermath fixed me with that shit that won't fail," then a second later, "Dr. Dre laced me with that shit that won't fail."

Initially, Tee was just as excited. He felt any day now he'd be Dre's next superstar and wrote about the many years he'd paid dues and women who'd rejected him. "Goin' platinum? I plan to," he said in one rap. "Run and tell 'em, King Tee's bailin' with Dre!" he said in another.

While busy with other projects, Dre had staff producers Bud'da and Stu-B-Doo work with him and Tee soon dedicated "Stay Down" to two dead Gs—a Crip and a Blood—and urged kids to stop the violence. "Speak on It" described crimes, gang signs, and rival gangs meeting in Leuders Park to arrange a truce. "Squeeze Your Balls" was about partying with gangsters in a disco. He rapped for the ladies on "Let's Make a V," alongside vocals by El DeBarge (who'd wanted to work with Dre since the *Above the Rim* period), and sounded great rapping near his guests Shaquille O' Neal ("Shake da Spot"), New York's Kool G Rap (over the Parliament sample on "G Luciano/King Tee finale"), MC Ren ("2 G's from Compton") and Killa Ben (really Sharief from the compilation song "L.A.W. [Lyrical Assault Weapon]," and featured on Tee's "Real Raw").

Before Tee knew it, Dre had produced a number of songs, and included more of the compilation's producers and talents. He had Dawn Robinson sing on "6 N'na Moe'nin," a Biggie-like tale of betrayal that included samples from B.I.G.'s songs "Warning" and "One More Chance." He then invited RC and Crystal to sing on "Step on By" and "Big Ballin'." He produced something called "Where's T," then gave him one of his finest tracks, for "The Future."

Dre also joined Tee and Dawn on "Monay," in which Dre confidently taunted his many critics. Instead of trying to get people to like him, he said haters sat on their ass griping about the next man instead of creating their own company. He said he worked hard since his days with the Cru, "and ain't a damn thing changed." He admitted that he moved from the ghetto ("the firin' range") and into a plush estate to escape "niggas with the problems always out to battle me." He told fans he didn't care about his old problems or detractors and would remain "a nigga talkin shit about his bullshit salary."

Dre's employee Ben Baller, who handled A&R duties for this album, remembered it sounded "fuckin' bangin' like a motherfucker." But when Tee was about a year and $600,000 into the project, Interscope began to critique his material, he recalled, since Dre's compilation "didn't really do what it was expected to do." Then Dre had second thoughts of his own.

After the compilation and The Firm, Dre needed to show he still had it. Though ads promised *Thy Kingdom Come* in summer of '98, after *The Source* gave an advance copy a three-and-a-half-mic rating, everything changed. The rating wasn't as bad as two and half mics—which meant something sucked—but it was also not a five, which meant all-time classic. And this, Tee felt, shook Dre's confidence in this work. Either way, King Tee soon joined Eve, RBX, Dawn Robinson, Last Emp, and the many compilation artists on the shelf. Then Dre hinted Interscope didn't like his material. "Let's do some more songs."

Tee instead pitched leaving and releasing it on his own imprint.

"I'll help you do that if you wanna do that," Dre said, "but if you wanna stay, you can stay."

Tee amicably split with Aftermath Entertainment. Dre let him take the completed album. When Tee opined it was outdated and considered a double album (one with Aftermath stuff, the rest new material) Dre graciously offered to produce two songs for the new one. "It's just about Interscope getting their money," Tee explained. "They want, like, five points." And it was only right since Iovine paid for the sessions, he added. "Everything is straight. I have no beef, nothing." Instead of Aftermath's next platinum superstar, Tee would be one of the many guests on Dre's next album.

By December 10, Dre learned the industry was about to undergo historic change. Until now, there had been a "Big Six," major labels that dominated music sales. But Seagram's bought Polygram and its imprints from Phillips for $10.4 billion. Now, Universal—Interscope's parent company—would account for 25 percent of all music sales here and in Europe. Universal now owned Island, Def Jam, Interscope, Geffen, A&M, Polydor, MCA and other labels, meaning it would profit from albums by many of rap's biggest acts.

And Universal wanted to make a few changes. For one, Geffen and A&M Records would become part of Interscope. Island and Mercury would be smashed together to form one company. And it would trim about $300 million a year in costs from various companies. "In the process, buildings will be sold, some 3,000 employees will be let go, and record labels will be gutted," the *New York Times* reported. Fifteen thousand employees—label presidents, promoters, A&R men, publicists—feared they'd be fired. Hundreds of bands worried they'd be among the two hundred dropped from contracts. Layoffs and dropping bands was nothing new in the cyclical industry, especially when a new owner came aboard, but this was a historic first. The changes followed years of labels signing acts for big money only to see them not release any new work. And when they did put something out, none of their music made the *Billboard* Top 40. At Universal, executives now looked over an act's previous sales. They repeatedly played their albums. They auditioned works in progress. They spoke with managers and A&R men. They met with the performers themselves and even attended concerts for fear they'd drop an act just when they created a surefire hit.

And if a musician emerged from personal tragedy or trouble with songs that had a new energy, that worked in their favor. But from now on, Universal wanted nothing to do with musicians that were coasting, in it only for the money and going through the motions, uninterested in what they were playing.

While changes were planned, artists delayed albums. Many employees put nothing but the bare minimum into promoting albums released that fall by Geffen, A&M, and Island Mercury. Sales were lower than usual for some acts and fewer of their songs popped up on radio. New groups were asked to accept new, less-profitable terms; two thirds of the acts signed to Interscope or the new Island Mercury would get the boot. Some would be able to take their unreleased works in progress to other labels, providing former labels received a portion of profits that let them recoup monies they poured into recording costs. And some acts were jittery since they didn't immediately know whether they would stay or go. That decision would be reached after they turned in their next album. Still others entered a sort of limbo, kept busy churning out demos of new material so label executives could determine their commercial viability.

For the next two months, Universal executives would trim the staff, cutting up to 75 percent at some labels. They would meet bigger stars arriving onto their rosters. They would also take a very close look at the lesser-known bands. Within sixty days, they'd know who would get dropped. "We're going to take our time," one unnamed executive told the *Times*. "At the end of the day, we'll be fair to both the acts we let go and the ones we keep."

At Aftermath during December 1998, Dre reached his own controversial decision. He said he was imagining where he'd be a decade from now and wondered which of his current associates would still be in his life; which were positive enough to merit inclusion. "That list turned out to be very small. But the list of people around me at the time could have filled the Forum."

At Aftermath he cleared the entire roster and began anew. Eve, Last Emperor, Dawn Robinson, King Tee, and most artists and producers from the compilation were out. And while he liked her work and style, so was songwriter Shari Watson. "Everything that I wrote kind of fell by the wayside because he lost his groups shortly after that."

King Tee understood why he did it. "Dre was gonna lose the deal with Interscope and that's why he put Eminem out and that saved it." A lot was happening at the time, Tee added; with some labels uniting and many black-owned imprints suddenly being shut down after mergers. Dre felt he had to deliver impressive results, and to do that he needed acts that could cross over, appeal to radio, and earn millions of dollars. "So the house got cleaned as far as employees and whatever else," DJ Ben Baller noted. Dre placed tracks for abandoned projects into the vault, near copies of everything he'd done. He also canned a number of label employees. "The sole survivors were me, Eminem, and Mel Man," said recent arrival Hittman.

But the firings led a few producers to rekindle rumors that Dre took credit for their ideas. King Tee said it was bullshit. Others did create beats in the studio but "Dre came in and added his shit and made it 'phat' and he took half of the fucking credit. So what? So fucking what?" Other big name producers did the same, he explained; they hired lesser-known cats with hot beats to help. "And they pay them the best." If these disgruntled ex-employees beefed, Tee added, it was because Dre forbade them from moonlighting; they got caught "doing outside shit," and he gave them the boot. "So that's why they want to come and say certain shit about Dre."

Dre also reached another decision. No more sampling. So many has-been musicians had by now sued more-famous rappers that a cottage industry of "sample clearance houses" had sprung up. Money hungry negotiators tried to pry top dollar out of producers' hands for dusty old records no one but a nostalgic rap producer remembered or cared about. Dre brought in new musicians, including Mike Elizondo, whose R&B band Buda Hat signed to Atlantic in 1996 but never released an album. "Dre was looking for new blood and wanted live musicians, rare at the time," Mike recollected. "He didn't want to risk someone else sampling the same song as him; he wanted something unique."

13

"My Name Is," released February 23, 1999, turned things around. Not only was it a huge hit with white music buyers—landing at number thirty-six on the *Billboard* Hot 100 and number eighteen on the Hot R&B/Rap chart—it also became the first rap video to reach number one on MTV's daily countdown show *Total Request Live*. It was a big change from October 13, 1998, when Eminem had released "Just Don't Give a Fuck" and filmed a low-budget video for it but saw the single (originally released on an earlier pre-Dre EP and backed with "Brain Damage") reach no further than number sixty-eight on *Billboard*'s Hot R&B/Rap chart. Before *The Slim Shady LP* arrived in stores, demand was so high Interscope shipped over one million copies to stores, which was rare for a debut.

Dre saw *The Slim Shady LP* enter the charts at number two and sell 480,000 copies its first two weeks. Then, with his month-old "My Name Is" video all over MTV, the white newcomer was offered slots on almost every major summer tour. *Rolling Stone* said he'd gone "from white trash to white hot," while *SPIN* called him "the most promising new rapper of the year," claimed his being played on hip-hop radio was "extremely rare for a white," and added, "All those years he spent fighting for his right to be white finally paid off."

Dre joined innovative black female artist Missy Elliott to praise, and vouch for, Em in a promotional clip. The clip wasn't a rarity, but Interscope buying commercial time on network television to air it in support of a rap artist, was.

In its review of *The Slim Shady LP*, *Rolling Stone* rated it four of five stars. "He's not only the first new protégé from Dr. Dre in years, he's the first new sound from Dr. Dre in years." He was also "a white MC in a rap scene that hasn't gotten any less black in two decades." His "loser anthems" were also as funny as comedian Rodney Dangerfield, the magazine continued. "Eminem has skills—he's a warp-speed human rhyming dictionary with LL Cool J's gift for the killer dis."

But rap magazine *XXL* published an article calling Eminem "a culture stealin' invader, and AmeriKKKa's Great White Hope, and all that shit," Em recalled. And a subsequent issue included a cartoon of Em's mother—a frequent target in his own songs—spanking him with "a Double XL paddle." *Billboard* editor in chief Timothy White then wrote *The Slim Shady LP* was "making money by exploiting the world's misery." And black hip-hop fans and artists wondered why everyone rushed to embrace Eminem while their own work went largely ignored. "It's some very awkward shit," said Dre. "It's like seeing a black guy doing country and western, know what I'm saying?"

Dre himself was cast as "Em's mentor," and seemingly included in features to say color didn't matter; talent did. And soon, a reporter asked Em how it felt to bring Dr. Dre "back to prominence." Em replied, "I wouldn't say I was bringing Dre back. I don't think he ever left." But then he added, since Dre saved his life, he was simply returning the favor.

While Em considered himself a hardcore lyricist, Interscope felt he was really video driven. "We thought it was a pop hit at first," said Courtney Holt, who oversaw Interscope-Geffen-A&M Records' New Media strategies. "'My Name Is' was a novelty song on the radio but the record had so much depth."

A large white audience already loved seeing him dress up as Bill Clinton and Marilyn Manson in his first video, "My Name Is," but Interscope still needed to convince people ("especially in urban communities") that he wasn't a one-hit wonder, so the label built an Em site and let fans battle over whether he was a real hip-hop artist.

Come time to choose a second single, Em suggested "My Fault," inspired by a friend's bad acid trip, and even prepared a clean version. Interscope, however, felt, after "My Name Is," this would make him seem like a novelty act. Instead, on June 8, 1999, they went with his duet with Dre, and Holt said, "'Guilty Conscience' with Dr. Dre established Eminem as a real artist."

◆ ◆ ◆

Dre was working on his next solo album. The media reported he was taking his time with a follow-up to *The Chronic*, but really, "They pushed my album back, like, six times." So he used the extra time to make it even stronger. He'd been at it for over a year, spending ten to twelve hours in the studio each night, and auditioning too many rappers to count. Before rapping for him, some of them talked until his ears fell off, but after ten seconds of lyrics, he knew whether he'd want someone on the album or not.

Dre's employee Big Chuck introduced him to Knoc-Turn'al, whose father, a funk musician, took him to Rick James concerts. During a four-year prison stint the young rapper had written 150 songs. But he wouldn't use any since he felt, "You have to keep moving on." After hearing Knoc-Turn'al rap four lines, Dre said, "Man, you dope. I give you two thumbs up and a big toe." He then walked Knoc right into the studio and added him to "Bang Bang," a song that claimed today's kids were too violent, and three other songs.

For music, Dre had Mike Elizondo play bass near a guitarist, keyboardist, and his trusty Akai MPC-3000 drum machine. If he wanted a certain note, he sang it. Between takes he talked other music besides rap. "He's hip to the Beatles, hard rock, classical music, jazz, funk, and R&B," Mike learned. Soon, he heard Mike adding psychedelic Mellotron keyboard riffs to his drums and he started coaching Mike on how to create bass parts, hooks, and melodies his fans wouldn't mind hearing for four minutes.

Dre also revived a few *Chronic* ideas. For "Murder Ink," set to a piano like the one from John Carpenter's *Halloween*, he wanted Hittman to perform the sort of fake reggae Daz, RBX, and Snoop had used in the past. "This is anybody murderer," Hitt chanted. Then for "Ackrite," he had Hitt rap about attending a beach party (with his gun) and asking women to sleep with him.

The *Chronic*-like approach extended to the inclusion of a strong woman rapper to take a few potshots at men, as Rage once did. Midway through "Let's Get High," Ms. Roq claimed she'd make guys put their faces down there. "Yeah, little dicks always runnin' they mouth," she rapped. "While a bitch is better off to masturbate and be out. All you bitches up in here know what I'm talkin about." Then he included a skit in which the raspy-voiced comedian Eddie Griffin denounced single mothers who caused breakups then poisoned kids' minds once the fathers left (over the poignant music he created for "Ed-ucation").

After Dre recorded one or two of his usual posse cuts, he invited M.C. Ren of N.W.A. to a session. When his last album, *Ruthless for Life*, tanked (he was "going through shit. All kind of problems"), Ren vanished from the public eye, focused on raising his four kids, and struggled to adapt to changing times. Other labels wouldn't sign him because they wanted innocuous, hook-driven rap when he prided himself on being "a hard moth-erfucker with lyrics." They wanted "some dancing shit" or a beat to ship right to Power 106, but he kept enjoying old KRS and Public Enemy records at home. Still, a friend said, "Dre wants you to come down," so he scrambled to get there and talked a little on Dre's posse cut, "L.A. Niggaz." Dre then cued up "Bang Bang" and decided to add Ren's rap over someone else's voice. But then the guy Dre removed said, "That's fucked up. You put Ren on there! You put him on there 'cause he Ren!" Dre supposedly restored his voice, removing Ren because the guy was sobbing ("little bitch shit").

Uncertainty had him scrapping songs, then bringing them back up on the computer. Some were amazing but Hitt remained silent until Dre removed "Blaww." Hitt—who appeared on it—urged him to leave it on but Dre said he preferred "What's the Difference."

"Man, take my verse off that shit, then," Hitt said. "I don't like 'What's the Difference.'"

"You sure? The verse is hot."

Hitt was sure so Dre replaced his verse with one by Xzibit.

Just as quickly, Dre confused everyone again with another snap decision. He kept playing the few songs he had in the can. The songs included as many new artists and styles as *The Chronic*, and everyone around him was enthusiastic about the album's direction. But Dre didn't like it. He surprised and confused those left around him by changing its entire focus in a day. He decided new artists should rap alongside Snoop, Nate, Kurupt, and other original *Chronic* players.

He reached out to Snoop, whose May 1999 album, *No Limit Top Dogg*, arrived in stores with three Dre tracks, debuted at number two, and sold over 187,000 copies in a week. After producing his hit "Bitch Please" Dre had directed a video for Snoop on a sound stage near Sunset and Vine. Dre was thrilled to hear Snoop would be involved. "Snoop is like my little brother," he shrugged. "We both know that we sound best when we're together." He was just as pleased when Kurupt and Nate Dogg agreed to appear on new songs.

But when he called The D.O.C., his old collaborator sounded surprised to hear from him, especially since he called during a period in which D.O.C. and Solar chief Dick Griffey were suing him for $75 million. "Because I never got no money from the Death Row shit," D.O.C. said, "and you know I used to own a portion of that motherfucker." As Dre spoke, D.O.C. wondered if the call was a reaction to the lawsuit. "Hey look," Dre said, "it's time to quit this shit." D.O.C. wondered if the call weren't something "maybe Jimmy Iovine induced." Whether Jimmy had told Dre, "Hey, call your boy, tell him to get off my nuts and come on over and have a drink with you and you all get back together."

Either way, he accepted Dre's invitation to lunch at a seafood place near the beach on Pacific Coast Highway but felt it was "one of those places where the 'WPs' go all the time. When I say 'WP,'" he added, "I mean white people. That's where the WPs go eat." At the table, Dre wanted to rekindle their friendship. D.O.C. was open to the idea (later settling his part of this lawsuit), but years of welcoming people into his life, only to see them attack, left Dre suspicious so he asked, "Can I trust you?"

"Yeah, you can trust me."

"Are you gonna come back up and take any more of my reels?"

He said he wouldn't.

Over drinks, Dre mentioned he was starting his next album and wanted help.

"Shit," D.O.C. cried, "it's not a thang."

With everyone ready to work, "Then we went to Reno and just buckled down," said Hitt. "We were there all at once." Dre was happy to see Snoop arrive at Granny's House Studio, but apprehensive about Kurupt and Nate. Would the old chemistry be there? When they grabbed pens and pads and got right to work, he relaxed. And before he knew it, they were cracking as many jokes as they had during the good old days. Soon, it was as if they had never split. Nate was in the booth singing, "Smoke weed every day," while another song found Kurupt chanting, "Come on, let's get high." Not one to be outdone, Dre rapped a lyric that claimed, "Yeah, I just took some Ecstasy."

Dre had already let his nostalgia for simpler, less violent times shine through on a few songs over the years. But "The Watcher," his collaboration with rapper Jay-Z, found him tackling the issue of aging head on. Rap legends were now called Old School, he noticed; and making way for "these new names and faces." But along with the stars, the nature of the music changed, too. Rappers now got "wrapped up in image and actin'" then got murdered. "I've seen 'em come, I've watched 'em go," he continued. "Watched 'em rise, witnessed it and watched them blow." He saw people get famous and lose everything in lawsuits. "Best friends and money?" he asked. "I lost them both/Went and visited niggaz in the hospital." His life had been far from serene, he said, so now, he'd "just sit back and watch the show."

The chorus was just as sobering. Everything had changed, he said. "People I used to know just don't know me no mo'." Then the next verse responded to claims he somehow sold out. "I moved out of the hood for good, you blame me?" He explained he did it so that gun-packing enemies wouldn't be near him. Fans would do the same if someone wanted them killed. "And choose a new spot if niggas wanted you shot/I ain't a thug: how much Tupac in you you got?" He wasn't soft, and would defend himself if he had to, but said he just wanted to enjoy success and be happy with his family.

The third verse was even more mature. He said cops still wanted to handcuff young black men. "They wanna hang us, see us dead or enslave us/Keep us trapped in the same place we raised in." This explained why rap was so angry and why young gangsters were "dangerous, to people who look like strangers." The world was so crazy now, he added, that these new young Gs were calling Dre and his peers "busters" and making him remember when he was their age and just as disobedient. Even so, he didn't like it.

While guests handled the tough talk, he worked with lyric writers to create verses that let him speak from the perspective of a weary rap veteran forgotten by an industry he'd done so much for. The new image was refreshing but no sooner had he programmed a dirge-like funk track and pecking guitar notes than he filled the song "Light Speed" with an ad-lib that would have been at home on the old *Chronic* album. "Hey, yo whassup? My name is Dre," he said. "Can I blaze some chronic witchu?" He claimed he still hung in Compton, but also mentioned "Firm fiascoes" and why he wore a tuxedo and did the tango in a video for his *Aftermath* compilation. Then he frowned on how "Rap tabloids write Dre's light in the ass" and repeated he was still ghetto.

As sessions continued, Dre saw old resentments bubble to the surface. D.O.C. felt Dre had successfully reassembled the original pieces of *The Chronic* but was sabotaging his attempt at a true sequel. As he saw it, the vibe was fucked up. "I mean, we weren't all equals anymore." He kept bickering with Dre's people. His entourage, Aftermath employees, and people in the studio were "all a bunch of ball lickers," he felt. And if they were "gonna suck nuts" around him, he'd say, "You're a dick sucka." As he saw it, these ambitious non-Dres didn't dare push Dre to make great records, despite hip-hop always being about who is the best. Dre's stuff was sensational, but D.O.C. still felt he was coasting; getting too comfortable; not wanting more than what he had. But Dre let him keep attending sessions and soon dedicated part of "What's the Difference" to him.

He started this song by looking back on when he made beats for N.W.A. and Cube and Ren rode around in a Mercedes Benz. "But sometimes the business end of this shit can turn your friends against you," he said. And this happened with The D.O.C. after his crash. But he wanted D.O.C. to know he was still his friend and that he felt the same about Eazy. He never got to say this to Eazy when he visited him in Cedars-Sinai, he rapped. "Fuck the beef, nigga, I miss you, and that's just bein real wit'chu." He still liked Snoop, he continued, but not the unnamed "fake-ass niggaz" that sold few records but insulted him in magazine interviews. "Until then, I ain't even speakin' your name. Just keep my name outta yo' mouth and we can keep it the same, nigga."

He also discussed his life and thoughts on a sequel to "Xxplosive," in which he compared his life to a movie; promised he and friends would soon be on the silver screen; and said the trend of carefree bragging about money had peaked. "What is this? Everybody's jiggy now?/Is the hustle that good in everybody's city now?" He ended this one by again reflecting on his past, this time on high school days when people traded clothes and he chased girls and made them carry his books. "I had 'em slavin, yo," he claimed.

The rhapsodic mood soured a bit once Dre learned Suge was preparing a competing *Chronic 2000* at Death Row with unreleased tracks, old *Chronic* numbers, and (one article claimed) "a Tupac Shakur sound-alike." As Dre told it, Death Row named their album *The Chronic 2000* after learning he planned to use the title in the near future. Death Row's version would drop in April but Dre's lawyer Howard King said he'd contacted Death Row "to say that we'd sue if they even thought about it. In the end, both sides agreed that we'd allow the other to use the title, and then let the public decide which one they preferred." But the mere fact there was controversy over the title inspired Dre to say, "Fuck it, *2001*." That should have ended it, but Death Row's distributor, Priority, threatened to sue if he used this title. "At first we just laughed, but it's serious business," said King. So on July 15, 1999, King sued Death Row and Priority on Dre's behalf, and explained Dre owned the title *The Chronic*. The lawsuit also tried to stop the manufacture and sale of Death Row's *The Chronic 2000*. "If we have to, we'll just seize all profits from their album," King explained, which would be unfortunate: "You'd think there would be some sort of honor between men, especially men that once worked together."

While his lawyer handled this matter, Dre heard from Eminem, who was in Detroit working with The Bass Brothers (producers he worked with since his debut, *Infinite*). "I have an idea for a song," he told Dre. "I just need some music to it." When Dre received the chorus, "Forgot about Dre," he invited Em to Granny's House Studio in Reno, where he got the song done in a few hours. He railed against envious critics and reminded everyone he made N.W.A., Snoop, and pot-related lyrics popular. He then admitted that critics

that claimed he went pop, or that The Firm flopped, caused him to lose
sleep. But if they kept messing with him, they'd make him become the old
violent Dre. After Eminem claimed everyone talked gibberish and acted like
they forgot about Dre, Dre continued his rap, saying he wasn't giving anyone
anything; he inspired all these new gangster rappers; and he still had a gun.
"What you think? I sold 'em all?" He griped about people rushing him to
finish his album, and hate mail and rap in general. "So give me one more
platinum plaque/and fuck rap! You can have it back." The song also further
positioned him and Em as the mentor and protégé described in articles. "All
right, hold up, hold up," Eminem cried midway through the song. "Stop the
beat a minute. I got something to say." Dre lowered the drums. "Dre, I wanna
tell you this shit right now while this fuckin' weed is in me."

"What the fuck?" Dre asked.

"I don't know if I ever told you this, but I love you, dawg. I got your motherfuckin' back. Just know this shit."

Dre raised the music again. "Slim, I don't know if you noticed it. But I've
had your back from day one." After Em claimed he'd kill for Dre—since
Em's lyrics usually included revenge fantasies about his wife Kim—Dre said
he'd point him toward the ocean so Eminem could dump her body in it.
Once they recorded it, Eminem kept stopping by the studio two to five days
a week, then told a reporter, "I don't want to boast but I think I got him
excited again. He is back on track."

Dre also had Snoop rap alongside younger rappers on "Fuck You," a slinky
number that started with a needy married woman falling apart on his voice
mail. After she said she understood he had to work, she sobbed that she
loved him and needed to see him. "I'd do anything . . . I'll be your perfect
woman for you." Dre immediately rapped, "I just wanna fuck bad bitches" to
make up for nights when he lacked female companionship, then had other
guests describe how they'd screw her.

For the next to last song, he collaborated with Scott Storch, a young white
ninth-grade dropout from Philly who played keyboards on The Roots' 1993
album *Organix*. Dre met him through Eve, also from Philly, and had already
included him on "Big Egos," and "Housewife." For this next work, Storch
fiddled with chords until he found a tone center, or melody, for Dre's bouncy

beat. Dre settled on a spooky piano riff, then stacked other sounds (including guitar and ukelele) onto every note. The end result surprised him since it sounded like a sample.

Dre then sat with Jay-Z to write "Still D.R.E." Along with his own hit albums for Roc-A-Fella, Jay's verses written for others were earning him some pretty good money. But when Jay allegedly delivered another conversational stanza about living well, driving new cars, and sipping bubbly, Dre wanted a rewrite that would let him tell his audience he was older but still had his chops. The lyric found him saying he'd grown a lot but was still close to the streets. If anyone thought he sold out, it continued, they better remember he still smoked weed, made beats, and didn't like cops; still wore khakis like a gang member; still loved the streets and called California home. "Since I left, ain't too much changed." The next verse then noted how well he was doing since Death Row fell; he lost some friends. "Kept my ear to the streets, signed Eminem," he claimed, and Em's album was triple platinum and selling 50,000 copies each week. "Still, I stay close to the heat," he went on. "And even when I was close to defeat, I rose to my feet." During the song's final moments, he said other things hadn't changed either: he still ruled rap; still liked seeing young blacks earn money; still hired friends; and still wanted to become even more successful. The song, and Snoop's turn on it, so pleased him he decided it would be his first single.

For the album closer, Dre rapped to a track created by producer Lord Finesse. Mel-Man met the producer of Biggie's haunting classic, "Suicidal Thoughts" while record shopping in downtown Manhattan, and told Dre, "Yo, that dude Finesse, he's so real." Dre replied, "A'ight, we'll send him a ticket."

During Finesse's three-week stay, Dre invited him to his home, introduced him to Nicole, Tyler, and Truth, and tried to collaborate on a track with him, only to abandon the idea. Finesse left to handle a few shows on the road, but returned with more music on burnable CDs (which had replaced demos on cassette). In the studio one day, Finesse prepared to audition some just as Dre left the room.

He heard Mel ask their visitor, "Yo you got that track?" Then, with the door ajar, heard some music play. He returned to the control room, heard a little more, then asked, "Can I get that?" Finesse said, "Hell yeah, you can get that. That's no problem."

Dre kept listening to the melancholic track when he was alone then reportedly worked with Eminem's pal Royce The 5'9 on a lyric about his murdered brother, Tyree.

Once it was finished, he faced the mic. "This one is for my brother, Tyree, R.I.P.," he said. The first verse asked God why he took Tyree so young and found him admitting he didn't know what to do and he was only half the man he used to be. God didn't have to take him, he continued. Tyree was the one that got him into the G stuff. Now, with him gone, he remembered their arguments and fights. "He had talent, too," Dre rapped. "I had plans on watching him grow." After leaving a few bars empty for a chorus, he rapped directly to his late brother. He knew he was probably "packin heat up there," and he'd seen his son the other day and said he'd help if he needed it. He still couldn't believe he was gone. "I done been through all emotions," from shock to a poker face to breaking down in tears and "showing all emotions." And if real Gs don't cry then "I'm realizing I ain't no gangsta." He missed him so much, he added, "sometimes I wish I just died with you."

When the vocal was down, he invited Mary J. Blige to sing on it. While Blige hadn't bothered hearing his R&B work on *Dr. Dre Presents The Aftermath*, she liked *The Chronic*, counted him as a friend, and showed up in the studio to ad-lib a few much-needed positive messages. "Listen, children listen," she sang. "I'm tryin' to tell you something good. Don't get caught up in the hood." He called this song "The Message," and frequently played it when no one was around. "I was so emotional," he said. "Even now I have a hard time listening to it unless I'm alone."

After creating over ninety-six tracks in sixteen months, Dre felt twenty-two were good enough. It took his engineers a while to collect everything into a computer program called Pro Tools but once they did, he spent a mere forty-five minutes sequencing the entire album.

"It's done?" Hitt asked.

"Yeah, we can go. Let's go listen to this shit."

Dre was so happy to leave the studio for a while he threw a party at his home. Then in August 1999, he moved Nicole and the kids into a bigger place in the Valley, a $4.9-million, 18,000-square-feet number in a gated community closer to L.A. From here, he put his 15,000-square-foot Chatsworth property on the market and turned his thoughts back to preparing *2001* for release.

At Interscope, executives asked for a cover concept. "I just want the album cover black with my name on it and the title of the record," he replied. And since his engineer took photos during sessions, "Make a collage and put that shit in the CD booklet and that'll be interesting. And that's it."

Interscope agreed the first single would be "Still D.R.E." so Dre shot a video that mimicked "Let Me Ride" and a few photos in his November 1992 *Source* article. He was back in all-black clothing and a ball cap, on the Compton streets, in a blue convertible, driving past noisy low-riders; but as a concession to modern trends, he set a few scenes in a dark strip club, too (with a gorgeous Mexican woman in thong swinging around a pole). And during post-production, he tacked footage of Hittman performing part of "Last Days," a song from his album-in-progress, onto the finale.

September found him taking the first steps to promote the new work. At the MTV Video Music Awards, Eminem rapped part of "My Name Is" on a stage decorated to resemble a trailer park. Dre walked out for "Guilty Conscience," before Snoop emerged from the fake trailer and replaced Eminem for Dre's oldie, "Nuthin' but a 'G' Thang." But Em inevitably drifted back on stage, to dive into the crowd of white fans slamming into each other in the "mosh pit" section of the audience, before leaping back on stage to bawl, "*Chronic 2001*, October."

Dre soon learned that all of his worry and losing sleep had been for nothing. If anything, the people he thought were hoping he'd fall had actually been dying to hear his next work. And when it arrived in stores in November, it was at number two behind the rock/rap band Korn's *Issues*. But his sales of 516,000 copies weren't that far behind Korn's 573,000.

He knew *2001* in some ways rehashed *Chronic* themes and that his musicians played what amounted to covers or soundalikes of old songs. But compared to everything else in the genre, it felt like "something different, something innovative, maybe even motivating for some producers and young artists out there."

Reviews were almost uniformly positive. Most also pretended *The Firm* and the compilation never existed. *SPIN* raved that his "ongoing commitment to formal excellence and sonic innovation in this art form may one day earn him a place next to George Clinton..." *Entertainment Weekly* felt his "G-funk is as addictive as it was back when over three million record buyers got hooked on *The Chronic*," and this new one "reestablishes his mastery of the form." *College Music Journal* wrote, "It's Dre Day now more than ever." *VIBE* named it 2000's Album of the Year, and said he hadn't "lost his Midas touch." *The Source* also loved it and called Dre "still the king of this shit here."

Rolling Stone meanwhile called it complex and impeccable and described Dre as being "at the gangsta crossroads." But it also claimed he created "an early seventies-era Marvin Gaye–style ballad" on "The Message" when he actually purchased the track from Lord Finesse.

Dre also had MTV behind him. Where the network once refused to air an N.W.A. video, it now scheduled a segment called "Dre TV." After flying to New York, he stopped by their Times Square studio and gushed, "It feels incredible just to be done. It feels, it feels, damn... it feels incredible, man." It was overwhelming but he was happy to be away from the studio, from buttons, for a while. And he was able to use these interviews to set the stage for Aftermath's next release. While the death of his grandmother three days after the video for "Still D.R.E." debuted plunged him into a period of family issues, beef on the streets, and "a snowball of shit," Dre still talked Hittman up during interviews as his "next protégé."

"He's the next person that we're going to groom and try to build into a superstar, super hip-hop star."

He told a mostly white audience Hitt could sing and rap, and appeared on *2001* as much as he did. "And he's a real cool, laid-back guy, you know, so I know, outside of the studio, he's not going to do anything to ruin his career."

"So it's just Eminem and Hittman?" a host asked.

"Eminem and Hittman right now. Taking it one step at a time."

◆ ◆ ◆

October 1999, Em returned from a European tour and called to say he needed new beats. Usually, Dre filled DAT tapes with ten to twenty unfinished instrumentals and only if someone rhymed on one would he "re-do it the right way." On the phone, he told Em, "I ain't really got no tracks but I'm trying to work on some new shit today."

Em asked about something playing in the background. "What's that?'

"What's what? You mean this?" He held the phone to a speaker and played something that evoked the quirky Casio-keyboard sound young producer Swizz Beatz tried on New York rapper Busta Rhyme's solo single "Woo-Hah." Later, French pianist Jacques Loussier would file a $10 million lawsuit that claimed Dre used his song "Pulsion" without permission and asked a judge to stop sales of Em's album and order all existing copies be destroyed. (The judge rejected the ideas.) The track sounded a bit corny, but Em liked it. "Send me that shit."

"You want this? This is some little shit we fuckin' with."

"Whatever, send me that."

Dre sent it and the next day Em had "Kill You" done. By now, Dre knew Eminem was trying to be as controversial as press clippings said he was. And the album in progress reflected this. He started it by urging producer Jeff Bass to say Eminem didn't care about anyone's gossip. They could "suck his fucking cock," he said. "Little did you know, upon purchasing this album, you have just kissed his ass," he added. "Slim Shady is fed up with your shit, and he's going to kill you." Eminem then said, "Sue me."

Em also let his manager Paul Rosenberg record a skit in which he pretended to be disgusted by the album. "I just . . . fuck it," he said. Then Interscope executive Steve Berman appeared in another skit named after him. Over Dre's music for "What's the Difference," Berman said Em had to re-record the album to make it commercial. "Do you know why Dre's record was so successful? He's rapping about big screen TVs, blunts, forties, and bitches. You're rapping about homosexuals and Vicodin. I can't sell this shit! Either change the record or it's not coming out." Em ended the skit by saying, "Alright, man; whatever."

His song "Marshall Mathers" meanwhile openly attacked "cheap imitations" of Pac and Biggie, rappers waving champagne and watches in videos, "sissies in magazines smiling," Detroit's Insane Clown Posse and some of his old fans in the underground rap scene (since they dared to imply his new blond hair and a duet with Missy Elliott signaled he'd "gone pop"). "Drug Ballad" meanwhile railed against bitch-slapping abusers and drunk drivers before Em pretended to be high on the euphoria-inducing drug Ecstasy ("We just met/But I think I'm in love with you"). Then he recorded "Kim," in which he pretended to scream at his girlfriend. "Quit crying, bitch! Why do you always make me shout at you?" He rapped about forcing her into a car, verbally abusing her some more, then slitting her throat. Amid sounds of gurgling he screamed, "You were supposed to love me! Now bleed, bitch, bleed!" Then he adopted a number of voices for another "Ken Kaniff (Skit)." This time, Em's rivals in the Insane Clown Posse were supposedly performing fellatio on him and he ordered, "Say my name." When one Insane Clown replied, "Eminem," he stormed out.

Weeks after sending him the beat for "Kill You," Dre started recording Eminem's songs for *The Marshall Mathers Album*. In the studio, he sat near co-producer Mel-Man and watched Eminem shout a chorus. "Bitch, I'm'a kill you!" he screeched. "You don't want to fuck with me! Girls neither! You ain't nothin' but a slut to me!" From here, he started in on fags again, saying they egged him on so he'd pull a knife and make them beg for their lives. Then he attacked *Rolling Stone* and radio hosts who wanted to argue about his lyrics. It was a far cry from "Gin and Juice."

But Dre played a few more tracks and one inspired Em to think, "Oh my god, this is ridiculous." Ready to call it a day, Dre said he could stay and record, then left. The next day, he heard Em's reference vocal, "Who Knew." Over Dre and Mel-Man's beat, Em tried to show a more sensitive side by rapping about how hard it was to be famous. He complained about being blamed for things like the Columbine shootings and, during the chorus, chanted he never knew he'd get this big. Dre told him, "Damn, you brought that shit to life. Let's get in and knock it out."

Then Em said he created the beat for "Criminal." "That's when I really got into drum sounds," he said. He wanted to preface it with a skit and spent an entire day trying to record a fictional bank robbery, working even after Dre walked out. Mel-Man couldn't get his line ("don't kill nobody") right, he said, "'cause he was so drunk." But Dre felt the end result was good enough to include on the album. "I did that skit by myself," Em said proudly. "I learned how from Dre when we hooked up on 'Guilty Conscience.'"

Dre and Mel-Man then produced "I'm Back," which went from gay-bashing and drug raps to another hollow chorus ("They call me Slim Shady/I'm back") to the issue of whether Em succeeded because whites wanted one of their own at the top. "Became a commodity because I'm W-H-I-T-E," he admitted. "Cause MTV was so friendly to me." But instead of going further, he resumed insulting Ken Kaniff, used a Rakim rhythm (from "My Melody") for a verse about the Columbine shootings, lambasted boy band *NSYNC, and told Puffy he'd love to screw his then-girlfriend, Jennifer Lopez.

After a while it all started to sound like one nonstop stream of invective, so Dre and Mel-Man reverted to *The Chronic* formula for "Remember Me?" They enlisted Sticky Fingaz, a former house music rapper turned bald gang-ster in Onyx, and RBX to join Em in chanting "remember me" four times, then had them each recite one of their best-known old lyrics. For his part, RBX rehashed a line from *The Chronic*'s "High Powered." Before Dre knew it, he learned Eminem was eager to tap into the excitement generated by Snoop's hit "Bitch Please," and his album's engineer Richard "Segal" Huredia remixed Dre's track for that hit. Dre agreed to join the original's lineup on the sequel. "Yeah, whattup, Detroit?" He rapped about the joys of "simplistic pimp shit," then said it was cool to see white rap fans in the mosh pit when he rocked "Guilty Conscience" at Eminem shows. Some of Em's fans were as rowdy as low-riding gangsters on Crenshaw Boulevard, he claimed, but his and Snoop's fans were actually from that street. And he and Snoop were the ones making people from Long Beach to South Central shout, "Whoa, not these niggaz again!" No one could harm them, he continued; they'd come a long way; folks shouldn't stare hard since he carried an Uzi every day. "Some-times it's like a nightmare, just being Andre." Snoop also agreed to appear on the song, and even tried to vouch for Em by calling him his nephew and announcing, "The Great White American Hope done hooked up with the King of the motherfuckin West Coast, bay-bayy!" But in the end, after recording various works, Dre had to admit that DJ Mark the 45 King delivered the best song. Titled "Stan," it was set to one or two sections of Dido's mellow "Thank You," and moved Eminem past the corny jokes. Like Slick Rick, he played different characters, including a deranged fan that demands someone answer his letters, before murdering his pregnant girlfriend. The song ends with Em, in a spare moment, finally receiving the fan's mail, and writing back. Dre felt it was the best song Eminem had ever done."45 King did his thing."

They submitted *The Marshall Mathers LP* to Interscope, and suggested the Dre-produced "I'm Back" for its first single. Interscope said, "Nope, this isn't it."

Em proposed "I Never Knew" but Interscope "nixed both of 'em." Nothing was commercial enough to fit the bill, the label said.

Dre understood, but Em was livid. "What do you want?" he asked. "Another 'My Name Is'?"

"Not exactly, it doesn't have to be that."

Dre had to wait until Em came up with something. The label booked a flight and hotel room for the rapper—later charged to his royalty account—and he boarded a plane back to California. During the flight, he felt he "was about to explode," and wrote "The Way I Am," about his frustration with the label, his comedic image, his mom (suing him), and his pop coming around.

In the studio, he asked Dre's keyboardist to play a piano riff, he made a beat using some of Dre's famous sounds, and he felt the result "was like night and day from anything we had ever produced." During his rap, he claimed weed helped make him "the most meanest MC on this, on this Earth." He breezed through a few usual themes then admitted he was tired of Interscope expecting him to deliver another "My Name is." Then, for the chorus, Dre heard him borrow a rhythm from Rakim's early classic, "As the Rhyme Goes On."

The month continued and Em kept sleeping in various hotel rooms. Finally, in desperation, he let Dre hear an old hook. Em said he didn't know if it was hot but Dre spent a week, four studio sessions, testing it on assorted beats.

By Friday, he and Em "had just about given up," Em recalled. Dre was going home. They had Interscope breathing down their necks and had to meet with them the next morning. Em, lying on a couch, asked Mike Elizondo and keyboardist Tommy Coster Jr. to jam and one riff soon had him leaping to his feet. "What was that?" As Em told it, he asked Tommy to play it high then low. "Right there." He ran and got Dre to come listen and they added drums.

Saturday morning, they met with Interscope (probably Iovine). "Well, did you come up with anything?"

Em played, "The Way I Am."

"It's a great song. It's just not the first song."

The label settled for "Criminal" but Em spent the weekend writing to Friday night's track, insulting easy targets. He hadn't liked watching Will Smith say, while accepting an award, "I didn't kill nobody in none of my records, I didn't use no profanity in none of my records...gangsta rap is wack." He liked it even less since he and Dre had contributed a cowboy-themed song for Smith's *Wild Wild West* soundtrack. So he wrote, "Will Smith don't gotta cuss in his raps to sell records/Well I do, so fuck him and fuck you, too." Then he attacked pop singer Christina Aguilera, who told MTV he was married when "I wasn't ready for the public to know that about me yet." He also insulted boy bands, mentioned TRL, championed Dre, and frowned on white kids trying to dye their own hair blonde. And though *The Slim Shady LP* was named Best Rap Album at the Grammy Awards, he claimed, "You think I give a damn about a Grammy?/Half you critics can't even stomach me, let alone stand me!" Monday, Dre recorded the lyric for what they called "The Real Slim Shady" and saw Em nod with enjoyment. But Dre wasn't sure about this song—it sounded like featherbrained pop rap—until his kids chanted its chorus. "That was enough for me."

◆ ◆ ◆

Away from the studio, Dre met with Cube, who spent two weeks in November telling him the time was right for an N.W.A. reunion. Dre, eager to get back to weighty themes, felt Cube was motivated enough. Soon M.C. Ren was back. But instead of Yella, Dre insisted on including Snoop. It was an odd choice, but he wanted to play it safe. Snoop was commercial and could add "that extra spice that needs to be there." The others had no choice but to go along with it, but Snoop sensed the project would involve criticism, debate, and "a lot of clashing."

Now that they all had solo careers, they couldn't just meet up in an apartment on Paramount and write songs like "Fuck tha Police." They had to arrange schedules. Dre had to promote *2001*, in stores only a month, while Cube was knee deep in his next album, *War and Peace, Vol. 2 (The Peace Disc)*. But Cube wouldn't let Dre move on to the next enthusiasm. "The only way we can do all of this stuff we're talking about is to just go do it." He offered a slot on the *Next Friday* soundtrack, and said they could get a new song done quickly, so Dre joined them for "Chin Check." But he insisted on having Mel-Man co-produce.

As usual, they prefaced recording with some smoking, small talk, and chess. "Nobody was talking about old beefs," said Ren. Old resentments lingered, yet there was nothing to do but move on. Mel was having a great time. "The chemistry is just incredible," he said. Dre meanwhile viewed the song as a "test run," Mel explained.

He gave them a track that was more Dre *2001* or Eminem than N.W.A., then saw Cube assume his usual role as lead writer. They were like "two field generals," Mel recalled. "They both lead: Dre as far as music, Cube as far as lyrically." "Chin Check" began with a woman calling 911 to report a home invasion. After a gunshot, Cube and Dre performed well-rehearsed banter. "What the fuck's up, Dre?"

"You tell me. You talk to Ren?"

Ren chimed in. "I'm right here, nigga. Release the hound."

Snoop then chanted his *Chronic* catchphrase, "Bow wow wow."

Cube pretended he was still a gangsta riding for his side in Compton and said God bless Eazy-E's memory. Then he claimed, if it weren't for him, rappers would still be "rapping like the Treacherous Three, fuckin cowards." He ended his short verse by saying "Fuck Jerry Heller and the white superpowers." Until the chorus, the song stayed true to their usual themes, albeit with simpler lyrics. But during the bridge, Dre gathered them around the mic so they could perform a few *Chronic* tropes. "I'ma smoke where I wanna smoke" he had them chant. For his turn, he offered lighthearted boasts about his skills, his ability to capture enemies and tie them up, and all the ladies he attracted. Then he got down to business again, having them lapse into a "Deep Cover"–like routine. It started with Cube saying, "Let's get together, make a record. Why the fuck not?" Ren repeated the question; then Dre; then Snoop. "And that shit was all cool, man," Ren said of the sessions.

Dre had just as much fun recording it, so they united again, for "Hello." And this one found him milking a recent lyric for all it was worth. He had each member say the line from "The Watcher" in which Dre claimed, "I started this gangsta shit and this the motherfuckin' thanks I get?" Ren claimed the world was a gun-filled ghetto. Dre remembered how haters claimed he fell off and tore *Chronic* posters off their walls. "Questionin' Dre's credibility? Wondering if it's still in me to produce hits? Y'all be killin' me." His rap said he didn't need to record anymore; he had a mansion and six cars so everyone could suck his dick; he worked hard to make it this far; he was a millionaire. "Motherfucker, I'm Dre, I don't need your respect. I don't need to make another album, bitch; I don't gotta do shit." But then he added, "Fuck the fame, I'm still stayin' the same, little bitch!"

Cube loved the song, and wanted it on his next album. Ren felt it was better than "Chin Check" but the vibe was different. "Motherfuckers be having a gang of niggaz now in the studios." Even so, they excitedly planned an action-packed video (a re-enactment of the siege at Waco, with N.W.A. inside and the feds trying to get them). They never filmed it, but Dre told a reporter *Not Those Niggaz Again* would be a hot project "if and when it happens." While fans continued to reject Snoop as a replacement for Eazy, he figured, they could have the album ready in a year then work out which label would release it, since he was signed to Interscope, Cube was still on Priority, and Snoop was with No Limit.

The others wanted to record more, but in December, Dre returned to promoting his own album. He had to keep the momentum going, and decided a remix of his album cut "Fuck You" would do the trick. While recruiting the women he wanted to include, he wound up pursuing another interest. He decided to call singer/songwriter Shari Watson, who had moved on after the purging of Aftermath in 1998 to write for L.A. Reid's publishing company. The thirty-year-old single mother was preparing to leave the business when he told her, "Come do this remix and start working again." She was reluctant until he offered good money. "You know what," she thought, "I'm gonna take this money that they givin' me and move back to Atlanta and go to school because I have a daughter. I'm gonna put my daughter through school out there."

He recorded her, Ms. Roq, and Cube's former artist Yo-Yo on the track, only to shelve it. But by three a.m. on Christmas Eve, he called her mom's house in San Jose to say, "You know what? As a matter of fact I think I wanna do your record."

"What the hell are you talking about?" she asked.

"I think I wanna do your album, I think I'm ready, I think you are ready. You know, let's do this."

He wanted to tap into the lucrative R&B market (which was booming with artists like Jennifer Lopez and Ashanti) but she was skeptical so he turned to someone in the studio. "Mike, I don't think she's feelin' me." Then into the phone: "Do you hear me?"

"Yeah I hear you." She just wanted to sit and discuss the logistics.

"Ooohkay."

Shari wanted to write her own songs, have a say, and not do anything to play herself. "I'm too old for that. I'm not about to be out here tap dancing and doing whatever. I have to be able to be me."

"You know what, I understand that. It's gonna be as much you as it is me. Let's sit down and let's put this together and whatever you don't want any-body to hear never has to come out the studio. We will keep trying until we get this shit right." He added: "I'll move you down here. We gonna get started on this record."

He immediately named her "Truth Hurts," and, before she signed anything, started creating a song. Then during her first day in the studio, he had her test her microphone level, taped her singing, and decided this song was done.

◆ ◆ ◆

By March 2000, he reunited with the new N.W.A. for an appearance on *Jimmy and Doug's Farmclub.com,* a Web site, record label, and USA Network variety show created by Interscope co-chairman Iovine and his good pal, Universal Music Group's chairman Doug Morris.

The group hadn't recorded anything since "Hello" but kept throwing song ideas around. Cube wanted to start the album in June. Dre got into an Oakland Raiders hat and traveled to the venue, where he told a reporter they wanted to "change the course of hip-hop again."

With cameras rolling, they performed "Chin Check." Like Cube, Dre paced the stage while rhyming. Low-key as ever, M.C. Ren stayed on the sidelines. After he said, "Release the hound," Snoop (in his Dogg House Records jacket), stepped forward to teeter from side-to-side and rap. They ran through it again then did "Straight Outta Compton," before Dre and Snoop performed "Nuthin' but a 'G' Thang."

Cube beamed with pride after the show. He told a reporter it was an honor to share the stage with megastars like Dre, Snoop, and Ren. It was "magic," he added. Dre, however, said, "It went really well considering that we didn't get a chance to rehearse or anything."

◆ ◆ ◆

It was during this period that Dr. Dre first expressed dissatisfaction with online file-trading. He learned one or two of his songs were being passed out on the web site service Napster and had his attorney Howard King file a lawsuit. By now, labels were opposing free music, while The Offspring, Limp Bizkit, Courtney Love, and rap legends Chuck D and The Beastie Boys sided with fans. King, already representing Metallica in their week-old lawsuit against Napster, filled Dre's April 18 lawsuit with the same accusations of copyright infringement. That was fine and dandy, but instead of speaking directly to fans or the media, Dre issued a statement. "I don't like people stealing my music." A day after he sued Napster, however, George Lucas sued him for using his THX sound to start *2001*, so Dre looked more than a little hypocritical.

But he continued his legal battle against the site and tried to explain that he was only trying to protect the value of his master tapes since they "come back to me after a certain period of time" and he wanted his many kids to profit from them in the future. He understood people wanted free music but noted it cost money to create. "Straight up, this is my job," he griped. "I bet you there's nobody at Napster that's workin' for free. So why you tellin' me I should?"

His battle against the site inspired many younger white music fans to feel he was as greedy as Metallica (they were already calling this group sell-outs and posting humiliating cartoons online). But Dre kept trying to say he didn't want to shut Napster down. He just didn't want people getting his music for free. "I know there's a lot of fans out there that I've lost because of this, but I got into this business to make a living at something I really love doing, and they were trying to stop that as far as I'm concerned." The battle didn't really affect sales.

In fact, his amazing run became even more impressive once Eminem's *The Marshall Mathers LP* arrived in stores. Dre executive produced and created music for seven of sixteen songs (including Em's hit single, "The Real Slim Shady") and saw it become the fastest-selling rap album in history. It sold a million copies in a week and by its second week, passed the 2.5 million sales mark, and topped the chart. "The Real Slim Shady" was just as popular, continuing its rise in the Top Ten.

In *Rolling Stone*'s review, writer Toure wrote, "Welcome to the summer of Shady." He called Eminem "the king of hip-hop" and acknowledged how strange this was. But instead of exploring why this might be, he likened the situation to "something out of science fiction" and claimed, "He is, simply, better than any other MC in hip-hop except for Jay-Z. Yes, better than Beanie Sigel, Pharoahe Monch, Snoop, Common, Prodigy, Xzibit, Redman, Big Pun, and all of the Lox."

He reserved as much praise for Dre himself. N.W.A. was fourteen years behind him, and seven years had passed since the original *Chronic* but "Dre is that legendary coach taking a third different team to a national title, still making your head hurt from all the nodding, still crazy dope after all these years."

At Aftermath in May 2000 Hittman was moving past the death of his grandmother and hoping Dre would release his own music. Dre, however, was focused on his first national tour as a solo artist. Hitt now felt, since

2001's release, his own career was "a casualty of Dre's success." Since *2001* made Dre the man again everyone wanted to work with or interview him. Even worse, Dre told him,"Yo, Hitt, Jimmy only hears a couple of songs that he likes."

Hitt's first thought was, "shit, then we need to go in the studio and knock some shit out, then." Then he suggested releasing album cut "Akrite" to influential DJs; or his own new work, "Hot Damn," during the summer so as to buy time. But with everyone going on the forty-date tour, there'd be no one at Aftermath to promote the single to radio. Dre then heard Hitt propose leaving the tour after early West Coast dates so he could keep recording. This way, when Dre got back all he'd have to do to complete Hitt's album was create five tracks. According to Hitt, Dre ignored this, too.

He was busy lining up talent: Eminem, Snoop, Cube, Cube's group Westside Connection, last-minute addition Kurupt (since he was in one of Dre's videos) and his stepbrother Warren G. And he also had Warren asking for a deal.

Since leaving Death Row, Warren scored a hit with his 1994 Def Jam debut, *Regulate . . . The G-Funk Era*. But 1997's *Take a Look Over Your Shoulders* didn't fare as well. Then he left that label when it merged with Universal in 1999. But with his latest, *I Want It All*, not doing too well on smaller imprint Restless, he was between engagements. "I got at Dre and tried to be down with his situation but we never got to talk to Jimmy Iovine," he recalled. Their talks ended once Dre said there'd also be a wait. Though his greatest success was six years behind him, Warren felt, "I'm an established artist. Why should I have to wait?"

Dre said he'd produce something for his next work, when the time came, then offered him a slot on the bill, which Warren accepted. Then Dre got back to thinking about the many hats he'd have to wear.

Every day was consumed by the thing. And he didn't even want to tour. He didn't like traveling so he hadn't hit the road in a decade. Touring also meant working harder for what amounted to a pay cut (In the studio, he charged people tied to his label $75,000 per track while outsiders paid $250,000). But Interscope wanted this to happen, so he said fine. And with *2001* nearing the 4.2 million sales mark of *The Chronic*, and Dre winning various awards, he kept talking himself into it. "Yo, why stop now?" he thought. Dre tried to regain control by limiting the jaunt to two months but saw the label cram his itinerary with dates, creating a grueling schedule that would have him on stage five to six nights a week.

Realizing he couldn't win, Dre focused on something he could control: what the actual show would present. Envisioning a four-hour package, he studied why other tours, not only in hip-hop, succeeded or failed. He worked out details and budgets with Magic Johnson, whose company was onboard as an investor. Then he hired the best professionals money could buy, people who worked on profitable tours by white rock acts Aerosmith and KISS. He even reportedly rented some of their old props and pyrotechnic devices. Exerting as much control as he would for a record or N.W.A. reunion, he meticulously plotted a concert in which each act's turn would feature enough video monitors, pyrotechnic devices, elaborate stage props, and equipment to fill a caravan of semi-tractor trailers.

The Up in Smoke Tour began in mid-June in San Diego. In arenas nationwide, audience members saw Snoop's protégés Tha Eastsidaz, Warren G., Mack 10, and others, do ten-minute sets. Comedian Alex Thomas warmed up the crowd with jokes about the ghetto, rap, and overpaid athletes while the road crew erected a set that resembled an ice palace. Once a huge icicle emerged, Ice Cube popped out and filled twenty minutes with oldies like "A Good Day" and "AmeriKKKa's Most Wanted."

Next came Eminem, who won a Grammy for *The Slim Shady LP* in February and had just been crowned fastest-selling rapper in history (*The Marshal Mathers LP* remained at number one on the chart for six weeks). Though his face was on the cover of *Teen People*—near a caption calling him "Sexiest Rapper Alive"—and his numerous Dre-produced pop ditties were all over radio, the white rapper struggled to show hardcore rap fans he hadn't sold out.

Mostly white audiences viewed his half-hour set as an exercise in frustration. He griped about no one understanding his debut and about being famous for the wrong reasons. He interrupted the crowd's singalong by abbreviating "My Name Is." "I never want to hear that song again." The crowd wanted to sing again during his other Dre-driven pop hit, "The Real

Slim Shady," but he made that an even shorter rendition, then had a giant pair of hands with raised middle fingers appear on each side of the stage, giving everyone the finger. From here, he brought out a woman-shaped blow-up doll, introduced it as his wife, then stabbed it a few times with a knife while the crowd applauded.

At this point, Dre played the crowd a seven-minute short film that evoked videos he once made with N.W.A.: he and Snoop cavorting with big-assed women in thongs; visiting a weed spot; blasting stickup kids in a liquor store. By the time it ended, technicians had the twenty-foot tall skull out on stage calling the audience "motherfuckers" and demanding *The Chronic.*

Dre steered the real '64 Impala low-rider convertible into view, with Snoop riding shotgun just like he did in old *Source* photos and the last tour. With an array of backdrops, videos, and fiery explosions, they breezed through *2001* numbers and Death Row oldies "Let Me Ride," "Gin and Juice," even Pac's "California Love" in under an hour. Some white fans got carried away, throwing joints on stage, so Snoop sometimes lifted them and started smoking in mid-song. For his part, Dre made like a bandleader during the swing era, trotting out Eminem, Xzibit, Nate Dogg, and Kurupt. Then, once this cavalcade of hooks, middling drum tracks, and radio hits drew thunderous applause, everyone cleared out and three black banners dropped from the ceiling. The first contained a red letter "N." The second had the "W." During one show, the third, the one with the "A," got stuck so a road crew member had to edge into view and move it a little. Once they saw the flag unfurl, everyone got excited. This was the N.W.A. reunion they'd read about for months. But after he, Snoop, Ren, and Cube did "Chin Check," Dre said, "More soon," then walked off stage.

Dre had mixed feelings about the tour. He was anxious to return to the studio. "It's almost like a high for me," he later admitted. And if he were away too long, he'd feel, "Damn, this could have been the day I came up with fucking 'Billie Jean' or some shit." But before long, the sight of fans in their forties near teens in the audience made him feel good about the trek, and about having a tour last more than a few dates. And while American newspaper reporters described rap shows as inherently violent, the Up in Smoke Tour played forty-two venues without incident. A few artists bickered and

Dre lectured the production crew once after pyro-blasts didn't go off ("leaving us standing up there looking fucking stupid") but other than that it was smooth sailing until he reached Detroit.

It was July 6, 2000, and Dre still remembered how the first N.W.A. tour ended there. They signed a contract saying they wouldn't perform "Fuck tha Police," and said, "Fuck that." "Boom; that was the end of the tour." Now, an arresting officer from back then was chief of police. But Dre arrived at Joe Louis Arena hours before the show. He was making sure all the props were ready, and talking with artists, when Detroit police arrived two hours before he was to take the stage. He listened to them say they'd cut the power off if he showed his seven-minute video. After the show, he told MTV it was wack that Detroit fans couldn't see the whole concert and claimed he'd never again play this venue, "because it's too much bullshit that goes on." The next day, he arrived at the Palace in Auburn Hills, thirty minutes north of Detroit. He was getting ready again when more cops arrived. "We've talked to the Detroit police," one said, "and we're not gonna let you show that shit here, either."

Dre finally had enough. That afternoon, he had his lawyer get an order from U.S. District Judge Nancy Edmunds ordering Auburn Hills to let him show his video. He thought that was that, and showed it before his set but saw cops waiting for him backstage. They claimed he was guilty of criminal obscenity, a law his attorney said didn't even exist, then arrested him. (Charges were eventually dropped in November 2000.) But they severely underestimated Dre. He was no longer that young guy shaken by the death of his brother. He had his lawyers sue Detroit for over $25 million in actual and punitive damages. He also named two cops and the Detroit mayor's press secretary. Then he told a reporter, "We had to sue 'em for fuckin' wit' our business. After that everybody let us do our thing. We had to set a standard of 'Don't fuck wit' us.'"

The incident did little to dampen Dre's enthusiasm for the tour and the money it was bringing in. Not even Suge's jailhouse interviews got him down. Dre's thirty-three-year-old former partner had been imprisoned for the last three years (sentenced to nine for violating probation by helping Tupac beat a Crip at the MGM Grand the night Pac was shot). With a

release date of his own secured—but not for a record, rather a release from
prison—he began to hint he was angry with Dre. In *The Source*, he implied
Dre was just another big-talking, jewelry-flashing black label owner letting
"white executives pump them up." He said *2001* was good but rehashed
Death Row's successful *Chronic* formula. He added, "But when Dre gets into
a fight or beat-down, Jimmy Iovine is not gonna get outta bed and go fight
for Dre, is he?"

Dre ignored the insults since it was a complicated situation. With Suge
now married to Michel'le and fathering her other children, he was also practically raising Dre's son Marcel. Because of this, Dre had visited Suge at some
point to smooth things over. While Suge told *The Source* their talk had been
positive, he still ridiculed Dre's attempt to fit in with the next trend by having
Jay-Z write his lyrics. He said Dre wasn't the street nigga he portrayed in
public and noted that people in Compton didn't even like him. He also revis-
ited his oft-quoted claim of Dre being a homo. "I ain't the one that called him
a bisexual and faggot or none of that, like other people," he said. "That was
done from Eazy-E and everybody else before."

He also insulted Dre's CEO image—claiming he was so inept Aftermath
went out of business after its first seven months—then implied that Dre
didn't want to be around black people anymore. "I like Dre," he claimed.
"We've always been friends. But he wants to be white. I can't do that. You can
live like a white person, but you can never go back." He called Magic Johnson
a few names, mentioned he held the rights to the band name N.W.A., and
said, about the tour, "It's good, but they should have kept it more in the community. And they're using the same props as we did in '92—the skull, the low-
rider car..."

Dre took it in stride but another event signaled some people felt he was
past his prime. In August 2000 amid awards, acclaim, and adulation, *The
Source* wanted to hand him and Cube Lifetime Achievement Awards during
a ceremony. Dre was nominated in five of twelve categories (including Album
of the Year, Single of the Year for "Still D.R.E.," and Solo Artist of the Year)
and decided to attend. On August 22, in the Pasadena Civic Auditorium, he
watched Eminem win Music Video of the Year for "Guilty Conscience," then
joined Cube to accept the night's top honor. "When they told me I was

receiving the Lifetime Achievement Award, I said, 'Damn, I'm only thirty-one,'" Cube said. "But when I look back at the work Dre and I have done in the last fifteen years, it is a lifetime of work." The self-congratulatory mood soon turned to horror after two rappers traded blows in the crowd, then fifteen to twenty men in red shirts promoting a Death Row collection of Snoop songs titled *Dead Man Walkin'* rushed the stage to reportedly try to get Snoop.

Some audience members threw bottles and CD cases. "It was out of control," said Lt. Paul Gales. Police stopped the show, and ordered 2,500 guests to leave. Backstage, Snoop stood near a tent with a circle of bodyguards, visibly dazed. "I can't speak on that right now. My head is in another place right now."

Dre didn't get to accept four other awards that night. And when producers asked him to return and tape a performance with his Up in Smoke entourage, he declined. Then, within weeks of the melee, Suge resumed insulting him and Snoop from his cell. "People say I was cruel for calling him a faggot, but what's pissing me off the most is that he was dishonest about it," Suge said now. "I don't have anything against gay people—to each his own," he went on. "Back in the day, we would have parties and he'd pretend to be with all these women. Don't lie to someone who is supposed to be your friend." Dre's associates shook their heads—he was married and had a bunch of kids. And fans had a good laugh, chalking it up to sour grapes. But Dre's image suffered another hit after he worked with Xzibit on his next album.

Once Xzibit's hardcore fans learned Dre would be executive producing they cried sellout. "So what I'm with Dr. Dre," Xzibit railed in print. "So what I'm with Snoop Dogg. So what." Dre busied himself with selecting the best works from the tracks X gathered from producers. As usual, if something didn't grab him in four short bars or less, he felt listeners, radio station programmers, and MTV would move on to the next record. He liked Xzibit's earlier producers—including his cousin Jinx—but felt a wider, general interest audience wanted catchy pop. Dre chose easygoing grooves by Rockwilder, EPMD funk-rap pioneer Erick Sermon, Battlecat, DJ Quik, Soopafly, and The Teamsters, but also felt—as with the N.W.A. reunion—there was room for Mel-Man, too.

And while Xzibit already had a good thing going—underground albums made him a darling of the rap magazines—Dre urged him to shorten his

verses and include more hooks and chants. Then he started suggesting
themes for lyrics. When X said the album title was *Man Vs. Machine*, Dre
saw the word "Restless" tattooed on X's body and said, "You should call your
album that. You could start a whole new lifestyle like that, roll with it."

Their sessions yielded works like "Get Your Walk On," which found X
urging the crowd to "back that ass up" and get drunk. "It's a party track," X
explained, something for the clubs. "DNA (Drugs and Alcohol)" included
the ubiquitous Snoop while Em appeared on another song. Where X usually
growled his insults, Dre had him make a few changes. "My tone, delivery,
and cadence is a little different from my earlier two albums," X shrugged. He
made *Restless* another *Chronic*-style work with the usual guests and themes
then insisted on creating it's lead single, "X," himself. He asked young white
co-producer Scott Storch (now wearing dress shirts with big collar points,
rose-colored glasses, and platinum jewelry) to help out but could not suspect
this would inspire a seven-figure lawsuit.

Though Dre was the producer—which in hip-hop meant creator of the
music, as opposed to simply taping an act's work—X let Storch bring him a
hot riff and cool beat. Unfortunately, producer/songwriter Mike Lowe
claimed Storch stole it from him after their August 6, 2000, meeting at Pep-
Soul Recording Studios in Philadelphia. In a lawsuit, Lowe remembered
Storch asking him to bring his "hottest stuff" so he could run it by producers
like Dre, to see if they'd buy them. Storch liked his track, "West Coast (Dre
Beat)," Lowe recalled, and asked him to go home and fetch the original disk.
He left, Lowe claimed, then Storch programmed identical beats and music
into his own keyboard and passed it off to Dre as his own creation.

Either way, in the studio, Dre enjoyed the orderly piano chords, smooth
keyboard line every four bars, and memorable chant Xzibit created for the
song. And when fans heard this song "X," they told each other Dr. Dre was
still one of the best producers in the game and inspired reporters to describe
Restless as "the most anticipated hip-hop album of the year."

This latest success made Dre more esteemed than ever. While he'd only
produced less than a handful of the songs, the very fact he was involved with
its creation helped *Restless*, upon its release December 12, quickly become
Xzibit's first million-selling work. Dre was delighted to see an album with

tougher sounds do well, and soon entered talks with his old hero Rakim. As he saw it, his production was what made his artists' albums sell. Eminem proved that, he felt. And the Xzibit album only confirmed it. When he heard Ra was between deals in late October, he remembered how much he enjoyed the four albums Ra recorded with DJ Eric B. from 1987 to 1992. He had quoted from them during N.W.A. and Death Row and, at the 1995 Source Awards, publicly mentioned wanting to work with him. Ra told another reporter he wanted it to happen but left music for two years, only to release two lackluster comeback works (1997's *The 18th Letter*—packaged with a greatest hits bonus disc, *The Book of Life*—and 1999's low-selling *The Master*). Dre didn't let the low sales affect his belief that Ra could still deliver a hit. As it was, he had just seen Eminem quote a few of his lyrics and sell copies through the roof. Though other producers or labels might see an aging rapper who was reportedly behind in child support payments, and whose best days seemed behind him, Dre knew his catchy sound would work wonders for his sales.

So when DreamWorks let him know Ra might sign with them, and asked if he would work on the album, Dre instead told Rakim, "Yo, come over to Aftermath." Now, Dre could barely contain his excitement. On the set of Em's video "Stan," he predicted, "This is going to be the biggest hip-hop record ever, straight up and coming at you from Aftermath, baby, so fuck all of y'all." Ra was one reason he stayed in hip-hop, he added, and working with him was "a straight-up blessing. I'm just grateful. I'm gonna step into the studio and make this the best record that I've ever made."

◆ ◆ ◆

With another project added to an already crowded plate, something had to give. Dre decided it'd be N.W.A. Between shows, his old friends wanted to record but Dre said he needed to know exactly who owned the group name. Cube felt these were distractions, and they should worry about making good music. "Once you do that, it's amazing how things work out." They all had enough money to put the album out without a label, he added. But just as quickly, Dre started having second thoughts about "Chin Check." Now, he felt it didn't sound as hot; he'd given them an old track and it sounded rushed.

During the tour, however, he tried to stay upbeat about it. He'd contacted Yella and got him to agree to contribute to the music once they left the road. They came up with a general concept for *Not These Niggaz Again* (violence) and even started working on general ideas (what Dre called blueprinting) in a mobile studio he hired to accompany their buses and tractor trailers. Hoping to release it the Fall of 2001, they knocked out a few ideas for beats and threw other ideas around hopefully, but too many people kept coming in and out, the itinerary was crammed with dates, and they couldn't really concentrate. Further, the bus broke down a few times and experienced other technical difficulties, so he put N.W.A. on hold. "We're gonna see how it goes," he said at the time. If it was "coming out hot, we'll continue it and finish it." They'd record after the tour, he added, and by then know who owned the group name N.W.A. "I think that's getting cleared up," he said then. "Everything's gonna work out."

But now, in late 2001, *Not These Niggaz Again* became another project that fell by the wayside. With reporters asking about it, Cube feebly said, "It's really on Dre. If he ain't puttin' the tracks together, I really ain't down to rap on nobody else's tracks." Then Dre claimed publicly that their work to date left him unsatisfied. They could try again, he said, but Cube was doing "a big special-effect movie," Snoop had to promote *Tha Last Meal* (an album he'd release December 19), and Dre had to work with Truth Hurts and Rakim. "I have no idea when that record's gonna happen, or if it's gonna happen."

Eventually, the truth got out. "I want to do the record, Ren wanna do it, and, of course Yella wants to do the record," said Cube. "But Dre doesn't want to do it." Ren said the same. "It was on Dre. We was ready." But he and Cube wouldn't "keep begging this dude to do no record." Though disappointed at this latest rejection—the first being the removal of his voice from "Bang Bang"—Ren said, "I ain't fittin' to cry over that shit." Meanwhile Yella couldn't even get Dre on the phone since Dre kept changing his number. "I haven't talked to him this year but I talked to him last year."

And then it was over, a year after Dre first described the album he then called *Not These Niggaz Again*. D.O.C. wasn't surprised at all. Knowing Dre, he said, it was bound to fail (and will never happen). The reunion for the tour was fun to watch, but they weren't equals, and without equivalence, they couldn't make great music. One guy would always think he was better. And none were hurting for money so they didn't have to do it. In addition, they didn't seem to want to spend time with each other. Even worse, "everybody except for the ingenious Mr. Dr. Dre realizes I'm a huge piece of that shit. Dre doesn't think so. He feels the piece I brought to the table can be manufactured from somewhere else or something, so you don't need to call me, but that's a huge mistake." But the worst mistake, he felt, might have been insisting that Snoop be part of the group. Snoop's voice on some songs worked but his face on an N.W.A. record would alienate fans. Eazy simply could not be replaced, he felt. Then they barely even mentioned Yella's name. Reporters had to ask about him. "You got to be equals, brothers, or you got somebody runnin' the show and thinkin' his word goes and soon as he gets mad and walks out everything shuts down," D.O.C. concluded. "That's a load of bullshit."

After abandoning N.W.A., Dre kept working with Snoop on his album *Tha Last Meal*. For one song, he had Mike Elizondo jam on guitar over a drum track until he heard something he liked, and to Elizondo, it constituted "some co-production." Either way, "Lay Low" started with another fake voice-mail message. "Ay, ay, Snoop what up?" Dre said. "This your nigga Dre. Ay, man, I was thinkin I ain't said shit on your whole motherfuckin' album. So check it out, put this on there: 'All you motherfuckin' haters out there can suck my motherfuckin' dick! And we still smokin'. What?!'" Whether he believed they'd do N.W.A. when he wrote this lyric is unknown, but the song found Snoop saying, "Snoop and Dre give a fuck about what y'all say/From the 'World's Most Dangerous Group,' N.W.A." After this no less than Master P, head of Snoop's label No Limit, praised Dre, too. "What's up, pimpin'?" he said. "It's P and Snoop. With Dre on the beat, this ain't nuttin' but loot." Dre felt his contributions to the album sounded like hits, and looked forward to seeing what fans and critics thought. But before its release in December, he saw yet another Death Row–related controversy erupt. This time, Death Row reportedly posted nineteen of Snoop's songs on its official site on November 27, near text that asked visitors to "take the Snoop Dogg challenge" and compare it to Death Row's own Snoop collection, *Dead Man Walkin'*. The new songs vanished quickly but reappeared in early December, before being removed again. Where he usually took a deep breath and kept on moving, ignoring Suge's slights, this time Dre found himself telling a reporter, "Why don't those people do what we are doing [and] move on? You live your life; let us live our life. I don't fuck with you, you don't fuck with me, and then everybody can just move on with their lives, be happy and chill with their families, and go on." This was petty, he felt. "Like, 'Yo, my record isn't selling, so I'm gonna try to fuck up what you try'na do.'" But from his cell, Suge had a quick answer. "Why would Death Row attempt to sabotage *Tha Last Meal* when we are partners with No Limit/Priority Records on this album?"

◆ ◆ ◆

In early 2001, Dre's amazing run continued. He looked back on the previous year as one of his most accomplished. True, N.W.A. fell apart, but his tour ranked as hip-hop's most successful, fans made a hit of the accompanying *Up in Smoke* DVD, his album *2001* sold over six million copies, he was mentioned prominently in reviews of Eminem's seven-million-selling *The Marshall Mathers LP*, and critics offered breathless praise for his cuts on Snoop's *Tha Last Meal* and Xzibit's *Restless*. At home, he was comfortably settled in quiet domesticity and he and Nicole were expecting their second child, a little girl they'd name Truly. Some people kept claiming he took credit for work he didn't do and Suge Knight continued to insult him during interviews, but in early 2001, he was shocked to learn he was nominated for five Grammy awards (including Producer of the Year). Eminem was up for four and *The Marshall Mathers LP* was competing with *2001* for Best Hip-Hop Album.

It seemed he'd win since, at the American Music Awards, Dre beat Em for the Favorite Rap/Hip-Hop award. And the media seemed to finally be rooting for him. After he granted an interview to the *Los Angeles Times*, he saw Robert Hilburn ask in print, "Will Dr. Dre get his due, finally?" "If Dr. Dre wins Producer of the Year honors at the Grammys tonight, as has been predicted by some, it will be a victory not only for the thirty-six-year-old rap titan, but also for rap music itself," Hilburn continued. The article let everyone know Dre should have won Producer of the Year way back in 1989 for N.W.A.'s *Straight Outta Compton*. "But few record industry powers and Grammy voters took rap seriously enough then to consider nominating him." Hilburn then noted that the Academy's respect for rap had grown by the time he released *The Chronic* but implied Dre was again slighted (winning one award for a single in 1994). But now that he'd produced some of Eminem's *The Marshal Mathers LP* and released *2001*, Hilburn felt, there was no way Grammy voters could ignore him.

Only after he was nominated did Dre reveal he viewed *2001* as his final attempt at being a rapper. "If it didn't catch on, I wasn't going to try another solo album." If it tanked, he would have given up rapping. And it wouldn't mean anything, either, since "The thing I'm proud of is the production. That's my thing."

By Grammy night, Dre was more excited than ever. But once again, Eminem was in all the headlines. As Em had predicted, many people took offense to his lyrics, and GLAAD (The Gay and Lesbian Alliance Against Defamation), the Family Violence Prevention Fund, and the National Organization for Women were objecting to his inclusion and calling his rhymes homophobic, abhorrent, and misogynist. But Dre avoided comment and attended the ceremony, joining Em on stage for various performances and cracking jokes throughout the evening.

But then they started handing out awards, and Em beat him for Best Rap Album. Then Em won Best Rap Solo Performance. Dre accepted an award for Best Rap Performance by a Duo or Group for "Forgot about Dre." Then Em surprised critics by trotting openly gay singer Elton John out for "Stan," embracing him, then raising both middle fingers to the audience. Finally, it was time for Producer of the Year, Non-Classical. Dre maintained a detached facial expression even when they said he won. "That was big," he felt, but instead of heading to the podium for a speech, he simply stood and raised his arms: "The perfect ending to my life story."

But right after the Grammy win, he learned Mike Lowe sued him, Scott Storch, and a few other companies over the music on Xzibit's "X." The lawsuit, filed in late April, asked for over $1 million in damages and claimed Storch stole his music from "West Coast (Dre Beat)." Lowe's attorney sent each defendant a settlement proposal, but everyone, including Dre, ignored it. They claimed he and Xzibit wrote the track. After being served with legal papers Dre quickly pleaded not guilty. But journalists kept reporting on Lowe's allegations and it renewed gossip in rap circles that Dre was simply a figure-head at his own company, including his name in credits for tracks he didn't even do. But such talk didn't matter to Vivendi. As the Universal parent company saw it, Dre was the man who helped *2001* and Eminem's *The Marshall Mathers LP* sell twenty-five million copies worldwide. Since it wanted to continue to be in on the profits and excitement, Vivendi raised its stake in After-math, reportedly handing Dre thirty-five million dollars.

14

As 2001 continued, Dr. Dre—thinner, and a bit weary under the eyes, inspiring some people to believe rumors he'd been dabbling with Ecstasy—had even more reason to be ecstatic. After years of trying to break into film, in April, he was handling preproduction on *The Wash*. Principal photography would start May 7, 2001, so Dre had friends help him learn dialogue and taped practice videos. He'd been trying for years, with a pilot, an N.W.A. script, and more, but managed only to land a cameo as a gun dealer in *Set it Off* and a crooked cop in *Training Day*. (He also recorded "Put it On Me," for the soundtrack, in which he asked, "Y'all ready to get dirty?" then rapped about getting a woman into a hotel room, playing music, handing her mushrooms, then screwing her "in every room.") DJ Pooh (who co-starred in Cube's *Friday*) had been inspired to write the film during the tour, when he saw Snoop's dressing room always noisy and crowded, while Dre's was quiet, with just his family around. "This is perfect," he told Dre. "It's the odd couple."

He soon presented his script, *The Wash*, since he never forgot the days when he'd drive Dre, who didn't have a car then, to N.W.A. sessions. In return, Dre showed him the ropes (which helped Pooh join the LA Posse, begin his production career, and segue into film with *Friday* and *Next Friday*). "I'm returning the favor and pulling Dre into film," he said.

While Dre aspired to crime comedies as trendy as those by Quentin Tarantino, no one was rushing to give him a starring role. New to the field, still learning about marketing and distribution, and eager to move beyond bit parts, he told Pooh he'd star in the movie, co-produce, and handle the soundtrack. He'd play Snoop's buttoned-down roommate and bicker with him once he becomes his boss at a car wash. He'd also have to carry the movie, since his story arc showed him going from broke and irresponsible to selling out once he receives a promotion. During casting, he suggested Eminem and Truth Hurts, then reported for work and ceded control to director Pooh.

Between takes, he rehearsed lines. Standing near a refrigerator, he said, "Okay, I'm supposed to go to the fridge? There's supposed to be some ice?" He opened the door only to see a bottle of Hennessey smash onto the floor.

In embarrassment, he retreated to his trailer, where an acting coach calmed him as much as the mellow Marvin Gaye CD, *What's Going On*, he was playing. He relieved more tension by griping about how his character didn't get laid, got threatened at gunpoint a few times, and had to ride the bus. Then he had to dance. It was as far from his image as he could go and he had second thoughts. But when Pooh called him to the set, he took his mark. He felt nervous but started moving when Pooh gave the order to roll film. With Funkadelic's "Knee Deep" playing, Dre danced stiffly and soon worked up a sweat. The take went on forever but he kept moving. Finally, he roared, "Goddamn, Pooh!" Pooh laughed. "Cut. My bad. I didn't want to stop you." Everyone had a good laugh, including Dre. But when a journalist from the *Hollywood Reporter* asked about the film, for whatever reason, Dre said, "I don't expect *The Wash* to be *The Godfather*. We only spent three million and went and had some fun."

◆ ◆ ◆

Originally, Dre hoped to make *The Wash* soundtrack an album-length reunion with Snoop (since Snoop kept pushing that *Break Up to Make Up* idea). But an October movie release slot made it inconceivable. So Dre kept working on a project that might have at times reminded him of the how harried he felt while creating the *Aftermath* compilation. He'd have to recruit others to help, and get his own contributions done while also starring in the film and, as co-producer, keeping an eye on the budget. In addition, he had to juggle acts and agreements with about eleven companies.

By now, his musicians carried beepers so that, if he wanted to work, they'd drop everything and scamper to the studio. Once his elementary drums were cycling, they jammed until he heard a catchy riff. After finishing a song, he'd play it at full volume, and nod along or reject it as weak. He'd have asked others' opinions, but by now, whenever he played anything, whether good or bad, people would face the speakers built into the walls and try to keep time with some supportive head-nodding. To them, everything was always great.

For "The Wash," Pooh helped him rehash Leon Haywood's "I Want'a Do Something Freaky to You" again. Dre then produced "Holla," by high-energy party-rapper Busta Rhymes, and got Knoc-Turn'al into the studio for "Str8 West Coast."

With the deadline nearing, Dre searched for collaborators, including Hi-Tek, Focus (recruited by his employee Mike Lynn), and female rapper Shaunta, who hailed from Compton. A day after hearing her nine-song CD for former label Atlantic he signed her, then teamed her with Hi-Tek for "Good Lovin'." Then, when he met unknown rapper Smitty on the set (where Smitty had sneaked in and waited sixteen hours to meet Dre) he recruited him to write a few rhymes. Next, he had Mahogany, who sometimes produced for Jay-Z's Roc-A-Fella and DMX's Ruff Ryders, create music for a duet with Knoc'Turn'al, "Bad Intentions." Dre had his musicians replay the group Eleventh Hour's "Hollywood Hot"—a sample Mahogany included on a beat CD his manager sent Aftermath—then let Mahogany take over while he recorded a vocal. And while Mahogany coached the flautist on how to play a riff, Dre urged Knoc-Turn'al to try a new nasal tone and just talk, not rap.

"Bad Intentions" found Dre urging clubgoers to pour drinks and smoke weed. He bragged about top-notch hoes coming to see him each week. He mentioned offering them an "X pill"—again fueling rumors he indulged in this drug (a claim Eminem also made during one interview)—then claimed he sometimes had ten women in bed at once. He described how they lay on their bellies while he penetrated them from behind then asked them to "keep them titties jumpin, keep the Henny [Hennessy] comin'." After this unseemly sex rap claimed everyone's women wanted to hang with Aftermath, he said, "Yeah, Aftermath, Doc Dre, five-star surgeon general." He thanked Knoc-Turn'al and Mahogany (for "droppin the instrumental"), and said "Aftermath gets the last laugh."

Since this would probably be the album's Dr. Dre single, he made this session last a staggering fifty-six hours. He was exhausted, but within a week, oversaw three other sessions that lasted nineteen hours each. Security guys started asking Knoc, upon his arrival at the studio, "Man, is it going to be another one of those days?" And Dre—at the center of a circle of agreeable security guards, conformable musicians, and a few trusted friends—kept quietly receding a little. During dinner breaks, while guests crammed into a room to smoke pot, drink Henney, and start partying, he sat in his chair at the board with his meal, chewed quickly, then cleared everyone out by quietly saying, "Back to work."

But he joined Snoop for "On the Blvd," for which producer Jelly Roll created the track. On the surface, this was another jovial buddy rap with Snoop. "The world ain't set for what I'm about to do," Dre rapped. "Ninety-six tracks mixed down to two." But as it continued, the lyrics seemed to address the recent incident at The Source Awards. Dre said out west people were always hunting. Snoop said, "But I won't wear no bull's eye." Within seconds, Dre added, "Y'all know how the story goes. We give a fuck about award shows." Snoop said he felt the same about hoes. "Real niggas own platinum balls," Dre went on. "I ain't got it on my neck, nigga; check my walls." Dre was so thrilled by its sound, he decided "On the Blvd" would be the first single. But his perfectionist tendencies led him to keep working on it right up until two days before they had to shoot a video. Late one night, he had singer Cocaine stop by. Dre shook his head. Radio might not go for that name, he later told a reporter. But the newcomer could sing and Dre had a deadline so he had him polish his vocals on the chorus. He played the track and told him what he wanted but Cocaine couldn't get it, so he sang it himself. Cocaine nodded, he understood, but also needed to warm up. A few minutes later, Dre heard

Cocaine say he was ready, slid the seat across the room to the mixing board, and said, "All right, everybody, let's make some music."

He also joined Snoop on *The Wash,* to once again warn people California was dangerous, to boast about his astronomical sales figures, and to say he now commanded an asking price of $250,000 per track. Snoop meanwhile managed to work in mention of his new Snoop Dogg clothing line.

While the schedule and deadline were demanding, Dre managed to deliver first-rate results. He had Mel-Man and Aftermath acts Shaunta, Truth Hurts, and rapper Joe Beast create "Benefit of the Doubt" and "No." Hi-Tek and Shaunta filled "Good Lovin'" with joyful Marvin Gaye samples. Eminem and his producer Jeff Bass delivered D-12's pro-drug "Blow My Buzz." Timbaland and white Southern artist Bubba Sparxxx presented "Bubba Talk." Other songs by Xzibit ("Get Fucked Up with Me"), Soopafly ("Gotta Get Dis Money"), a few newcomers, and singer RC (who sang on Focus' track, "Riding High") were just as absorbing. But when he asked Hittman to do something, the rapper declined. It was a situation in the making, Dre knew, but it had to wait. He had too much on his plate, spending every waking hour in the studio; working with strangers; having to cede so much control; no time to sit and live with the material and improve it. And at home, there was not enough time with Nicole and the kids. It was hard to concentrate on anything. People opined he'd get it done, don't worry; but what was actually being created felt a bit haphazard. He was spending so much time in the studio that *Time* reported, "If he didn't go to the parking lot for the occasional car-stereo listening test, he'd have no idea whether it was night or day." But the deadline required he get right back in that stale room where some contributors were recording stale music about stale themes. Still, he had to get it done. He had to see it not only as an artist but a label head with a deadline to meet. And for all he knew maybe people would like it. Once songs were coming together he leapt into creating the score. Along with Funkadelic's "(Not Just) Knee Deep," The Ohio Players' "Funky Worm," Blondie's "Rapture," and Eric B & Rakim's oldie "I Ain't No Joke" he and his session players created four original pieces.

He could have used a break at this point but he threw himself into a few lucrative outside productions, including one suggested by Jimmy Iovine. Eve, who left Aftermath, sold two million copies of her 1999 debut, and wowed critics with a turn in *Barbershop*, was creating her second album, *Scorpion*. She wanted to collaborate with someone, so Jimmy Iovine said, "We're going to get Gwen. Let's get Gwen Stefani, let's get her." Eve asked if Stefani, the thin blonde in the Madonna mold who fronted No Doubt, would do it, and Jimmy said, "Let me handle it." Dre recorded their parts separately, and set them to another tame pop track. But the resulting single, "Let Me Blow Ya Mind," helped *Scorpion* sell a million copies and earn Eve two Grammy nominations (for Best Album and the single). "Basically Dre saved her shit," said DJ Ben Baller.

Xzibit, four songs into his fourth album, *Man Vs. Machine*, wanted his help, too, so Dre gave him a CD with thirty-eight beats (some for Xzibit's album and some for Dre's next work, which he said would be about "the Internet"). "He actually didn't really need that much of my involvement, because he hustles," Dre said. "Xzibit is not one of those that needs to be baby-sitted." Even so, he showed up to add final touches "or do what I feel is needed to the songs, and that's that." Then when Mary J. Blige said, "Dre, I need a nice hot sound," he gave her "Family Affair," a string-laden radio hit. "She went to Dre and Dre crunked her single," said Baller. And since Warren G's career needed a boost Dre surprised Warren by joining him for a song. Warren was just beginning to accept that Dre and Snoop were consciously deciding not to involve him with production for their albums. "I guess they look at me like Little Warren, you know what I'm sayin'. I mean, I don't understand it myself." At the same time, Warren was going in circles in an industry now dominated by a handful of majors. Though he'd left Def Jam after Universal bought it, he was now taking "a pay cut to go with Universal. I really respect their machine," he added. And he hoped to pull a Dre and rehash his big-selling debut with a sequel called *Return of the Regulator*. Dre rapped alongside Warren on "Lookin' at Me" (the first time both spoke on the same record) but surprised him again when he just as quickly said he couldn't do it. "Jimmy Iovine and them wouldn't let it happen," Warren recalled. "That kind of fucked with me, but I ain't trippin'. I understand how this game go."

Dre kept moving. He spent two days with Busta Rhymes, who left Elektra after four albums for Clive Davis' new J Records. After Mel worked on one new song, Dre played a track. Busta nodded along, so Dre said, "Yo, look what this beat got us doing in here. We're breaking our necks to it. You should just call this shit 'Break Ya Neck.'" Busta used the title. Then Dre got him to do "Truck Volume" and brought out a Doors-inspired track he created during one lunch break. Next, he handed him a third beat on CD and sent him to another room to write while he coached keyboardists and guitarists. "He'll have, like, an orchestra going on in the studio," Busta said.

They got the songs done but Dre kept working on "Truck Volume" after Busta returned to New York. He felt the Vox organ needed a few strings. "I need louder cellos," he told an engineer. As the guy raised the volume, Dre muttered to himself, "Cellos make everything sound evil." Then he told a reporter from *Time*, who was on hand watching him record, "The cellos are real. I don't use samples."

Once they were done, he listened to it a few times. "More reverb here." The engineer complied. Dre heard it for the twelfth time and felt the two-second echo he requested was off. "Now it sounds like he's in the Grand Canyon." Reaching for a phone, he called Busta in New York. "I don't think we should add any more to it. Nah. All the breakdowns and all the instruments sound full enough. I'll call you if there are any changes." He hung up, heard it again, then said, "Put that on a CD real quick. Let me listen to it in my truck." Only out there, with the volume up high, did he decide it was good to go.

Time printed an article describing him as the top producer in the business, instead of as someone struggling to regain the control he had to surrender to meet the deadline for *The Wash*. The rush, and long sessions, took their toll, and in the end, like some cruel joke, it seemed to be all for nothing. The deadline he'd rushed to meet was in September 2001. *The Wash* soundtrack was in stores on time but the nation didn't feel like partying much after terrorists in hijacked planes destroyed the World Trade Center's Twin Towers, murdering thousands; attacked the Pentagon; and inspired the president's declaration of war.

The singles "The Wash" and "Bad Intentions" sat in stores. They also didn't chart on *Billboard*'s Hot 100. The album itself stalled at number nineteen on the *Billboard* 200. But Dre didn't much care. He too was shocked and saddened by recent events and on September 20, with the nation still reeling, donated $1 million to KPWR (Power) 106's Power of a Dollar Relief Fund.

Five days later, *The Wash*, his official debut, arrived in theaters. It was a decent film, with a great performance, but like most pop culture products released during this dark period, it also went ignored. The media was focused on war and trying to make sense of that day. And at Aftermath, plans for an overseas tour with another recording studio trailing tour buses, ended abruptly. "Everything was on halt," Hitt recalled.

15

By October 2001, Dre saw the situation with Hittman reach its sad, but inevitable conclusion. Hitt's view of Dre had soured a little. He wanted to follow up on the buzz after *2001*, but Dre got so busy promoting his own album and career that nothing ever happened. "Eminem's album did so good and then 'Forgot about Dre' really had everybody sayin' 'Oh shit,'" Hittman recalled. "So they rushed to put that album out." Next, Dre had to go on tour. Then he executive produced Xzibit's *Restless* and mixed Snoop's *Tha Last Meal*. "Then it was Grammy time and he wins Producer of the Year so he gotta go out and be Producer of the Year." With everyone willing to pay top dollar for a track, "he wanted to take advantage of the Mary J's, and do production with all those other people."

While Dre was busy, Hitt worked with Mel-Man, Battlecat, and Dre's usual guests Knoc-Turn'al, Truth Hurts, and Em, on new songs. He also helped Dre blueprint his next album, which he said would be called *Detox*. Originally, Dre wanted it to be about the Internet, but couldn't find time to record it. Still, he went from running ideas by trusted insiders to playing Hitt ten beats and outlining concepts. In response, Hitt wrote and recited early drafts. Dre liked what he heard but also knew Hittman was itching to release an album, and that Interscope needed to feel his work met their commercial standards before they'd agreed to release something. "Fuck it," Dre said when Hitt let him hear lyrics. "We gonna put that on your album."

But before he could devote his full concentration to the project, he had to do *The Wash*. While Dre felt his success would keep people interested in every act on the label, and help sales of artists like Hitt, Hitt felt Dre didn't consider his debut a priority. "And that's where the conflict came."

At the same time that Hittman became dissatisfied, Dre also had to work on Rakim's project, Eminem's next single, and Truth Hurts' debut. Furthermore he had to handle duties at Aftermath. Despite huge sales, Aftermath was actually a small outfit, with one president, a general manager, and "basically a bunch of assistants for other people," said Hitt's DJ, Ben Baller.

When he'd squeeze in sessions with Hitt, he then saw the artist reject what he felt were viable ideas. Hitt now felt that, in the hands of majors like Interscope, hip-hop had devolved into a cookie cutter formula: "Yo, this is your song for the hood, this is your song for the girls, this is your song about your homies." He didn't want his album, *Big Hitt: The Last Days of Brian Bailey*, to present the same. During this period, he said, Dre told him he didn't hear a single. "They been holdin' it up because of that," Hittman told a reporter. He proposed "Last Days," something Dre's pop audience already enjoyed during one video, and Dre said all right, then changed his mind again, becoming "ultra critical."

Dre kept suggesting other ideas but Hittman ignored them. Then he came to feel—like King Tee before him—that Dre cared too much about magazines and ratings. He wanted to discuss these issues at length, and remembered Dre saying Iovine was the one who wouldn't release the music yet. He tried again, but heard new employees say, "Yo, talk to me 'cause Dre got a lot of shit to do." Finally, in October, he booked a week in the studio. He agreed to re-enter the post-merger limbo in which labels kept acts busy churning out demos, in order to determine their commercial potential and decide whether to drop them or not. He arrived at the studio and suddenly heard unnamed people claim, "Yo, we waitin' for the engineer." One day, he sat for an hour among "niggaz holdin' their balls, playin' video games," then left. During the next week no one from Aftermath called to reschedule. Even worse, on a Sunday night, his phone rang and a female singer asked, "Yo, did you hear you got dropped?"

"What you talkin' about?" he replied.

"Look, just check into that shit."

For three days, he couldn't reach anyone on the phone. Finally someone said, "Yeah, you got dropped; Jimmy dropped you, basically." He left Aftermath so quietly most label-mates didn't know he was gone. Aftermath then delayed in signing his walking papers, he claimed, to the point where other labels lost interest in signing him. "I definitely think they put some difficulty into the game."

◆　◆　◆

It was a brand-new year, and this one would be even better, Dre thought. It started with the *Los Angeles Times* asking twenty-two label executives who would sell the most records over the next seven years. In January, they all said him, with one going so far as to say the thirty-five-year-old Grammy winner might be the industry's greatest talent. Dre was delighted and "livin' pretty good right now. Let's just say I haven't even spent all my N.W.A. money yet," he added. But his image continued to come under fire from Marion "Suge" Knight.

After his release from prison, Knight appeared on BET and told an audience a hilarious anecdote. He claimed Dre once approached him at Death Row to say, "I want to be white, Suge. Can you help me be white?" He faced Dre like, "Is this nigga really serious?" he added, then replied, "You can date a white woman, move to a white neighborhood, but I can't physically make you white." The audience loved it so he repeated this claim to another reporter, adding, "That's why he married a white woman and signed Eminem."

Then he told *The Source*, "If Jimmy tells Dre, 'Hey, nigguh boy you will do this,' Dre will say, 'Yes, sir, boss.'" Before long, a number of rap-related web sites were reporting that, during a recent trip to New York City, Suge appeared on radio and told listeners Dre once admitted he was bisexual, Dre was a rat, and Dre had a letter "W" tattooed on each ass cheek so it'd spell "Wow." No one really believed any of this, but Suge added that once, while changing, in boxer shorts, he saw Dre staring at his groin. Once he got the image-smashing anecdotes out of the way, Suge then voiced the true reason he was angry—the restraining order Dre allegedly filed against him. "I thought that was for battered wives."

Dre avoided a war of words and focused on working with new acts. While reporters wondered where the Rakim or Truth Hurts albums were, Dre was hatching a plan that could potentially make Aftermath the most exciting and profitable label in the business. Hittman was gone, but he had a stable of enthusiastic and talented young artists raring to record, including female rapper Brooklyn, twenty-year-old Joe Beast from Pittsburgh, nineteen-year-old singer Antonio from New York, Shaunta from Compton, and a singer named Amy. Then he learned about a skilled nineteen-year-old rapper from Compton named The Game.

◆ ◆ ◆

A guy named D-Mack reportedly passed Dre a demo and he liked what he heard. Then he learned more about the rapper. Born Jayceon Taylor, Game was raised in a foster home in Compton and originally aspired to a career in athletics. But by Winter 2000, he and his older brother Fase ran dealers out of a dope spot in an apartment in Bellflower, California, on the outskirts of Compton. The disgruntled dealers returned twice to try to rob them. Then at two a.m. on October 1, 2001, someone knocked on the door. "The way we had it set up, we shut down at twelve a.m., the whole spot," Fase later recalled. Game, playing a John Madden Football game on a PlayStation 2 console, went to answer the door. "I was greedy," he later admitted, looking to earn a potential "quick three, four hundred dollars." Three men ran in, two of them armed. The unarmed one ran for Game's gun on a nearby table. Game tussled with him on the floor while another gunman fired eleven bullets, six of which missed. But one tore a chunk of Game's chest off. Another ripped into his stomach. A third hit his leg, bringing him down while he ran down a hallway. For fifteen minutes, he lay face down on a floor, waiting for them to finish the job. Finally, he rolled over, crawled to a bathroom, pulled himself up, and turned on the light. His tank top was soaked with blood, he claimed. But he lifted it to see where they hit him and blood splattered onto the mirror. He said he called the cops, gave his address, then lapsed into a two-day coma. But his older brother Fase said, "He ain't spend no days in no coma. What was it, a thirty-minute coma? He was out of the hospital the next day." Either way, Game claimed that while recuperating in bed for five months, he heard Jay-Z's *Reasonable Doubt*, Notorious B.I.G.'s *Ready to Die*, and music by N.W.A. and Pac and thought, "Damn, I could probably do this shit." At the LA Summit in 2002, the tall, brown-skinned rapper performed for Snoop's sidemen Goldie and Tray Dee (The Eastsidaz) and met entrepreneur JT The Bigga Figga, whose Get Low Records had released an amazing seventy albums in eleven years. "He didn't have a demo or label," JT recalled, so he took him to a studio in Fillmore, California, and knocked out twenty-two tracks and a few performances for a DVD. "All I want claim to is the songs that me and you do," he told Game. "Whatever you do on your own after that, it's on you. Get your money, cousin."

Once Dre heard Game's demo, he wanted to meet him. The young rapper arrived while Dre was working in the studio. Dre told him he liked his freestyles and wanted to sign him. Game was thunderstruck. Soon after the deal was signed, Game started viewing Dre as something "like the father I never had." At the same time, Aftermath saw JT of Get Low Records offer Game's first songs. When the label rejected them, JT felt Game was behind it, thinking he might be angry about having a big debut with Aftermath and a completed album with Get Low. "It's fucking their story up," JT said publicly. "They wanted the story to be that 'Dre found him; he's from Compton, from Eazy-E's block.'"

Whatever the case, Dre couldn't work with Game anyway. He was busy with other projects and seemingly enthusiastic about everything but his own album, *Detox*. Two years after he first mentioned it, people wondered if this would end like *Helter Skelter* or *Not These Niggaz Again*. With artists second-guessing him, and Interscope now suggesting projects he should do—along with *The Wash*'s failure to emerge as a hit even after the nation moved past the terrorist attacks—Dre had begun to question his own decisions. But now he was confident again. While only blueprinting, he felt five tracks could work, and one could easily be the first single. "It's going to be a breath of fresh air," he promised a reporter, "and I'm not going to stop until I feel like it is that way." But other people continued to show little faith in him despite his impressive track record. "He's talkin' about workin' on a record called *Detox*, he told me," D.O.C. said during this period. "Well, he's gonna have to bring something other then that same 'ol shit he's been doing if he think he's fittin' to move the crowd now."

Then Dre began to wonder if, at thirty-seven, with about eleven children (including stepson Trevor), he wasn't too old to be rapping about low-riders, parties, and weed. "I mean, that's played." But he overcame these crippling and useless doubts, ditched the Internet concept, and decided to rap from the perspective of a hired killer, and to have his regulars act as guest stars in this "hip-hop musical." He spent six months "getting ideas together," considering how to present the narrative, and gathering sounds. He impressed Truth Hurts with the few ideas he let her hear. It was all "a little more future than what Dre has been doing," she said, yet still ghetto. He had her sing about crooked cops (with an astonishing vocal arrangement), then invited King Tee onto another song (letting Tee choose a beat and telling him, Tee recalled, "he's trying to come quick with this one"). But just as quickly, he filled another song with downhearted recollections of past glories over Roy Ayers' bittersweet "Everybody Loves the Sunshine." Before he could really make headway, however, he had to help Interscope wring another commercial hit out of an increasingly jaundiced Eminem.

While Dre took his time with artists, Eminem moved on with his career. In addition to his own roster of acts and a label called Shady Records, the troubled white rapper now had his own Dre-like operation in Detroit. Like his mentor, he worked on the best equipment; hummed melodies to two full-time musicians; had two engineers track, edit, and mix his sounds in Pro Tools; and managed to churn out a beat tape every two or three weeks. At the same time, he was making the move into film. He had accepted a minor role in *The Wash*—playing a disgruntled young white guy who wanted to shoot someone at the Car Wash—but was now in talks to star in a big-budget Brian Grazer production. Dre had long discussed such a film with Em but now it was a reality. Grazer (whose credits include *A Beautiful Mind*) had arranged a meeting with Em's manager Paul Rosenberg after seeing one of his videos on

MTV. Now, Curtis Hanson, of *L.A. Confidential*, was in the director's chair, Em was playing a rapper named Jimmy trying to make it in Detroit's rap scene, and on the set, Dre watched from the sidelines and vetted ideas.

Whether Dre felt Eminem was outpacing him while he remained mired in projects that never seemed to yield gratifying results is unknown. But the balance of power between the two had clearly shifted. Em was no longer the hungry young artist willing to be molded so as to earn diaper money and rent. He was the fastest-selling rapper in history, a working producer—even Jay-Z bought a track for his hit *The Blueprint*'s "Renegade"—and running his own Interscope-backed label, which would release the soundtrack to his movie, *8 Mile*.

From the sidelines, Dre watched Em handle most of the production for his next album, *The Eminem Show*. Instead of accessible pop, he was sampling Aerosmith's chestnut "Dream On," singing an apology to his mom ("Cleaning Out My Closet"), and rapping about his turbulent marriage, legal woes, and run-ins with other groups. He included Nate Dogg on a song, and Truth Hurts on what she called "a spin-off of Rockwell's 'Somebody's Watching Me.'"

Eminem took a three-month break to film *8 Mile* and cut down on his partying but kept writing for fans who preferred somber "Stan" over "The Real Slim Shady's" featherweight pop. He was by now openly saying his past hits disgusted him. "Like 'My Name Is'. I fucking hate that song anyways." He also said that if the label wouldn't let him show fans he was a real MC, "then I'm quitting." With fans already going nuts over his self-produced "Cleaning Out My Closet," featured in trailers for *8 Mile*, he didn't really need Dre or anyone's opinion. But he sometimes called to ask what Dre thought of new songs. "He won't sugarcoat it," Em felt. "His honesty is one thing that I've appreciated the most, ever since he signed me." And when reporters asked about the album, all Dre could say was that Em's production skills had improved. "He's singing a lot," he explained. "He's singing and doing a lot of his own choruses and harmonies."

Inevitably, Interscope said it didn't hear a single and wanted Dre to get in there and deliver some good party music. Dre created three songs at a commercial facility in Reno, before working in Eminem's new studio in Detroit for a week and a half. "It was like the old Motown style of working," said Elizondo, "with a group of us creating the music and tracks in the same room."

Though much had clearly changed, Dre and Em tried to revive their old image of teamwork and unity on "Business." Dre cried, "Marshall! Sounds like an S.O.S."

Eminem replied, "Holy wack unlyrical lyrics, Andre. You're fuckin right!"

"To the Rapmobile! Let's go!"

But Em was visibly bored. "I had been in a slump, thinking, 'Where is hip-hop gonna go?'" He told everyone he was tired of the same crews and sounds. What could Dre say or do? He wrapped sessions and flew back to Los Angeles, to add final touches. Interscope scheduled *The Eminem Show* for release. When reporters called to ask if Em was getting heavy, Dre said no. "The shock value of Eminem is definitely gonna still be there, but it's just getting better." Then an Interscope rep rushed to say his first single, "Without Me," would evoke those for *The Slim Shady LP* ("My Name Is") and *The Marshall Mathers LP* ("The Real Slim Shady"). Rakim contradicted them ("Put it this way: He stepped the skills up") but Dre and Interscope kept promising a fun-loving album. Em meanwhile remained in the doldrums until manager Paul Rosenberg handed him 50 Cent's latest CD, *Guess Who's Back*. Em, who loved every note, took the underground self-released work to Dre and asked if he'd want to collaborate on the project. Dre already had numerous albums to finish. But with Eminem drifting further out of his orbit—producing his own music, filming a movie, working at his own Interscope-backed label Shady—he answered, "Yeah, let's give it a shot."

◆ ◆ ◆

Born Curtis Jackson, 50 Cent was a former dealer with a competitive streak. He learned song structure from Jason Mizell, "Jam Master Jay" of Run D.M.C., then signed a $65,000 deal with Columbia Records. His novelty rap, "How to Rob," rubbed many artists the wrong way—he joked about robbing Big Pun, Ghostface Killer, and Jay-Z, among others—and his name became even more well known when superstar Jay-Z told a concert audience, "I'm about a dollar, what the fuck is 50 Cent?" With other established acts firing back, rap fans wanted to know more about the brash young newcomer. But on May 24, 2000, before Columbia released his album *Power of the Dollar*, a shooter ran up on 50 while he sat in a car in front of his grandmother's home in Queens and shot him nine times. "All over the place," he recalled, "My pinky, the face, a lot of leg shots." During a thirteen-day hospital stay, he signed a publishing deal and received a $125,000 advance but his label figured he'd been shot in the face and couldn't perform. "They freaked out," he said. After losing his deal, he spent a month off his feet then traveled to Pennsylvania, where he lived with his girlfriend and their son, Marquise. "He literally had a bounty on his head," his producer Sha Money XL said, but he kept recording more songs in Sha's basement studio.

He returned to the industry with his backup group G-Unit, a bulletproof vest, and his self-released debut, 1999's *Power of the Dollar*. His album-length mix-tapes began to dominate New York radio. Universal, Jive, J Records, and Capitol were among the labels interested in signing him when Dre and Em called at nine p.m. on a Friday night and told him to be in California the next day. He made it to a release party out there and briefly met Eminem but had to wait until Sunday to meet Dre.

That day, Dre blasted one of 50's tapes while driving his Lamborghini to an editing studio, where Em was working on *8 Mile* footage. Pulling up, he turned the volume down, left the car, and walked up to 50. "You ready to make history together?" Before he could answer, Dre listed the songs he wanted on the album. Before their meeting ended, he offered champagne only to hear 50 say, "No thanks." By the time 50 returned to the airport for a flight back home, Dre knew he'd sign with them. Attorneys drafted up a reported $1-million, five-album contract, and Em scheduled studio sessions in Detroit.

◆ ◆ ◆

Maybe it was a sign of changing times. By Spring 2002, many rappers seemed to have "getting shot" on their resume. But some rap fans were disgusted by all these guys in head rags, tattoos, and tank tops, claiming they survived gunfire.

Even so, Dre was excited. And other artists were amazed by the attention 50 generated within the Shady/Aftermath camp. Em's artist Obie Trice reacted to the delay of his own album by telling a reporter, "He had the momentum, the buzz, all that shit from New York. He's been shot nine times, yes, yes, get what I'm saying?"

50 meanwhile spent $300,000 registering the trademarks 50 Cent and G-Unit. He immediately formed G-Unit Records—he didn't even wait until he had a multiplatinum album with Interscope—then pitched Jimmy Iovine on the company even though Eminem and Dre already owned his next five CDs. "I could be in there and be the guy under them," he said of the duo, "or I can make myself almost the equivalent of them." Interscope agreed to distribute his imprint.

Then Dre saw Em and 50 record so many songs Em had enough for the *8 Mile* soundtrack, including 50's popular "Wanksta," "Places to Go," and a duet with Obie Trice ("Love Me"). Dre meanwhile got Rakim's "R.A.K.I.M." on the album and let 50 rap over a track intended for Rakim ("Me I Call the Shots Round Here").

◆ ◆ ◆

Dre saw *The Eminem Show* emerge as one of the year's top three albums—alongside the mostly sung *Nellyville* by St. Louis crossover rapper Nelly and singer Ashanti's eponymous debut. At the same time, he continued to be in business with Vivendi Universal, which had nine of the year's top twenty rap albums and rosters that included Aftermath, Murder Inc.'s Ja Rule, Def Jam's Jay-Z, Eminem, and DMX. "In large measure because of hip-hop, the Universal Music Group distributes one in three records sold in the United States," the *New York Times'* John Pareles noted. So Dre was in no danger of being in the poorhouse.

But with sales dipping, magazines losing credibility, and labels churning out mindless pap, a darkness crept into the music and culture. Other acts now looked to a white audience for salvation, since they believed whites bought about eighty percent of all rap albums, and believed also that their own people were haters. "It's sad, because that feeling is mainly towards my black people," Ja Rule told the *New York Times*. "When my white fans come around, I don't feel uneasy, like they want to harm me. But when I'm around a whole group of black people, a defense comes on. That's the tragedy of this."

In *Rolling Stone* black freelance writer Kris Ex claimed, "With *The Eminem Show*, Eminem just may have made the best rap-rock album in history." He claimed Em was "quickly becoming an expert beatmaker" and added, "Dr. Dre's three contributions ("Business," "Say What You Say," "My Dad's Gone Crazy") are hard to pick out without production credits." Then he ended the review with the sort of phrase one would expect from a label-approved press release. "*The Eminem Show* makes it clear that Mr. Just-Don't-Give-a-Fuck still won't leave. He can't leave rap alone. The game needs him."

Though pleased to see *The Eminem Show* top the *Billboard* Top 200—and "Without Me" reach number two on the Hot 100—Eminem was more enthused about 50's album. "We're lucky to have him."

Dre agreed. "I'm ready to see what he is gonna do."

He got his chance when 50 arrived in sunny Los Angeles to work with him. 50 was friendly, and polite, but suspected Aftermath might try to commercialize him. Unlike other acts, he had already seen the public and New York radio embrace his ideas. He was independent, a proven talent, and someone not prone to fawning over name-brand talents. If anything, he kept soliciting beats from unknown producers (sifting through 600 CDs, each holding thirty to forty beats).

Dre, however, had his own idea about how 50 needed to sound. He dug out an old drum track with horn stabs that evoked club music of the bygone 1980s. Another artist had already given the six-month-old track a thumbs down but 50 started writing to it and within an hour let Dre and co-writer Mike Elizondo hear his chant: "Go Shorty, it's your birthday/we're gonna party like, it's your birthday."

After tightening up the drums and strings, Dre recorded "In Da Club" with an ear toward making changes. Finally he saw his chance when 50 rapped, "My flow, my show brought me the dough/that brought me all the fancy things." Leaning into the talk-back mic, Dre said, "Do it a bit lighter." 50 sang it like a chorus, so they moved on, completing the song in an hour.

Dre kept playing tracks for the choosy artist. But after one or two songs, Dre noticed 50 liked a key-heavy, somewhat Pac-like sound and played another noncurrent track with heavy organ chords that evoked The Yardbirds. "No one knew what to do with it," 50 recalled, but he wanted it so Dre left the control room while 50 wrote "Heat." They got this done in about an hour with Dre again requesting changes. But when 50 rapped a softer, almost ballad-like work called "21 Questions," singing a few lyrics, Dre didn't want it on the album. "How you goin' to be gangsta this and that and then put this sappy love song on?"

50 replied he was multifaceted, not tied to just one image.

Within five days, they completed seven songs. Dre then sat with 50 and Enimem, adding things, trying mix ideas, and getting six ready for the album and one for a mix-tape.

His involvement didn't end there. While 50 recorded on his own in New York, Dre critiqued CDs he mailed after each session. Then 50 and Eminem sifted through forty-eight songs, twelve by Dre. Though 50 had his favorites, "they made the final executive decision," he said. They put the sixteen best (only four by Dre) onto *Get Rich or Die Tryin'* and 50 left the sessions feeling Dre was "one of the illest producers I've ever worked with."

◆ ◆ ◆

Back at Aftermath, artists still waited to release albums (including the venerable Rakim) but Dre spent September 2002 negotiating with Ice Cube. Now a full-fledged movie star, Cube said, "We're in the process of making it work." He hoped to have a Dre-helmed album in stores within a year, and parroted Dre's line about how it "could be the best album I ever released," but negotiations dragged on. Still, Dre was enthusiastic. And since he was supposedly working on *Detox*, they discussed releasing both works during the same period and embarking on a huge tour.

During the negotiations, a reporter asked about the N.W.A. reunion. They wouldn't let it go. Neither could Cube. He said it was over, but then, just as quickly noted his presence at Aftermath could make it "more and more realistic."

But a creeping malaise seemed to settle over Dre. And it only intensified after October 29, 2002, when he saw Eminem's *Music from and Inspired by the Motion Picture 8 Mile* sell a staggering two million copies its first day in stores and soar right to number one. Just as quickly, Eminem's gritty movie *8 Mile* took in $55 million at the box office during its opening weekend, and inspired talk that Em should win an Academy Award.

Dre meanwhile still hadn't released any music by new artists, and after three months had yet to agree on terms with Cube. Still, in early December, he recorded a few beats, handed them over to Cube, then said, publicly, "I haven't heard him on the mic just yet. He's got a couple of tracks that I think are banging, so I'm just waiting to see what he is going to come with." At the same time, he tried to work with female artist Brooklyn. Like Hittman, she had her own ideas about what was best for her. She resisted the *Chronic*-style guest-crammed format and wanted her old producers to re-create songs on her original demo. Until now, Dre had her work with Focus and outside producer DJ Scratch and liked Scratch's track, "I Still Stay" ("Dre wants that to be the first single," she said). But in the studio, he didn't seem to know what to do with her. He had her rap over a *Detox* track he bought from young producer Just Blaze, then tried to tap into the mix-tape trend 50's success created by having her sing over the instrumental version of Shady Records act D-12's "Fight Music." Finally, he included her on 50 Cent's "In My Hood" (which he produced) then decided, for reasons unknown, that her album *Name & Address-Brooklyn* needed to be delayed from its planned March release.

While he grew more detached from various projects, he learned kids, radio, and MTV were going crazy for "In Da Club." 50's single was at number fifteen on the Billboard Hot 100. Then, three weeks later, February 6, 2003, *Get Rich or Die Tryin'* sold 872,000 copies in under a week, topping the *Billboard* album chart. Demand for 50 was so high even his independent album, *Guess Who's Back*, sold close to 20,000 copies that week.

In its review, *Rolling Stone* praised *Get Rich* and claimed, "By now, 50 Cent's coronation as the new king of hardcore hip-hop is all but assured." And 50 was king because Eminem called him "the illest motherfucker in the world," his songs were all over MTV and radio, and "even casual pop fans" knew he'd been shot a few times, it added. As for the music itself, "Dre,

Eminem, and a handful of lesser-known producers are at the top of their game here, concocting these alternately club-ready and spaced-out tracks out of dark synth grooves, buzzy keyboards, and a persistently funky bounce." Dre was happy to see his name included, and saw 50 become even more successful. Interscope had to add another 400,000 copies to the million already shipped to stores, and during its second week, 50 recalled, "My record showed almost no drop." With *Get Rich or Die Tryin'* on its way to becoming 2003's very best selling work, Jimmy Iovine began helping 50 create a movie called *Locked and Loaded*. As with *8 Mile*, Dre wouldn't appear in this one, either.

◆ ◆ ◆

The Source had run their famous cover story in 1992, just when Dre needed a deal. Then it ran positive features about Death Row and, when Dre left empty-handed, another face-saving cover story. In 1998, it had been first to give Em national coverage in its Unsigned Hype column and since then had nominated Dre and Eminem for a number of Source awards. But in 2001, the masthead started listing rapper Benzino (born Raymond Scott, and formerly known as Ray Dog of Boston gangsta rap group The Almighty RSO) as a co-owner. Ray had also recorded a solo album, *Redemption*, on which he claimed Eminem opened the door for the white takeover of rap. As Ray saw it, black creators didn't receive as much media coverage.

The Source, once a semi-respectable monthly, but now staffed by the same sort of trend-chasing critics used by *Rolling Stone*, then printed an essay, "The Unbearable Whiteness of Emceeing: What the Eminence of Eminem Says About Race," and included a cartoon that showed Benzino holding Em's severed head in one hand. Em struck back with his mix-tape, "The Sauce," and since then they'd been talking lots of trash about each other. By February 2003, Aftermath and Shady Records pulled their ads from the magazine and one unnamed *Source* employee told reporter Josh Tyrangiel, "It's insane for a rap magazine to antagonize the number one rapper the way we have. I can't believe Dave (owner of *The Source*) would be doing this if Benzino wasn't in his ear all the time."

Interscope (which came with Shady, Aftermath, and G Unit) also pulled its ads. Then other labels under the massive Universal Music Group umbrella (including Def Jam, which hosted Roc-A-Fella, and Geffen, home to acts like Common and The Roots) followed suit, leaving the magazine struggling to make ends meet and launching even more attacks against what it (and other black artists) now called "The Machine," the white corporate takeover and domination of rap music. Soon, *The Source* dragged Jimmy Iovine into the fray, printing a story that branded him a devil and including a photo that showed cartoon devil horns protruding from his trademark ball cap.

As 2003 continued, Dre found himself dragged into another problem— 50's pre-existing feud with rapper Ja Rule. A father of two from Queens, Rule recorded for Murder Inc., a Death Row–styled label also distributed by Universal, and was sort of a singing Tupac. Only instead of political lyrics, he was content to draw white fans by singing and rapping in videos with Jennifer Lopez, Mary J. Blige, and Mariah Carey. 50 and Ja had feuded since the late nineties when Ja rubbed 50 the wrong way, 50 claimed he'd stolen Ja's chain, Ja claimed he stabbed 50 in a studio, then someone shot 50 nine times. And now, Ja addressed Dre in *The Source*. "Suge just chased you the fuck up outta here, so what, you think I'm the sucka? If you're gonna be authorizing 50 Cent to spew records on me, then I wanna do what I gotta do to take your company under. And that goes for Dre, Em, or whoever." Next, he spoke out against Dre on a mix-tape. While Nas' "Made You Look" (a hit set to the sort of samples Dre used to use) played, Ja rapped, "Gay Dre Young: Suge told me you used to take transvestites home/No wonder Feminem be cross-dressing in pumps and tight little dresses."

With the rap media—and even MTV—reporting on every word, and some people hinting he should strike back, Dre considered avoiding comment. Already, Death Row was insulting Aftermath on albums like *Too Gangsta for Radio* (which included a skit that claimed Dre liked to take drugs and sodomize young male rappers seeking deals with his imprint). Now, 50 and G-Unit were up against Murder Inc. Suge was friendly with Murder Inc. Murder Inc. now hated people at Violator (which represented 50). Ultimately, these feuds were bad for business. And Dre was a proud man—even if his output had diminished over the years and so-called protégés were doing as well, if not better than he was.

◆ ◆ ◆

During this period, the problems kept coming. The next one involved singer Truth Hurts. In February 2002, while working on her album, Dre had chosen her first single. It was created by DJ Quik (the Compton-based producer). One morning, Quik had his TV tuned to a Hindi channel while brushing his teeth. He heard some music "and before I knew it, I was grooving," he recalled. In the next room, he saw a woman on TV belly dance to a cool melody. "So I pushed Record on the VCR." After he added drums he tested the groove with one or two rappers before playing it for Truth, who said, "Man, I've never heard anything like this." In the studio back then, Dre listened to her copy and thought: It's simple—a drum track, a bass line, and an Indian woman singing. But it's incredible. "This changes the game right here," he told her. "Tell Quik to call my phone right now." When Quik did, he told him, "I love this track. I think it's gonna be her first single." In addition to her album, Dre was looking for ways to position Rakim as relevant to a younger audience that included many whites who might not be into his quasi religious lyrics. He invited Ra onto the song, "Addictive," even though Ra, a devout Muslim, wasn't crazy about its title. Dre was so excited about this work, Truth recalled, he then created a second version. "Dre did the remix without me," she remembered, and while her own songs generally didn't excite her much, when she entered the studio this time and heard his track she literally jumped for joy. "He took another part of the Indian sample and added it to the beginning and to the middle." He also made it "more club" and had Rakim open with a rhyme hotter than the original. "It's just amazing," she felt. She couldn't get over how great it sounded. "Dre did his thing on that one."

After that, Dre executive produced her debut. She wanted creative control but he sifted through submitted tracks, felt something by new discovery Hi-Tek fit her style, and told her, "I want you to write for this track." He also brought in other songwriters. And when other producers arrived to turn their demos into records, he sat right near her in the studio until they left, which is when he'd add extra touches and make tracks useable. The longer he worked on Truth's album the more people around Dre wondered if the album would ever see release. But Dre kept taking his time. "I'm not about to be out here sideways ever again," he told her. He once let others do stuff for the compilation and release it under his name only to see it fail and reflect poorly on his good name. So since then, he told himself, "No. From this day forward, I gotta do it like this and I got to feel it one hundred percent or I cannot put it out."

After creating twenty-one trial and error songs, he still didn't know which direction to take so he recorded two or three songs a day, staying in the studio from three in the afternoon until ten the next morning. But by April 2002, they had about fifty-four songs done, and room for only fifteen. He then decided, of these, only three would be Dre-produced. He began to whittle the songs down, deciding what the public would hear and view as her best. Then he told her Interscope would ship her album to stores in June. Truth wondered if Eminem's latest (scheduled to be released a week earlier) would affect sales, but he said, "Nah, we won't have any issue with that, trust me."

He released *Truthfully Speaking* on June 24, and saw it debut at number five on the national charts. But within a month, an attorney representing Saregama India Limited, a ninety-year-old Calcutta, India–based music and film studio, contacted Aftermath and Interscope about the music on her single, "Addictive." Saregema's attorney Dedra Davis contacted Dre's legal counsel to say the single unlawfully used the company's music (from the soundtrack of a Hindi movie) and the original singer, she recalled. Aftermath and Interscope told her they had tried to locate the track's owner, but couldn't since the company supposedly changed names a few times. Davis then sent Universal Music Group a cease-and-desist letter but the label conglomerate ignored it, she continued. Then (despite claims the copyright holders were hard to find) Davis said Universal India asked for and received permission to license the same song for an unrelated cover version on June 12, twelve days before *Truthfully Speaking* arrived in stores. "Producers, if you are going to use someone else's work, ask first," Davis said in print. "If you can't find them, don't use the work. What is done in the dark, does come to light."

Dre figured attorneys would handle this problem and by mid September, turned his thoughts toward recording an even better follow-up album. He liked Truth's personality and confidence and also how she accepted his vision for her music. "I definitely will be a bigger part of the next one," he said publicly, "now that we know exactly where we are going." Truth, who had finished touring a little, told someone else, "They want it out by next summer. That's how Dre works."

But everything changed a week later, when Dre, Aftermath, Interscope, and parent company Universal were sued by Saregama for over $500 million. In the copyright infringement lawsuit, Saregama said "Addictive" sampled their twenty-year-old hit without permission. "When you hear it, it's like, 'Oh my God, they didn't even try to get original with it,'" said attorney Dedra Davis. "They didn't try to change it up or anything like that." The lawsuit recounted the chain of events—the cease-and-desist letter, Universal India licensing the song for a cover—and claimed "the defendants clearly and admittedly knew their activities were, and currently are, infringing on [Seragama's] copyrighted work."

Saregama's wanting $500 million (including legal bills, punitive damages, and profits from the single and album when *Truthfully Speaking* had only sold about 273,000 copies) brought Truth's career to a grinding halt. She hadn't created the music—it was part of Dre's vision for her career—but when asked about the lawsuit, she repeated Universal's claim of not being able to find the song's copyright owner. No one ever got back to them, they kept calling, and now that the song was a hit, they called back, she said. "That's what happened."

The situation worsened on February 3, 2003. Bappi Lahiri, composer of the song, convinced a judge to stop Aftermath and Interscope from selling the single until he received song credit, since, he claimed, "Addictive" illegally sampled four minutes of the original. The composer's lawyer accused Universal of "cultural imperialism" and asked for over $1 million (from profits of Truth's music and losses he claimed to have suffered). Once Lahiri got an injunction, Universal could either pull the music from stores or send retailers a sticker crediting Lahiri to affix to each copy. Though Truth vividly recalled Dre creating the remix, Dre's attorney Howard King told a reporter, "Because

Dre didn't write, produce, or perform on the song, but the album happens to be on his label, he was named as a defendant. He had zero to do with the creative elements and the use or non-use of any particular work."

Either way, by March 2003, Truth Hurts left Aftermath. But Dre's label had nothing to do with it, she explained. "It was really with Interscope." She didn't like that Interscope wanted to delay her second album. As her attorney got involved to negotiate an agreement, Dre didn't have much to say, she recalled, so she told him it'd be best if she left. Since her debut was filled with "so much of Dre's spirit," and various producers ("like the Timbalands"), she felt her own talent went unnoticed. At her own label, she hoped to become known "not just because of Dre's name" but rather her own ideas.

During this same period—Spring 2003—Compton rapper Shaunta also left Aftermath. She'd signed in 2001 and worked on her album during the following year, but felt the label lacked artist development. Dre included her on "Good Lovin'" for *The Wash* and publicly said, "Along with *The Eminem Show* and *Truthfully Speaking*, I hope to release the debut album from Shaunta next year," but he focused more on 50's project. She kept recording, finishing about thirty songs, but Dre never finished her album. Then she tired of the office politics. D.O.C. had earlier referred to the "non-Dres" around him, and Hittman spoke of new employees preventing him from speaking with Dre about his album. Now, Shaunta described a place where people indulged in poisonous gossip behind her back. She soon felt, to make it at Aftermath, "You just gotta learn how to suck dick and politic." After sitting on a completed album for six months, she finally left. Just as quickly, rapper Joe Beast was also dropped (after steering Dre to a track for *Detox*). Hearing he was gone, Obie Trice said, "That's some bullshit, man."

Dre meanwhile worked on music for the *Bad Boys 2* soundtrack, perhaps hoping this would bring him closer to his dream of conducting an orchestra and scoring a major motion picture. The assignment, as described in the media, called for him to program drum machine beats over which a composer would add strings, and the album would be released not by Aftermath but rather Sean Combs' Bad Boy Entertainment. Either way, Dre was soon distracted from this project by yet another dismaying situation, this one involving his mother.

Over the years, he saw less of Verna. At one point, he heard her say, "I wish we would go back to being poor." This way, they'd all be together again, "which means more to me than money." One person claimed Dre's wife, Nicole, didn't want his mom stopping by the house. Even so, Verna would sometimes drive up to the gate. She wanted to see her grandchildren, but assumed they wouldn't even answer if she rang the bell, so she just drove away. Dre himself might not have known about these visits. At any rate, he didn't completely leave his mom behind. Sometimes, he'd credit her during interviews for inspiring his love of music. And he let her move into a home he owned in Hidden Hills, fifteen miles north of Los Angeles. He just couldn't drop everything and see her as much. "Now, he's so busy and he's married now," she said. When they did have lunch, she felt privileged to be near him.

He was shocked, however, to hear she'd been arrested. According to the police (and press reports), on a Monday night, between the hours of seven and nine, fifty-four-year-old Verna had a guest over. For whatever reason, she pulled a gun and fired a shot. The guest wasn't hurt—or identified in press reports—but rushed to a phone to call the cops. When deputies showed up and cautiously entered the home, Verna wasn't there. But someone else found her car—and a pistol—at a nearby gas station. If she thought the incident was over, however, she was wrong. The very next day, the deputies and alleged victim returned to the home, and the cops placed her under arrest. Someone paid her $50,000 bail and she was released but when reporters called to ask his opinion, Dre had no comment. What happened next, however, was even more controversial.

◆　◆　◆

As long as a facility had a good engineer and a lounge with a kitchen, Dre was happy. He worked with the same people, played new rhythms with stock sounds, and stockpiled ideas. He also used the same old tape, microphone, recording equipment, and instruments (the SP1200, the Akai MPC3000, and keyboards by Korg, Rhodes, Wurlitzer, Moog, and Roland). "We have a routine for writing and recording," said Elizondo. "We would show up at the studio at three pm, almost like a day job."

Near the Solid State Logic 8000 board, engineer Veto (Mauricio Iragorri) made sure everything was ready when Dre walked in. Dre would play a few drumbeats, choose a keyboard, then create what he called a song skeleton. Next, he'd sit with artists and make sure lyrics included a few of his ideas. It was always the same, and Rakim felt this was one reason they experienced creative differences.

Since he'd signed his former idol to Aftermath, Dre worked to bring Rakim into the modern age. When he needed a new manager, someone at the label suggested Zach Katz (who repped producer Hi-Tek), and when Jay-Z wanted to include a sequel to the *2001* number "The Watcher" on *The Blueprint 2: The Gift & the Curse*, Dre included Rakim and heard Jay describe them as rap's holy trinity.

The differences between their approaches were obvious. Where Dre's verse claimed he was still on top of the game, reminded everyone of his fall and rise, and said, "Haters wanna stop my reign. But the music lives in me, every drop in my veins"; Rakim railed against drug dealers, greed, and the fact that, in his neighborhood, "the number one cause of death is money." Dre's themes were pretty serious but lighthearted commercial fare compared to the social ills Rakim was describing.

But in the studio, Dre stopped feeling nervous about directing him and started suggesting concepts. And if Ra wanted music by DJ Premier, he invited the producer to fly from Brooklyn and hand deliver tracks.

Dre first met Premier (born Christopher Martin) during the N.W.A. days, when he saw him selling mix-tapes at Texas A&M. Dre met him again in the early 1990s, and played him *The Chronic* at Premier's usual studio, D&D in Manhattan. In response, Premier trashed beats he'd just created for Gang Starr's *Daily Operation* and started all over again. Since then, Premier had produced classics for Biggie, Nas, Jay-Z, Jeru Tha Damaja, and KRS-One. But the differences between him and Dre were as pronounced as those between Dre and Rakim. Where Dre felt comfortable being what some acts called the clean up man, arriving at the tail end of a project to create the sort of dance rap Interscope could market to a white audience, Premier felt major labels signed garbage, and wanted to co-opt rap as they had rock and R&B. "They trying to water it down and turn it into something else that's not hip-hop and that's

what it is: 'Something Else.' It's another type of shit that you are hearing now."
Even so, Rakim wanted him on the album so Dre did, too.

In the studio one day, Premier shuffled toward Dre and Mel-Man with
some DAT tapes and zip drives. Dre nodded along to one DAT then faced
Mel. Instead of just saying what he felt, he seemed to have Mel act as a mid-
dleman. "Yo, we dig the Funkadelic chop you did but we gonna get Scott and
'em to redo the bass line," Mel said. "Is that cool, ma' man?"

"No question, I trust you and Dre."

Dre relaxed, and when Premier pulled ten old albums out of his bag, his
eyes widened. The albums contained beats and riffs he hadn't heard in ages.
He reached for them, looked them over, then decided he needed some coffee.
It'd been a long day so he got some from the tiny kitchen adjoining the
studio and came back in while Premier was telling a reporter, "Me and Dre,
we opposites but we bring each other up." He said Dre inspired his use of
live bass and drums while he had Dre wanting to use the SP1200 sampler
again. At this, Dre lowered his cup. "Cats forget I used to do the grimy,
James Brown–sampled shit." He didn't have to say anything, but he added
that he'd used this device on two songs for Rakim (and one he tried to create
with Primo) to remind people of how he started.

Competitive as ever, Dre then played the writer "Cruel World," and
watched for his reaction to West Coast rapper Ras Kass and Xzibit's guest
turns, a sped-up Donald Byrd sample, and three layers of filtered drums. But
while Dre wanted the spotlight clearly on him, Premier mentioned, "I loaned
Dre a Roy Ayers live bootleg record I copped in Germany. He owes me for
them drums, kid."

After Premier's visit, Dre had Rakim join Truth Hurts in a video for
"Addictive," before Truth left the label. On the set in L.A., Ra ignored four
belly-dancers around him and rapped a lyric that started with an old line
from an eighties's hit. This was a more glitzy situation than the normally
low-key intellectual was used to, but when a reporter asked about his own
album, he said, "I couldn't ask for a better producer."

Dre, however, was frustrated. He wanted "something new and fresh out of
him." Ra was tired of waiting for his music to be released but Dre vowed to
keep recording until he achieved his goal. Ra agreed to rap on what he called

"West Coast tracks" but felt Dre could meet him "a little more halfway as far as who I was and what I wanted to do."

They managed to record "When You Die" but Ra's philosophical rap was too heavy for the festive track. And when Ra refused to rap about themes the younger set might prefer (hoes, parties, marijuana, automobiles, fictitious gangbangers), he said Dre became less enthused, and soon had employees or Rakim's manager relay his call for more street themes. Then during one studio session, Ra recalled, Dre sat in his swivel chair, and said, "Well, that's what I want you to talk about, Ra."

But Ra refused to fill fifteen songs with "the ghetto miseries," so Dre moved on to other projects and Ra spent weeks sitting around, waiting for other producers to submit music. Soon, he considered leaving Aftermath. Dre continued to talk up the album and to privately hope Ra would come around to his way of thinking. He really did want it to be the best thing either had ever done. He also did what he could to get Ra's name in front of a huge mainstream audience that probably didn't even know the respected hardcore rapper even existed.

When an MTV reporter stopped by to film a segment, after his grand entrance in a silver-and-black Ferrari, Dre rushed to play tracks from *Oh My God* at full volume. But relations soured when Aftermath rejected all of Premier's tracks. "Yeah, that's true," Premier said, and they did it when the tracks didn't have any vocals on them, which he felt would have made it difficult to gauge how they'd really sound.

Rakim grew even more disenchanted when Aftermath's staff rejected tracks from other East Coast producers he wanted on his album.

Still, Dre looked forward to finding time to finish the album. Outside of the third annual BET Awards in June 2003, where 50 was the main attraction, Rakim said, after almost three years on Aftermath, his album was coming soon. "Me and Dre, we about to do full-steam on it." They'd have a single out by fall, and an album shortly after that, he added. "We finally got everything on track like we wanted." Sixteen songs were done, he continued, and after Dre did seven more, they'd pick a first single. "He can bring the best out of me, and I want to make sure that I bring the best out of him."

Whether the comment about someone having to inspire him to do his best was too much for an enormous ego to bear is unknown, but within two weeks, Dre decided they'd never get it together in a way that'd please them and Interscope. On July 16, Rakim's manager Zach Katz announced on Aftermath's web site that the rapper and Aftermath had split. "He's already shopping a new deal. They mutually decided to go their separate ways."

Dre's core audience, and Ra's fans, were shocked. The rap legend tried to return to DreamWorks again, in vain. Dre said he could use the material they'd done but—like King Tee during his own departure so long ago—Ra felt it was dated. Instead, he and Premier planned to recruit classic New York producers Large Professor, Pete Rock, and Showbiz. Said Premier, "It'll be done our way."

Five days after Rakim's departure, Dre's audience learned Big Chuck (senior director of A&R for seven years), Mel-Man, and newer producer Neff-U had left Dre's label, Aftermath Entertainment. *The Source* feature "Before & Aftermath" arrived with a headline that read, "Some of Dr. Dre's closest associates have broken ties with Aftermath," and were "ready to expose some of the label's secrets" and "get the credit they deserve." It was "the interview Aftermath does not want you to read."

Big Chuck was quoted as saying he convinced Dre to sign Eminem; he arranged Jay-Z's contribution to "Still D.R.E." and he took Mel-Man and Neff-U with him to start Drama Family. "Dre wants people to praise him all day like his name is in the Bible, and I can't do that." Readers learned Chuck first met Dre in Detroit during the 1980s, when he was with N.W.A. and Chuck worked with Big Daddy Kane. And when Dre created the *Aftermath* compilation "and everybody counted him out," he said he "was the Krazy Glue in the situation." But over seven years, Dre had changed for the worst, he felt.

After an undisclosed disagreement, Chuck called Dre, Dre said he'd call back, and instead the general manager told Chuck that Dre felt they should part ways. "He wasn't man enough to holler at me." The general manager, Chuck said, then told him Dre felt the A&R man hadn't brought him anything hot in three years. Chuck told this employee he'd recently enlisted Neff-U; he brought Dre the *Training Day* script, and, while playing Eminem's tape in Dre's house in late 1997, "I told him he had to sign him." He even urged

Dre to release 50's hit with Snoop, "P.I.M.P. (Remix)," he said. "He fought me for it and we kept it. Now look at it: It's a smash."

After implying Dre was severely out of touch with audience tastes, Chuck said Aftermath artists were being mistreated, going without credit for their music. "It's like, 'Take this money and be cool.'" It happened to Neff-U a few times; and while Mel-Man received co-producer credit on *2001*, "He didn't get that paper."

Next, Neff-U said he created stuff for *The Eminem Show*, and the beat for Dre's famous Coors Light commercial. "On 50 Cent's album, I did 'Back Down,' 'If I Can't,' and I played on 'Heat.'" He expected co-producer credit for "If I Can't" but saw *Get Rich* liner notes credit everything to Dre, he said. "They are fixing that as we speak."

Although Dre was a great producer, Chuck said, "As a person he's a piece of shit." Even more shocking was his explanation for why Aftermath didn't release more albums. "Well, you got one person who wants to be a superstar. He'll sign these artists and keep them on the label for a year or two. I guess it's a tax write-off." But seeing Aftermath artists grow demoralized broke his heart, he said. "They go in the studio and record then he gasses them up and drops them." It even happened to Rakim, whom Chuck used to manage. "How do you sign him and then stick him in the studio with a whole bunch of C-list producers? That's disrespectful."

He said that, while the media kept claiming they were working together, Dre would give the rapper a track and "not even sit in with him." And if Ra's work wasn't in stores yet, he said, it was because Dre, despite his image, wasn't calling all the shots at his own label: Unnamed investors had too much say over Aftermath's artistic side and "These seventy-five-year-old men" dictated what they wanted. "You got these motherfuckers A&R'ing a record and that's bullshit." Now Chuck would work with Punch ("who wrote Dre's verses on 'What's the Difference?' and 'Big Egos'") and Mel-Man (calling himself Hillstorian and a key player).

Although many rap fans knew *The Source* had it in for Dre—especially since Interscope and various labels had pulled their ads—many people were by now willing to believe the claims made in "Before & Aftermath" and even Yella weighed in on whether Dre actually produced his own beats. At Aftermath, his old friend said, Dre's staff created, then brought him tracks. "He can say: 'I like this, I like that.' Whether they keep their publishing and all that was up to them. If they sold him the tracks, that's their mistakes." Producers might be disgruntled because most articles credited Dre for everything, he felt. "They should handle the deals like 'I want publishing, I want this and I want that. That's the deal.'" But in the end, he claimed, Dre didn't steal beats. "I know Dre since the early eighties and he's stealing nothing."

When the issue wouldn't just go away, Dre reportedly addressed the article and other controversies during a rare interview. He said Mel-Man was like a brother. "Mel ain't left Aftermath and he ain't gone be leavin' Aftermath. Period." He claimed *Detox* wasn't stalled. He had twenty-six tracks but only liked five. Then he said, of *The Source* feature, "Yo, for real that shit is straight lies."

He reminded an interviewer of how Aftermath told *The Source* they wouldn't grant interviews, then saw them feature 50 on the cover anyway. "We ain't fuckin' with them no more: me, 50, Em. No one from Math or Shady fuckin' wit them. And as far as Big Chuck and Neff-U concerned, those cats right there are my brothers like Mel." In fact, he'd spoken with Chuck on the phone a day ago, he claimed, and while Chuck was creating a new label he said he'd always be there for him. "And Dre always gone help him with production or money. Anything he need he just has to holler."

◆ ◆ ◆

In June 2003, Dre saw 50 keep making moves. *Get Rich* continued to outsell every album, in any genre, released that year. At *Billboard*'s third annual R&B/Hip-Hop Awards that month, 50 was up for awards in ten different categories (Eminem only in five). But 50 didn't stop there. He liked signing deals and making money as much as he did recording new songs, so he hired Chris Lighty of Violator to represent G-Unit; he hooked up with the William Morris Agency and, while Dre dreamed of entering mainstream film, he had Jimmy Iovine working as hard to get a 50 Cent movie into theaters as Iovine had to make Eminem's *8 Mile* a reality. 50 also signed a $2-million deal with ringtone company Zingy and a licensing deal with Ecko

Unlimited for G-Unit Clothing (which earned $55 million in a year). Then he turned around and inked a $20-million deal with Reebok for a G-Unit sneaker line (which sold about four million pair). Away from the label, he bought former boxing champ Mike Tyson's fifty-room estate in Farmington, Connecticut, for a reported $4 million. To top it off, he was already at work on a new album in his home studio.

During the summer of 2003—the exact dates are unclear—Jimmy Iovine had a suggestion. Why not add The Game to 50's G-Unit group? Much time had passed since he signed him, and Dre had yet to release any music.

Dre had worked with Game for two years but 50 figured "creatively they were stuck a little," and more than a little eager to have the newcomer ride his commercial coattails. Game later denied ever being in danger of being dropped, but 50 insisted this was so. "Why else would they let me be a partner on a project that [Interscope] had for two years?" Either way, Dre was supposedly working on his album, but reached for the phone and called 50. Game was elated. While he languished at Aftermath, as ignored as other young artists Joe Beast and Brooklyn, G-Unit already had "a crazy buzz and they selling albums," he recalled. With members hailing from the East Coast and the South, he figured his West Coast image would help them appeal to rap fans in every region.

Once the year's best-selling musician let Game into his crew, Interscope suddenly felt excited about Game's project, and even more so when they learned 50 flew him out to Connecticut and "we recorded like nine records at the house in Farmington."

Game couldn't believe his luck. In the studio, everyone on G Unit was creative. No one had writer's block or any other excuses. They were freely throwing ideas around and coming up with great music that today's kids would dig, and buy. And 50 was just phenomenal "'cause he's real melody-driven, so it's usually him coming up with the song format." Where the After-math sessions he managed to book had basically amounted to nothing, now, he said, "We're knocking out three songs in a matter of an hour and a half." When they wrapped recording, Game excitedly played his new work for Dre in Los Angeles. "Dre liked them," 50 said, "and I just got him re-motivated and he went in and finished up the album."

Now that The Game was involved with G-Unit, in August 2003, Dre saw him appear in 50's video for "In Da Club." In this clip, a black Hummer reached the fictional "The Shady/Aftermath Artist Development Center" in a desert; a shirtless 50 worked out in a high-tech gym; 50 was then shown performing his dance-happy single for a crowd in a nightclub that included The Game.

The camera pulled back through a two-way window to reveal Dre and Em, in lab coats, jotting notes and nodding approvingly. Between takes, Dre told a reporter, "50's album, in my opinion, is going to compete with all the classic hip-hop records that have come out over the last ten years. *Illmatic*, *The Chronic*, *Marshall Mathers LP*, it's right up there. And that's no bullshit."

As if having to pass the torch weren't enfeebling enough, Dre looked over and saw Suge arrive on the set with a large entourage. Over the past few years, Suge had hurled quite a number of insults. But the outspoken father of five had also suffered his own stunning reversals. He and Death Row now faced numerous lawsuits; he divorced Sharitha Golden and was court ordered to pay $735,000 in unpaid child support. The IRS said he owed about $6 million in personal income taxes; a bank repossessed his ninety-foot yacht; another saw him skip mortgage payments and wanted to take Death Row's building in Beverly Hills; the Staples Center canceled his lease for a luxury box since he allegedly missed a few payments to them, too; and he was selling Can-Am Studios. He married Michel'le, he still had the building on Wilshire and over twenty-four vehicles in its garage, but the label wasn't as profitable.

Even worse, the *Los Angeles Times*' July 31, 2003, edition reported, "Someone is gunning for Marion 'Suge' Knight." By hiring so many members of different gangs, the paper added, Suge wound up in the middle of their feuds, "and unwittingly made himself a target."

During the Summer of 1996, Suge had supposedly fired a bodyguard, since the man wouldn't return two label-owned cars. Other bodyguards tried to abduct and kill him, shooting him in the ass, but he escaped, vowed revenge, and teamed with another Blood who already disliked Suge. Since then, police felt, he and his new friend—neither ever identified—had been methodically killing Suge's close friends.

Suge's bodyguard Aaron "Heron" Palmer was first. He was stopped at a red light in Compton on June 1, 1997, after leaving a Death Row football game in a park. Two men leaped out of a blue van behind him, opened fire, then left. Heron, thirty, died then and there. "Until that moment, nobody ever had the nerve to take out anyone in Suge's inner circle," another law enforcement official said. "This was no ordinary murder. Someone was sending a message."

On April, 4, 2000, killers tried to get Suge's friend, "Poochie" Fouse. He was sitting in the passenger seat of a white van on a dead end street in Compton when two men ran up and opened fire. They killed the man sitting behind the wheel and left Poochie in a wheelchair for three months. Then someone was killed in front of the home of Suge's closest friend, Alton "Buntry" McDonald, on March 25, 2001.

With time off for good behavior, Suge was released from prison that August. But by April 3, 2002, he learned Buntry was dead. The thirty-seven-year-old was at a gas station one afternoon, about to fill his tank, when two men appeared and shot him four times in the chest. Then, in October, Suge's friend Henry "Hen Dog" Smith, who designed Death Row's logo, sat in a Jeep near a chicken stand in South Central with a Death Row chain around his neck and his girlfriend's baby napping in the back seat. Someone aimed a gun, fired six shots, killing him, then rode away on a bike.

One night in May 2003, someone tried to send some sort of message by shooting up the front of Death Row's building. No one was hurt, and Suge laughed about it in print, but the *Los Angeles Times* felt, "Still, the bullet-ridden facade is a reminder of how far Knight has fallen. The lobby at Death Row's offices is barren these days, the hallways empty. Music executives duck Knight's calls."

Then, on July 24, "unknown assailants" went back for Poochie Fouse. They drove behind his motorcycle on a Compton street then shot him ten times in the back. Now, cops felt two gang members wanted Suge dead, one of them the bodyguard he allegedly fired in 1996. "If I was Suge Knight, I'd be worried someone was out to get me," said one gang investigator. He added: "If I was in his shoes, I'd be looking over my shoulder everywhere I went."

But Suge told people he wasn't afraid, and for whatever reason, seemed to blame Dre for difficulties he encountered while attempting to conduct business while on parole. "Didn't help with Andre and them snitching on me. He went and told the police, my P.O., that he feared for his life. Said I been by his house, chased him, all kinds of shit. And I ain't seen him."

Now, despite the fact that he was practically raising Dre's son Marcel, one condition of his parole was that he avoid being in the same place as Dre, or contacting him through third parties, e-mail, pagers, or two-ways. Though Suge left the set of 50's video without incident, director Philip Atwell said, "I don't know what the intention was or what was going on, he was just there. I don't know what that was supposed to represent. We just kept shooting, that's all I know."

In November Dre faced yet another setback. On November 18, at a press conference, *The Source*'s embittered co-owners, rapper Benzino and white publisher David Mays, played reporters two old Eminem demos they probably obtained from some old friend. While Em had (in 2001) said he wouldn't use the word "nigga" in a rap, one tape ("Oh Foolish Pride") had him rapping, "All the girls I like to bone have big butts. No they don't, 'cause I don't like that nigga shit. I'm just here to make a bigger hit."

The Source owners next played a thirty-second excerpt. "Blacks and whites they sometimes mix," Em rapped. "But black girls only want your money 'cause they're dumb chicks." Then: "Never date a black girl because blacks only want your money/and that shit is funny." Benzino then told reporters, "Don't make this right now a double standard. We gotta treat this the same way you treat Mike Tyson, like you treat Kobe Bryant, like you treat R. Kelly, like you treat O.J. Simpson."

Em quickly issued a statement. "Ray Benzino, Dave Mays, and *The Source* have had a vendetta against me, Shady Records, and our artists for a long time," it read. "The tape they played today was something I made out of anger, stupidity, and frustration when I was a teenager." He wrote that he'd broken up with his girlfriend ("who was African-American") and reacted "like the angry, stupid kid I was. I hope people will take it for the foolishness that it was, not for what somebody is trying to make it into today." As usual, Dre avoided comment. It was an appalling situation, inexplicable. Even *XXL*, extremely supportive of Dre and Interscope artists (now that *The Source* was in disfavor with the two), asked, "What's the truth? Who knows?" And in an interview, Em said, "I'm not disputing that it's me."

16

A way from the studio, in early 2004, Dre's still trying to sign Cube (whose *Barbershop 2* was another box office hit). Cube's anxious to record but a year has elapsed and they're no closer to agreeing on terms. "So until we do, I'm considered a free agent." Ultimately, Dre sees Cube leave the table and team with popular Southern producer Lil' Jon for *Laugh Now, Cry Later*. He says if Dre ever wants to collaborate they will. And if not, "I will keep it moving." The reunion will happen, he explains, if Dre tells them, "Yo I'm ready to produce this N.W.A. record." But for now, he won't discuss it anymore. Neither will M.C. Ren, who hasn't called Dre since 2000. "I don't even talk to him right now. He do his thing and I do mine."

During this same period, Snoop asks Dre to produce stuff for his first 213 album with Warren G and Nate. "He didn't get down with us," Snoop says. With other labels and stars outdoing him, Dre's struggling to finish his album but also maintain Aftermath's presence in a crowded market. He already has the 50 market covered with Game, so he can search for someone with a name and willingness to try new things. He sees these qualities in Busta Rhymes, who has just left J Records. "We haven't signed the papers yet, but the deal is done," says Busta's manager Chris Lighty. "They have been working together for his album for the past few weeks." Dre welcomes him to Aftermath by producing twenty songs for a debut he hopes to release by June or July 2004. Then he considers *Detox*.

He's had Game join 50's artist Lloyd Banks on a few songs but set them aside. He's come a long way from the days when he said it would be about the Internet. He changed the concept to an album rapped from the viewpoint of a hired killer like the one in the Donald Goines novel *Daddy Cool*, then stopped discussing it publicly. But at one point—possibly 2001 when they were working together on *The Wash*—he told producer Mahogany, "I'm thinking of making the album like a movie, like having sixteen-bar jazz pieces, live instruments." And by then the concept had changed again.

The story he described evoked the movie *Very Bad Things*, in which "four dudes were having a bachelor party in Vegas, doing drugs, sex, etcetera. Then something tragic happens with one of the hookers." Since Dre's last single "Bad Intentions" was about sex, partying, and excess, Mahogany believed *Detox* would open "with one last party and something tragic happens to make him want to detox." The producer wanted something on the album— the royalties will be amazing—so he sifted through jazz grooves and presented a twenty-two bar loop by War he felt could fit Dre's storyline.

At another point, they were experimenting with psychedelic sixties' rock. During a lunch break in 2001 Dre told his players he enjoyed the Doors keyboard on a VH1 documentary he'd watched the night before. In response, Scott Storch rushed over to a keyboard to play his own version, Mike played bass, and Dre, near a turntable, added a break beat, and felt it was done. Since that session, the direction stayed with him and Focus said, "We were doing psychedelic sixties rock music with dark chords."

During this period, probably 2002, Dre played Focus a few basic tracks and said, "Go do you." Before he knew it, Focus brought him obscure loops by groups like The Association. "Everyone was throwing ideas at him," Focus says. During 2003, Focus had seen producers come out of the woodwork to offer tracks. Rapper Joe Beast was on the label at the time, and played Dre a futuristic one by J.R. Rotem. Whether Joe wanted it for his own album is unknown, but Dre wanted it for *Detox* and had the label cut the check, front and back end, within twenty-four hours, Rotem explains. And not only that,

Dre actually recorded a vocal on it and had Denaun Porter, Em's early producer and D-12 band-mate, do the chorus. He sounded incredible, younger
than he had in years, while describing his days with Eazy, Snoop, Em, and
50, Rotem feels. Denaun Porter agreed. While playing the song for Eminem
back in their hometown Detroit, he said, "Yo, this nigga is out of his mind.
If he come back like this he's gonna shut the game down." But Dre was
already having second thoughts, trying an alternate version with Game and
Busta Rhymes.

During 2003, he sketched dozens of beats, rhythms, and song skeletons.
None had titles and nothing was final since he wanted to create over a hundred then choose the best. So far, he'd come up with jarring piano riffs and
intriguing vocal hooks, and settled on a good fusion of his usual clean pop
sound and deeper, personal material. But he'd take as long as he needed to
create twelve or thirteen potential singles that would top previous albums.
Like *2001* he'd include his usual guests, teaming with Eminem for a song
and hoping to have Mary J. Blige, 50, Eve, and The Game contribute. If not
the final, Storch says, *Detox* will be one of the last Dre albums, and a classic.
During this period, he received a twelve-track CD from Denaun. A week
later, though only seven in the morning in Australia (where Porter was traveling), he called to say, "I want seven joints." Porter was delighted. Dre would
use two on Xzibit's "Multiply" and 50 Cent's "P.I.M.P.," and invite Porter to
contribute to *Detox*. But when Porter arrived in Cali from his home in
Detroit to work on the album, Dre was too busy to devote time to it.

January 2004, Dre keeps working to make *Detox* "the one they remember
me for." Though he's spent years developing ideas, he tells a reporter, "I'm
actually just starting." He wants the album out by year's end. His keyboardist
friend (and co-defendant in the Mike Lowe lawsuit over Xzibit's "X") Scott
Storch tells reporters it's the most advanced rap album anyone will hear.
Now, his process includes sitting with producers to hear loops and ideas.
After each meeting his producers return to their own projects, and compile
more ideas for the next gathering.

Dre meanwhile has musicians replay the ones he likes, Hi-Tek recalls. One
day, Tek plays him something he created back in Cincinnati. It's an anguished
piece based on an eight-bar section from a soul record and some crooning by

unsigned singer Dion. He adds a hard beat and bass line to make it even more soulful, gothic, and hard and says, "To me that's Dre's sound, too." Dre enjoys it so much, he puts it on the shelf, considers signing Dion (eventually he does) and tell Hi-Tek he indeed captured the "*Detox* sound."

He'll record a few songs, then claim he has to handle duties as Aftermath's primary producer and top executive. Then if 50 Cent needs music, he reminds himself he's a producer first and gets in there to knock some out. But after 50's album, he rushes to work with Obie Trice, then Em's group D-12. The reality is, working with other artists means being able to bounce ideas off them. He can create music faster, and have a pretty good time. With his own stuff he stays there until he has a headache, revising something over and over. So he's in no rush to record for himself.

He has Denaun Porter of D-12, Virginia's Nottz, and Hi-Tek submitting tracks, and if he accepts some and doesn't release them, they wonder if he'll use them on the album. He doesn't want anyone hearing his new stuff, and definitely doesn't want tracks with sounds people have heard from other artists. And though he's commissioning music from others, Porter explains, "As far as creating, it's really Dre. He starts the ideas, everything."

Now, Dre isn't really inspired by anything out there. All he likes are the artists he invites into the studio, and not only because he is working with them and their records will pull in money, either. They're bringing hot ideas and inspiring him to try new things. They aren't like the cookie-cutter acts in stores, on MTV, or being praised in magazines. "There's nothing out there that's really different," he now feels. "There's nobody doing or saying anything that I haven't heard before."

Dre keeps working on *Detox*, spending entire days and most of some nights near the equipment or mix board. He'll keep recording a part over and over, or mixing a song until he feels "like a butterfly-type feeling." He wants his last album to be perfect, the same as with everything else on his label. And since he is the boss, "Nothing leaves this studio until I get that feeling."

He settles into a routine. He stops going to clubs or parties. After waking up, he'll hit the gym, then arrive at the studio around three. He has a nice system, right down to lining up five MPC3000s—four with drum sounds and one for sequencing the keyboard.

He now has fewer players around—he hopes to have just Mike Elizondo do all the playing and engineer Veto record and handle technical stuff. He starts each session the same way, laying down at least two or three instrumentals he can later sell to an artist. Next, he invites vocalists in to record their songs.

He is a businessman—he made that determination a long time ago and as a result won't act on something unless he first considers whether it's a good career move—but sometimes he feels like an artist. He thinks up an idea, rushes to get it on tape and knows it'll be a hit. But then there are weeks where he keeps trying to work on something, changing it, adding things, trying certain vocals or other artists, only to decide it won't work no matter what he does.

They stay there anywhere from two to seventy-nine hours, with him leaving the room occasionally to huddle with visitors. Maybe he breaks for a meal or some coffee. Whatever the case, he returns to his Aeron chair and continues developing ideas until he has a hit, or finally hits a creative wall and decides to revisit something later. Outside the studio, he is an older guy with a wife, about eleven kids, and tons of critics. In the studio he feels as energetic, as young, as in charge as he did when he started twenty years ago. "I still feel it," he says. "I love music."

Dre likes how he sounds, and what he writes about, but in February he's just celebrated his thirty-ninth birthday. He feels even sillier getting up there in front of teens to rap about what are basically juvenile pursuits. Parties, pot, and low riders are all a far cry from his daily reality: the studio, meetings, dinner with Nicole, hanging with the kids at home, and maybe watching some MTV or VH1 before hitting the sack. He also tells himself *Detox* will detract from other albums. He has enough artists already, but just finished another round of signings. "I decided not to do it," he says. "I didn't think it would be fair to all the artists I want to work with." He tells himself he is so hard on himself with high standards, and the music so structurally and thematically complex, he would have easily spent nine or ten months recording ideas and maybe even longer revising them and getting them right. In that time, he can knock out two or three albums for his artists. "I mean, if I didn't have a label to run, and a lot of artists to put out, it would be a different story, then I could just totally concentrate on self."

He has to keep building his company, and getting some of his artists' works in stores. In bed with Nicole, he says he wants to just produce; not rap. And as soon as he says it, a huge weight leaves his shoulders. He'll hand *Detox* tracks created with his players, or purchased from other producers, to other artists. He'll tell reporters he'll never record another studio album again. He'll give up. It's easier. It's over. No more rapping. "I don't think anybody's going to be mad about it after they hear what I'm doing," he says publicly.

◆ ◆ ◆

He really doesn't need to rap. The Vivendi deal alone reportedly brought in $35 million. And he still hasn't gone through his N.W.A. earnings, as he previously said. Furthermore, he's still in a good spot. Even without an album out, he reportedly earns a respectable $11.4 million during one year. Artists connected with Aftermath pay $75,000 per track. He receives a five percent production royalty and label profits from sales of albums and singles by 50 Cent, G-Unit, The Game, Lloyd Banks, D-12, and Obie Trice. And outside gigs (like Eve's and Gwen Stefani's latest duet, "Rich Girl") pull in about $250,000 a pop.

Even so, he doesn't feel good about abandoning what would have been his final album. Others are just getting used to the idea but privately he is debating whether to return when he starts working on Eminem's fourth album, *Encore*. He and Em have enjoyed a pretty good run. On the past three albums, Dre produced eleven tracks, including "Guilty Conscience," "Role Model," "Kill You," " The Real Slim Shady," and "My Name Is." He vouched for Em when he needed it and Em helped with his comeback *2001* and the 50 Cent deal.

But the blonde rapper has changed during the past two years. In his relatively short career, he sold over forty-three million albums worldwide, but after *The Eminem Show* and *8 Mile*, the thirty-two-year-old lowered his public profile, put his film career on hold, and handled his divorce, some lawsuits, and a few weapons charges. And while standing before a judge at one point, he realized the judge could lock him up and keep him from his daughter. "It slowed me the fuck down." He received probation, but still told himself, "I'm never fuckin' up again. I'ma learn to turn the other cheek."

He has replaced partying with boxing, and a new focus on "becoming an adult and trying to just become a businessman." *The Source* resumes its attacks, but he focuses on his label, his clothing line, Shady Ltd. (which brings in about $1.5 million), and his next album. He's been working on it since the day after he completed the *8 Mile* soundtrack, and by late 2003, had eight songs, or half of it done, but someone leaked early versions to bootleggers so he had to start over. As usual, reporters wonder if he'll deliver more irreverence (as "Slim Shady") or heavier material. And as usual, Dre says, "I really like Slim Shady, I like him talking shit and pissing people off. That's where he's gonna go next, talking shit and raising eyebrows."

Em is tired of the image but he accepts that Interscope, and many of his fans, want lightweight singles, and comic antics over heartfelt themes.

As always, Em, on his own, made the new album's first five to seven songs dark and emotional. He rapped about his mom ("Never Enough"), how he despised his ex ("Puke," sung over Queen's shopworn "We Will Rock You"), and how he missed her ("Crazy in Love"). He told his kid he loved her ("Mockingbird") then apologized for the tape *The Source* played reporters (his penitential "Yellow Brick Road"), and tried to end the beef with the magazine and Murder Inc. ("Like Toy Soldiers").

But when Dre arrives in Orlando, Florida, to record, he knows what Interscope expects. As usual, Interscope feels Em doesn't have a single in the stuff he created in Detroit. So for two weeks in Transcontinental Studio, Dre and Mike Elizondo create music for the lighter material the label, and Dre, prefer. "We were able to come up with ten to thirteen tracks per day," Elizondo remembers. "We had two rooms going; one room where we would write the music, and another room where Em would write to the tracks. He ended up writing nine complete songs in just two weeks, which was amazing."

"Evil Deeds" finds him agonizing over childhood issues and how others soured his fame. "Never Enough," with 50 Cent, has him just rapping without his Slim Shady or Marshall Mathers personas. "Mosh" frowns on the war on terror and says President Bush should "go fight his own war, let him impress daddy that way." And on his title track, he tells fans, "And don't worry 'bout that *Detox* album/ It's comin'/ We gonna make Dre do it."

But then something changes, as if Em stopped caring. He starts smashing old themes together. Amid "Rain Man's" fart jokes and pop culture references, he says, "I don't gotta make no goddamn sense. I just did a whole song/and I didn't say shit." "Ass Like That" finds him using the voice of a sock puppet and chanting an odd chorus: "The way you move it, you make my pee-pee go, D-doing doing doing." Dre gives another simple beat and Em delivers something called "Big Weenie." Then he ends *Encore* with a skit in which he blasts his audience with a gun then kills himself (echoing Biggie's suicide ending on *Ready to Die*).

In his fifth floor office at Universal's West Coast building, Jimmy Iovine sometimes plays upcoming works on his powerful stereo system with an ear toward making changes. Jimmy also likes talking with artists about "how we are going to make their records better," he says. Part of his job calls for him to "push them in directions they might not see or might not even want to go at first, and that can cause tension, but that's just part of the creative process." If he doesn't tell artists the truth the relationship is finished, and he can't just say everything sounds good. "The most important thing is to tell them when it's not great." While playing upcoming releases, he tells nearby employees which tracks work and describes changes he wants in a chorus or instrumental. But as a reporter notes, "He also keeps looking around the room for reaction to the tracks because he believes strongly that hit-making takes a team."

Even with Dre at the helm, Interscope doesn't think the album has a single. Em tells Dre he understands you need one to draw crowds—especially with file-sharing eating into overall sales—but it doesn't always have to be upbeat and trivial. His somber "Lose Yourself," he reminds him, "wasn't a cheeseball, you know what I'm sayin'; 'meant-to-be-fun' song." Yet, the *8 Mile* soundtrack sold two million copies in a day. Whether Dre understands or agrees, he doesn't say. But he acknowledges that it isn't only up to them. "Between me, the label, and Dre it's got to be a mutual decision."

With Elizondo, Dre creates some cheery keyboard and bass and sees Em write a hook in thirty seconds. Then he raps about Michael Jackson, yells like

Pee-wee Herman, makes bizarre noises, and raps that he doesn't have all the lyrics done and doesn't even care. After this, Dre wraps recording. Em feels the song "Just Lose It" is inane (his political "Mosh"—the only serious track he recorded with Dre—is better), but Interscope decides it will do. Em accepts the decision. "But it's not the song off this album that's going to speak to me as a hip-hop listener."

❖ ❖ ❖

Now that he is done with rap, Dr. Dre doles *Detox* tracks out to artists he is working with. Usher's song "Throwback" includes a beat Just Blaze sold to Dre in 2001. "The whole concept was him telling hip-hop she's gonna want him back when he retires," Blaze recalls. But he abandons that, has Brooklyn rap to it, then sets it aside, unused. Though old, the track helps Usher's album *Confessions* become one of the year's biggest hits, and keeps Dre's name out there. Obie Trice's "The Set Up," meanwhile, uses a Dre track with congas that, Focus says, he planned to release as one *Detox* single.

Then he gets down to business with The Game's album. Dre is excited. Not only is Game street, he raps like early Nas and Jay-Z. He includes West Coast gangsta details and wraps himself in N.W.A.'s legacy. He wants to call his album *Nigga Witta Attitude* and even quotes old N.W.A. lyrics on some of their samples (the "Amen Brother" drum loop from "Straight Outta Compton"). He eulogizes dead rappers and, unlike 50, doesn't have any problems following him to Aftermath. If anything, Game is mild-mannered. He talks tough but doesn't want to beef with anyone. He tells Dre he considers him like a father, takes direction well, and shows up ready to work. And if Dre keeps him in the booth all night recording vocals, he doesn't complain.

Dre removes his lyric from "Where I'm From" (originally the first Focus track he rapped on), and lets Game have it. Dre also reportedly gives Game a Hi-Tek track (the hard gothic thing with singer Dion) for his song, "Runnin'." Then he turns another *Detox* track into Game's "Here We Go Again" and learns, Focus remembers, Game leaked it on a mix-tape.

He is recording Game's verse on a song called "How We Do," when 50 walks in and says, "Yo, son, I gotta get on that." 50 starts his verse right after

Game's ends and Dre says it is too long. After 50 half-sings a hook, Dre decides this will be Game's first single.

While he feels good about abandoning *Detox*, he rises from his seat during one session, enters the booth, and raps on a Game song. Then he says, "That's it." But while recording Game's "Higher"—supposedly another track for his aborted album—he gets back on the mic and says, "Look out for *Detox*." He can't leave. He tried.

◆ ◆ ◆

50 wants him to executive produce his next album. *Get Rich* was 2003's best-selling album. 50's G-Unit Beg For Mercy tour pulled in $4 million. He got $14 million in royalties from *Get Rich or Die Tryin'* alone and $8 million from a contract renegotiation. He also got royalties from albums by G-Unit (3.5 million sales worldwide), Lloyd Banks (2 million), and Young Buck (a platinum debut), and one million pair of G Unit sneakers (about $6 million). But publicly, he describes "In Da Club" as his biggest hit and promises, "My album will be predominately [sic] Dr. Dre–produced." Dre says he'll do it, and that he'll produce more songs this time, since they'll start from scratch.

But 50 is raring to go, and, without Dre, creates fifteen songs in his home studio. Dre keeps working on Game's CD, but soon sees 50 arrive for sessions. He placed the completed songs aside. Choosing tracks in the studio is frustrating. Dre plays a track but wants to move to the next. 50, however, sits up. "Look. I need this beat."

Dre doesn't think much of this work. "Yeah, that was cool, but . . ." He plays the next.

"Wait a minute. This one. Give me this. I know what to do with this. You can stay in the studio and make records if that's what you want to do." Dre goes back to the beat he skipped over.

But before they can make serious headway, he has to meet a deadline for Game's *The Documentary*. He is mixing the album, which will be released first, and joining Game in publicity photos (looking leaner than ever, less weary and haggard than in 2000, and back to leaning on cars on Compton streets and wearing black dress shirts, matching jeans, and ball caps). With

Dre handing him tracks, the young rapper is openly bragging about how everyone wants to work with Dre, but Dre has handed him six or seven tracks. "I got more beats on my album from him than Eminem or 50 ever got."

While Dre was working, 50 and Game experienced a few creative differences. Though Game was involved with Aftermath, G-Unit, and Interscope, 50 felt he knew what was best for Game's career. So when Game tried to get his name out there by appearing on a New York DJ's mix-tape, 50 called while he was working out at a fitness center to ask if he recorded with one of the many rappers he was feuding with. Game said no, but learned that after his session, the DJ did include a verse from 50's rival.

This blew over but during the summer, Game wanted to join a New York rapper on a song and in his video. 50 decided the audience should first see Game in a video for his duet with him, "How We Do." They next disagreed over 50 targeting rappers like The Lox's Jadakiss and Fat Joe for abuse on his mix-tape number, "Piggy Bank." They had offended him by working with his rival Ja Rule, but Game wouldn't attack them.

Before Dre knows it, 50 has collected tracks from other producers and left California in a huff. "I can't sit there while he's tied up on another project." He claims he waited for months to work with Dre but that he was neglecting *The St. Valentine's Day Massacre*. He also claims Cali-based Interscope favored local boy Game since the West Coast hasn't enjoyed a huge success in years. 50 manages to get the new album done—and includes only three Dre-produced works—but becomes even more disgruntled once Interscope alters the release schedule in October. Since Eminem has a new one arriving in a month, they want it to sell as many copies as possible. So they delay Game's debut until January 2005, and move 50's holiday-titled work from February to March.

◆ ◆ ◆

In November Eminem's single "Just Lose It" draws fans to *Encore* when the entire industry is coping with catastrophic sales dips, layoffs, illegal file-sharing, and near-empty arenas during the summer concert season. *Encore* is far from Em's best—in fact he seemingly sabotaged most of it in an effort to destroy a career he felt he could no longer control—but still helps create the industry's 1.6 percent rise in sales when most other CDs are flopping. But sales of four million are half that of *The Marshall Mathers LP* or *The Eminem Show*. And, despite the fact that it includes more Dre beats than ever, some reviews call *Encore* his worst work.

Despite this, Dre appears on MTV in November to promote a batch of new albums. With 50 and Game on either side of him, in Avatar Studios, he announces *Detox* will happen. "Definitely," he says. "I'm back into it right now." He'll start in January and "hopefully I will get a fall release." And with albums by Busta and Eve also arriving, he'll try "to control the whole year."

He is just as confident when he arrives at the second annual VIBE Awards on November 15. It is being held in Santa Monica, and along with receiving a prestigious award, he'll get to watch Game perform. That night, when he enters with his wife, Nicole, he sees heavy security, private body-guards, and LAPD uniforms on the premises. He leads Nicole to a table where 50 and G-Unit members sit. And when he turns his head, he sees Suge and his entourage sitting not twenty feet away. From here, one person claims, "Suge proceeded to mad dog him for most of the evening."

Dre ignores him. This Suge and Dre thing is exactly like what he sees developing between Game and 50 and he is sick of it. Several performers take the stage to perform but, the show's executive-producer Jimmy Henchman says, there is tension since Suge and Dre are in the same hall. "Some people felt a little uncomfortable, people who knew the history."

Three-quarters of the way into the show Snoop and Quincy Jones—an inspiration and friend—walk on stage to present the VIBE Legend Award for lifetime contributions to hip-hop. Suge supposedly rises to his feet, strolls to the back of the room, and stands near an LAPD officer.

At 7:25 p.m., Dre stands near Nicole, ready to take the stage. He has come a long way since the days when he got Lisa pregnant and didn't know what to do with his life. He has seen a number of sounds and styles come and go. "Planet Rock," the Run-DMC era, N.W.A., the days of Public Enemy promoting black unity and black advancement. Then the Vanilla Ice and Hammer days, the savagery of Death Row and the killings of Tupac and Biggie in a six-month period. The costly videos and materialism era during

which fans and artists submerged their anger about the murders. The
Eminem phase and claims of a machine inspiring so many lackluster works.
And now, feuding magazines, lower sales, and the lingering Southern strip
club sound.

He always did his own thing, what he felt would best help him, his artists,
and the entire genre. He experienced a number of ups and downs and made
a few fearsome enemies, but nights like this make it all worth it. People are
always eager to believe the worst about him but sometimes his race can get
over a self-hate that inspires infighting and actually recognize someone is
trying to help.

He is near the table when a young black guy approaches to ask for an auto-
graph. With the crowd waiting expectantly, he has to get up there to accept the
award but agrees to sign one. But the guy punches him in the face. Before he
can react, the younger guy reportedly hits him again. Whether he's about to
defend himself or not is unclear, but private security try to grab his attacker.
And despite all the bad feelings about release dates and Game's career, 50 and
people with G-Unit leap to their feet. A few group members lunge at the guy,
a twenty-six-year-old parolee from Los Angeles named Jimmy James Johnson.

As Johnson scrambles for help, Quincy Jones tells the crowd it "messed
up" his rap. Then, disgustedly, "I can't believe this." Security tries to break
up the melee. Cops drag noncombatants from the room and lock the doors.
50 and Lloyd Banks stand in the middle of the free-for-all. So does their
Southern G-Unit member, Young Buck. Some group members throw chairs
at the cops; three men hold knives. Johnson runs into another man's arms.
The man tries to shield him, and Johnson himself grips the leg of a cop on
stage, but Young Buck lunges over the human shield and dips his knife into
Johnson's chest.

Within minutes, fifty-six cops arrive (including thirty already patrolling
the Awards). Dre's attacker Johnson is taken to a nearby hospital, where
doctors treat him for a collapsed lung and list him in stable condition.
Other officers spray the group with mace and the battle spills behind a
black curtain to backstage.

Dre isn't hurt. And he doesn't feel the usual embarrassment. He's long
outgrown that Dr. Dre image or needing anyone's approval. He spends

fifteen minutes reassuring his wife that he is fine. The police quickly restore calm and the audience is allowed back in but everyone looks shocked and appalled. They can't believe what they've just seen. "When they punched Dre, they punched the whole industry in the face," says one executive. But the show goes on and Dr. Dre accepts the award. Facing the crowd, the supporters and the haters, and Suge, he says, "They can't stop me. I don't care." He leaves the stage amid thunderous applause.

While leaving, Suge denies all involvement. "One thing about me, if I do something, I'ma claim it," he tells a reporter. "I'm not a idiot. See, an idiot would go out there and do stuff." But Dre's assailant, Johnson, soon claims he attended the Awards with Suge's entourage; Suge supposedly paid him $5,000 to hit Dre; and Suge also allegedly forgave his brother's debt in exchange for humiliating Dre. We will have that explanation in court, his attorney tells the *New York Post*.

Suge's lawyer responds to Johnson's story, "There is absolutely no truth to it." Johnson eventually pleads guilty to felony assault and receives a one-year prison sentence, and three years' probation. He is also ordered to stay away from Dre for three years. Young Buck, meanwhile, pleads not guilty and later reaches an undisclosed plea agreement that satisfies his attorney. Dre retreats further from the public eye. He has really had enough.

◆ ◆ ◆

Dre finishes mixing 50's album, now called *The Massacre*, and works on *Detox* with renewed purpose. Instead of simply building tracks he now puts vocals to music. But Snoop reaches out to suggest an album-length reunion again. "You need to can that *Detox* record and just get on this *Break Up to Make Up*." Snoop feels fans want them together. "They love it when we bombed out, doing what we do. You getting old but you still gotta keep that young flavor." Dre hears him out, but doesn't change his plan, so Snoop leaves feeling *Detox* isn't "coming out right right now because don't nobody wanna hear him not getting high."

By this point, *Detox* has become sort of a running joke in the low-selling rap magazines. Writers are mentioning Brian Wilson's *Smile* and Guns N

Roses' *Chinese Democracy* to imply he is slacking off. As usual, they ignore that he has to keep interrupting his work to handle other duties. And since the setup at the VIBE Awards, they have something else to gossip happily about. But just as many people celebrate his vision. Though the interest-conflicted magazines praise him as the genre's latest king, Kanye West openly discusses producing hits with an ear tuned to Dre's sonic experimentation.

When he finally meets producer Kanye West a month after the VIBE Awards, Dre learns he is a fan. Hailing from Chicago, West has produced hits for Roc-A-Fella Records, popularized sped-up soul samples, and scored a huge hit with his single "Jesus Walks." But he also grew up enjoying Eazy's *Eazy Duz It* at age ten, marveling at how Dre changed the beat five times during some N.W.A. songs, and feeling Dre's albums play like movies. And in a home studio at his mom's crib, he worked to understand how Dre layered instruments on 2Pac's "California Love," and was even more inspired by *2001*'s "Xxplosive," calling it the song "that I got my entire sound from." He filled Jay-Z's "This Can't Be Life" (from *Dynasty*) with similar soul grooves and hard drums and admitted it was "a direct bite." Dre is flattered, and likes West's music just as much, but is really there to ask if he'll produce Game's song "Dreams." Weeks before the album's release, he is still working to make it better. West not only agrees to do it, "I was begging him to mix my next album."

After the last-minute addition, 50 and Game set differences aside and perform together on MTV's *Total Request Live* in January 2005. Game's first single, "How We Do," becomes a huge hit. Radio plays it, rap magazines put Game on their covers, and Game is hired to promote Puffy's profitable Sean John clothing line. Dre's name is back in all the articles, for a more positive reason.

And Interscope ships 700,000 copies of Game's debut to stores, only to see it sell 400,000 in a day (January 20). By week's end—despite the entire industry's disastrous twenty-percent dip in sales from 2000—*The Documentary* sells 587,000 copies, more than the other nine Top Ten albums combined, and tops *Billboard*'s Top 200. "How We Do" is at number five on the Billboard Hot 100, and film producer Joel Silver, Game recalls, "wants to sign me for, like, five movies."

Though Dre produced only six songs, *Rolling Stone*'s review emphasizes his involvement. "Like any decent Dre affair, every song has a well-massaged hook and some immediate appeal, and verses that don't waste a lot of time getting to the point," it writes. It notes that "50 Cent looms large on key songs," and "takes over the album's killer single, 'How We Do'" but adds that Dre has made this an "A-list" effort by piling on hooks ("a simple keyboard part, a spare 808 beat, and strings that manage to sound both stressed-out and catchy"). The album will appeal to both black and white listeners, it adds, but feels like "a Dre/50 Cent side project" to tide fans over until "50's new album in March."

In early 2005 Dre keeps out of the public eye, but helps Game prepare a video for "Dreams." He arrives on the set in an Aston-Martin Vanquish, and soon considers signing another rapper. After a mutual friend introduces them, Dre asks newcomer Bishop Lamont, "You got some hot shit?"

"I think it's hot."

He asks for a CD.

The friend hands one over.

Dre says he'll play it in his car while driving home to "wifey." Then within weeks, he pops up on local station Power 106 to discuss his birthday, and says he wants to work with Lamont. While 50 and The Game keep taking potshots at each other, Dre decides to work on Lamont's *The Reformation* and *Detox* at the same time. He plays Lamont a few *Detox* tracks, then records him on its "Intro." The signing comes at a good time, since the long-running drama between 50 and Game is about to reach its somewhat inevitable conclusion.

On Saturday, February 26, both are in New York giving interviews to draw people to their albums. Game's debut is now at number two on *Billboard*'s R & B/Hip-hop chart after six weeks at the top, but he is popular as ever. Fans are just as excited about 50's new *The Massacre*. The gunshot survivors are both doing well and earning money for their kids, but 50's ego gets the best of him. They are on rival radio stations at the same time and while Game tells one DJ he has no problems with 50, on another station, a host asks 50, "Where does he [Game] stand with your camp?" 50 quips, "Across the street or around the corner. He's not in my camp. Not after being that disrespectful."

50 is angry because Game said he has no aversion to recording with 50's latest target, Nas, a major influence on Game's own style. By now fans are gossiping about who is better but Game tries, at this point, to take the high road. He tells one station Young Buck is cool, while Buck tells another Game is a wimp. "He's just a rapper, he don't live it, man. He's not what he says he is. He's one of them dudes that throws his bricks and hides his hands."

Inevitably, a listener calls in to tell Game they are insulting him on another station. "I'ma let them talk," he says. "I'ma play the background, let that man do what he do and keep it Compton." When the next caller says he won't be successful without 50, however, he tells her to "suck it." He wraps things up then leaves with friends, and 50 and crew trot in with their handlers for their own interview. And 50 gripes about Game some more.

He says his voice on Game's "Hate It or Love It," "Westside Story," and "How We Do" explained why everyone loves him; that he's gone without credit for writing Game's "Church for Thugs," "Special," and "Higher"; that he let Game have songs he once considered for a 50 Cent EP. "I muted my vocals and gave him records."

The interview continues, along with his complaints. "I did so much on his record," he fumes. "I did six records." And he diverted time and energy from his own *The Massacre*. "He'll wake up when it's time for him to do his next record." And this one, he predicts will only sell 500,000 copies. These sorts of comments are nothing new from the relentless self-promoter. In fact, for many, it is the best part of the show. But then he involves Dre.

Though his crew leaped in to help at the VIBE Awards, 50 says, "I love Dre, but if he's confused with what direction he wants to go in after this, my next album will have the same twenty cuts this album has on it, but it will be sold as a double CD. It will fulfill my requirements with Interscope Records. It will be the end of my Shady/Aftermath [deal] and I will move forward in my career as a Shady/G-Unit artist." After he basically threatens Dre in public, the interview is cut short.

50, Lloyd Banks, singer Olivia, and Tony Yayo are escorted from the studio.

Now the media is filled with reports of a shooting outside of the radio station. Game and his crew returned while 50 is on the air. Denied entrance, they argue with men leaving the building. Someone pulls a gun and Game's twenty-four-year-old Compton friend "Peanut" is shot in the left leg (and reportedly grazed in the leg and shoulder).

When cops arrive, they see members of both entourages leaving and a dark sedan abandoned with the engine running. Then, within the hour, someone stops by Violator Management (50's co-managers), and fires a few shots, shattering the glass front door, and leaving six holes in the lobby wall. Cops are investigating both shootings while newspapers prepare front-page stories with both rappers' photos. Interscope meanwhile cancels 50's in-store appearance at the Virgin Megastore in Times Square. A week later, both rappers shake hands and donate money at a press conference and try to show everyone—especially the cops—that the feud is over.

◆ ◆ ◆

By March 2005, 50's voice is on three records in *Billboard*'s Top 10. 50 has reportedly earned $50 million after taxes in 2004 (according to *USA Today*), sold eleven million copies of his debut, and helped Interscope promote his work to the point where Iovine says, "We learn so much from him. I think 50 is the modern recording artist. He understands how things work and what his audience does and wants. He's what the industry is going to look like in the next five years."

Game is another big moneymaker but telling reporters the feud cost him money, and a "shoe deal" with Reebok. "50 hated me out of that," he adds, by describing Game's Black Wall Street label as a California street gang stockpiling assault rifles in Game's home. "They took my deal away." He signed with another company but claims he then lost his tour insurance. "50 fucked off a lot of things for me," he claims, but it won't stop him. "All I need is Dr. Dre, and I don't need nobody."

At Aftermath, producers who recorded with both avoid choosing sides. "It's just sad that they're beefing," says DJ Khalil. "If Dre wants something for Game, Game got it," says Focus. "If Dre directs me to 50, 50 got it."

The media looks to Dre to say something, but he doesn't. With reporters and fans wondering if—as 50 had said—Dre will sever ties with Game, the young rapper reportedly leaks a *Detox* duet that makes it seem Dre leans toward his side. The duet, "Here We Go Again," starts with Dre's usual sample of a bouncing low-rider, and another precise "X"-like track and finds Dre addressing his own controversies ("Is Dre making the beats? Do he write his own flow? I get dough. I'm the Aftermath CEO"). Then for the chorus, Game asks, "You motherfuckers still hatin'? Take a vacation."

Then Game claims he left G-Unit, as opposed to getting the boot. "I left the group 'cause the group was too crowded/Now watch Game finish his second album without 'em." As 2005 continues, the feud becomes even more juvenile. At a huge concert in New York one June night, Game has two pals wander on stage. One, in a rat costume, is "supposed to be 50 Cent" while the other, in a hairy gorilla suit, represents G-Unit. Game's entourage members (in black tees that read "G-U-not") knock them to the floor and pretend to stomp them out, while Game screeches, "They kicked me out the group. I didn't ask to be kicked out." He asks 55,000 people to chant, "50 Cent can suck my dick. Tony Yayo can suck my dick." But when they won't, the show ends with Game storming off stage.

Privately, Dre tries to resolve this. "He made a few phone calls, 50 didn't take his advice and neither did I, but we grown men who make our own decisions and I think that at the end of the day, Dre and Em did the right thing by standing back and focusing on their lives and their families," says Game.

The feud continues and turns fans off even more. And soon, Game tells reporters he is shopping a distribution deal for his label Black Wall Street. "I'm not a hundred percent sure it's gonna fall under Aftermath/Interscope." 50 meanwhile has by now created products that have pulled in about $500 million (at least $41 million in 2005). But during interviews, he darkly speaks of turning G-Unit into an actual record company like Interscope. He wants G-Unit directly under Interscope, not Aftermath. "Like the Universal Music Group with Def Jam, all of that under the same umbrella." Dre or Aftermath go unmentioned when he describes his future plans. "I control the business, I make the decisions," he tells a financial reporter. "If I fail, it'll be my fault."

Eventually, this nonsense ends with Game and Interscope deciding he'll leave Aftermath for Geffen Records. Fans and reporters imply Dre booted him out, but Game later says he left because a contractual clause would pay

50 a royalty from all future Game albums while he is connected to After-math. "I didn't get kicked off, I left. If I wanted to work with Dre, 50 would have made money off my album. I can't let him do that." Thus, the battle ends quietly, with 50 resuming work on his next CD.

By 2005, Dre learns, the industry is making 20 percent less money then it did in 2000. The market continues to collapse under the weight of so many derivative acts and feuds. Despite 50 and Game's recent successes, the overall numbers are discouraging. But Dre continues to work on Busta's CD.

The Big Bang makes *The Chronic* sound primitive. When Dre uses a chord, chances are it contains five tracks of strings and reverb. But amazing as Busta's sound is, Denaun Porter explains, *Detox* will be ten times better "because it's for himself. Dre expects so much from Dre that he ain't puttin' out no bullshit."

In his seat at the board, Dre scrutinizes every line. At one point, he makes Busta recite one word for two hours. And when the song is done, he hears the result and says, "You know, Busta, you could've said this a little better. You could've said it this way. I don't know if I'm really feeling that line." After a session, he rides around with a song, takes it home, tries to see if, days later, it has the same impact. Two or three days later, he'll start revising it.

They've been at it for over two years. And thirty-four-year-old Busta isn't happy when the first one passed. Then after the second year, he thinks, "This shit is getting a little crazy." But Dre let him hear the results and Busta is pleased. Instead of the "high energy, buffoonish, animated Busta Rhymes" white labels preferred, Dre keeps adding new songs, removing others, fine tuning everything, and incorporating Busta's ideas. Then they see guests line up to make appearances. Once the great Stevie Wonder hears the late Rick James is on Busta's nostalgic "In the Ghetto," Wonder joins him on "Been Through the Storm."

Then Busta calls producer Swizz Beatz. Usually, they discuss anything but music. "But this one time, I guess he needed my help," says Swizz. He has a track for Eve, who thinks it is hot, but lets Busta include it on his song, "Touch It."

Since it is by an outside producer, Dre wants a copy. Usually, he lives with something for a week or two then says they need to make a few changes. Busta, impatient and used to getting his own way, has to remind himself that after six albums, he wants new results and will only get them if he tries new things. Thus, Dre is able to fill every song with startling new ideas, concepts, rhythms, and vocal styles. And this approach—this quest for something new—extends even to Busta's guest Raekwon of the Wu-Tang Clan. Rae's group had once been considered for Aftermath—Iovine ran the idea by Dre after member Ol' Dirty Bastard suggested it—but instead of the entire group, Dre wants Rae on Busta's song. And instead of the usual loud, wordy boasts, he works to wring a new sound out of him, having him speak quietly over a mellow groove. The results so please Dre he invites Rae onto his roster.

Then Busta's patience pays off even more. While producing a song called "Imagine," which ponders what the world would be like had rap never existed, Dre leaves his chair and gets on the mic to recite one of his most accomplished twelve-rhyme verses yet. "He don't rhyme on nobody's shit," Busta says.

In the booth, he raps that people would have had hard lives were it not for hip-hop. They'd starve like peasants in the art house movie *City of God*. They'd be in prison or "tryin' to get that dollar on some shitty-ass job." Biggie would probably be with his son and Pac would probably be alive, too, but many people would leave the ghetto for a jail cell, not a tour. Then after prison they'd return to a dead end life of crime. And no one would own the fancy jewels they keep waving in the faces of their cash-strapped fans. "From the East to the West Coast, everybody fucked up," he says. He ends the song by reminding everyone they've been blessed with this opportunity called hip-hop.

◆ ◆ ◆

By December 2005, during a New York photo shoot, Busta decides to cut the dreadlocks he's grown since December 1989 (when he was seventeen). But the haircut makes him look even more like 50. Where he once wore futuristic costumes or baggy tracksuits and outrageous hats, he is now lifting weights, flaunting tattoos, and appearing in decidedly 50-like publicity photos. And where past works showcased comedic and quirky speed-raps that evoked Slick Rick, his new album presents a tougher image. Dre by now has 170 songs done, but has to quicken the pace after someone leaks "I'll Hurt You" to radio. Once fans are excited by a leak, Busta explains, "the quicker your release date gets secured." Aftermath swiftly releases "Touch It," and it becomes an instant radio hit (that will spend thirty weeks on the chart). Dre meanwhile starts choosing which songs will actually appear on *The Big Bang*.

Busta wants the Dre-produced "This How We Do It Over Here"; "Been Through the Storm" with Stevie Wonder; and "Legends of the Fall-off"; which features the music Dre once planned for Ra's unreleased "When You Die." Dre agrees with these choices so Busta is ecstatic. "I got a whole new beginning," he says. "New money, new label, new cars, new crib, new support system of staff to promote my new shit, new album, new look, new everything."

Unfortunately, he is dragged into a controversy of his own after someone murders his bodyguard on the set of one of his videos, and police officers in New York tell reporters he isn't being as cooperative as they'd like. Dre stays out of it, as usual, and focuses on what is important: making *The Big Bang* stronger so it will sell more, and benefit everyone, including Busta. In May, he releases Busta's second single, "I Love My Chick" and sees it land on radio. Then in late June, *The Big Bang* becomes Busta Rhymes's first work to debut at number one on the Hot R&B/Hip-Hop Albums chart.

But despite taking three years to create, it's first week sales of 209,000 are less than the 212,000 Busta's 1998 work, *E.L.E: Extinction Level Event*, sold during its second week. And with some fans rejecting Busta's slightly 50-like new persona, *The Big Bang* spends months crawling toward the 500,000 sales mark. The album comes and goes quickly but Snoop is concerned. That only six Dre tracks appeared on it, and one revamped an old idea for Rakim, is a shame, he tells a reporter. He wonders if Dre's songs will stand out, become singles, and earn great reviews. "How many of them songs is gonna really help Busta Rhymes do what he trying to do? To me," he continues, "the best-produced tracks on Busta Rhymes album is Swizz Beatz, DJ Scratch—other niggas man, not Dre." That Dre didn't produce anyone's entire album anymore makes him feel "that energy isn't there no more." After noting how Dre did everything on *Straight Outta Compton*, D.O.C.'s album, *No One Can Do It Better*, his own debut, *Doggystyle*, *Eazy Duz It*, and *The Chronic*, Snoop adds, "His energy, man. When he did the whole thang, look at his results. Three, four, five million. Eminem's first record, whole thang."

EPILOGUE

Dr. Dre doesn't have to do anything if he doesn't want to. His resume includes many of the genre's high points and—for better or worse—most influential works. With N.W.A., he helped popularized gangster rap and said things about the police that many black fans couldn't. When that ended with friendships ruined, he discovered Snoop and delivered a new sound with "Deep Cover." At Death Row, with Suge, he introduced even more new stars on *The Chronic* and inspired a generation of rap producers and albums like The Notorious B.I.G.'s *Ready to Die*.

This would have been enough. He already had classics like "Fuck tha Police" and "Real Niggaz Don't Die" to his credit. And *The Chronic* yielded Top Forty hits like "Nuthin' but a 'G' Thang," "Dre Day," and his Grammy winner, "Let Me Ride." But he delivered Snoop's multimillion-selling *Doggystyle*, his Top Forty hit, "Keep Their Heads Ringin'" (nominated for a Grammy) and the music on Tupac's "California Love."

He was already in the history books when he left Death Row, and had Suge insulting him, too, but he didn't stop. He came right back with "Been There, Done That," to unite the coasts. When some fans rejected the R&B image and sound he used for *Dr. Dre Presents . . . The Aftermath* and *The Firm*, he didn't let prattle about him losing his career stop him from shifting gears, finally taking the reins, and coming right back with Em's "My Name Is" and his own hit, *2001*. By this point, he could have walked away. He had a mansion, a supportive family, and a business that basically ran itself. But he leaped right into starring in *The Wash* and recording a few songs for its soundtrack: "On the Blvd.," "The Wash," and "Bad Intentions."

He was looking forward to finishing his final album, *Detox*, but became sidetracked by projects he hoped would help other artists. He included Rakim on a song for Jay-Z. He dueted with Knoc-Turn'al on his album. He worked with Eve and Cube, and recorded something for the *Bad Boys 2* soundtrack. But after popping up as producer on albums by 50, Eminem, and Game, he stepped out of the public eye. And since then people have been talking. This time, however, the media and some close friends have seemingly switched roles. The media is on his side. While reviewing Game's album, *Slate* echoed sentiments felt by many. "*The Documentary* is more a product of the Dr. Dre assembly line than anything," *Slate* reported. "At the ancient age of forty, the former Andre Young finally has his hit making formula down to a science—just plug in a new rapper and clear some wall space for the platinum records."

Snoop however, feels "he's at the end of his career where he don't really have that much time to be developing and spending all that time creating. That's why all the new acts that he gets never come out." If they do, he adds, their albums have only minimal contributions by Dre. "It was never a time, when you was with Dr. Dre, and he didn't do your whole fuckin' record."

Snoop stops by when Dre is working on *Detox*. At the same time, Snoop is trying to position himself as the king of the West Coast. He urges Dre "to make this record sound like something. Get all the niggas that ain't from the West out of there." He tells Dre that, with his high profile and track record, he can stop pandering to other regions. With West Coast talent they can "bang it like we did on *The Chronic*." But Dre won't change course, not even when Snoop predicts this approach can result in an "instant four million sales off the top." Snoop then analyzes why the Up in Smoke Tour succeeded. The crowd loved that, excepting Eminem, "it was all West Coast." They want Dre supporting the West.

Dre says he'll invite others onto the album once he gets things rolling.

"You need to get them in to get your shit rolling! You need to have a vibe of where you're going, and then you can say 'Well I don't need ya'll no more, I need him, or I just need him.'"

Dre sits through the advice then sees Snoop, in print, say, "So, Dre, if you're reading this, come back home. Let's put this shit together and let's get this *Detox* record sounding good." Then Snoop repeats his belief that Dre is losing his drive.

At the same time, people keep claiming he stole credit when he openly told many reporters his music sometimes involved collaborators. And many songwriting credits include their names. "It's just drama," says D.O.C. "That's all it is." He's seen Dre create the music, he adds. "Anybody should be happy to be affiliated with this dude, because it's something really different about his ear and shit." Dre decides to ignore these critics, to stay out of the media and focus on what's important, his music. He surrounds himself with his usual collaborators and keeps knocking out ideas. He still has Mike playing bass, but now he also records guitar and keyboard parts. Veto still engineers and makes sure everything sounds crisp and clean. Dre also still keeps starting sessions by laying down one or two instrumental tracks before calling vocalists into the booth to record raps, some for their own albums, some for *Detox*.

With the media already describing Bishop Lamont as his new protégée, he also keeps working with another new artist. From Philadelphia, G.A.G.E. had worked three years to get the deal. His manager originally tried to go through Mel-Man and traveled to Cali to meet with him but when Mel left, they kept passing demos to Jay Bible, Dre's old pal from Compton. "We sent him about two hundred and fifty songs," G.A.G.E. recalled. "He [G.A.G.E's manager] was a little nervous, because you only got one shot with Dre." In March 2005, G.A.G.E. was ready to move on. Dre suddenly received a six-song demo. While playing it, he liked the voice and lyrics. "He also likes the way I enunciate my words, because you can understand what I'm saying." The next day someone called G.A.G.E. to say they booked a flight and a room in a Beverly Hills hotel. The night before the meeting, an Aftermath employee said Dre liked the music but wanted to see if he had "star quality; if you ready for the game; if you got the look." He added, "Dre's gonna stare you down; he's gonna be hard on you." But the next day, Dre was calm. "We don't really need to talk," he told him. "I'm feelin' your stuff; you feelin' the Aftermath stuff. Let the lawyers ping-pong back and forth until we both happy with the situation."

Before returning to Bishop's *The Reformation* and *Detox*, he tells employees to book sessions for G.A.G.E.'s debut, "My Life." During one, G.A.G.E. (working by himself since he doesn't know anyone in the area) is shocked to see The D.O.C. crossing the room. "He still hangs with Dre on a daily basis," G.A.G.E. reports. And now, D.O.C. says, "I just wanted to come check on you." From here, he keeps helping G.A.G.E. the way he once did Snoop. And he's happy with Dre. He finally got rid of the yes-men, D.O.C. feels. Now, if he says a beat isn't that hot, Dre actually listens. "You never see him with no jewelry on, no flashy rims; nothing," says G.A.G.E. "And he got more money than the people with all that stuff."

Some days, Dre listens to the beats G.A.G.E. wants on his album. He isn't as picky about vocals as reporters claim. "Nah, he's harder on you when you bring him the music." These, G.A.G.E. explain, have to be perfect. If a few bars don't catch his ear, he turns to the CD Shredder he now keeps on his desk and shoves the demo right in. When D.O.C. sees him shred a few, he holds his tongue. Dre can improve them, and hand them to other artists, "But it's his art, I can't tell him what to do with his shit. I don't even try, cause it won't work!" And before G.A.G.E. can get discouraged, Busta calls to say he shouldn't take it personal. "It's gonna be a lot of songs that everybody around you think is excellent," Busta adds. "But trust me, it'll work out for the better."

As Spring 2006 continues, Dre continues to avoid the media and stick to his familiar schedule. Before the studio, he hits the gym. He runs into artists like Bishop, Busta, and Stat Quo (Aftermath's way into the lucrative Southern market) there but focuses on building his strength, knocking out more pull-ups than anyone around him. And in the studio, he keeps working with D.O.C. on *Detox*. As usual, D.O.C. still wants to launch a comeback, even after his last solo album, *Deuce*, flopped. "I think Dre could make you a star," he feels. "If that's what he wanted to do." This time, Dre says he'll executive produce his next one once they knock *Detox* out. Then he tells him to call it *Voice Through Hot Vessels*. It's an odd title, some people feel, but D.O.C. jokes, "You can call the muthafucka whatever you want! I just wanna do one over your drums."

Dre stops everything when he hears in April that Em's friend Proof has been killed (he was shot right after he shot someone else in the face in a Detroit nightspot). Dre flies to Detroit for the funeral. In the crowd of almost two thousand, he sees Em, 50, Lloyd Banks, the group D-12, Young Buck, members of Naughty by Nature, Obie Trice, and Xzibit. So much has changed so quickly, he realizes. Death Row no longer exists. The imprisoned drug dealer that claimed he gave Suge $1.5 million for Death Row sued for over $100 million, and won. And when Suge was slow to pay, a court took the label away.

Xzibit meanwhile decided to record a darker album without Dre. He included political themes, didn't sell as many copies, but still hosts a popular show on MTV. Eminem has been laying low since Interscope rushed *Curtain Call*, a greatest hits work, into stores. Busta is still coping with the fact that a bodyguard was murdered on the set of one of his videos. 50 keeps feuding with Game, but wants to make it in acting. He's also quietly recording another album.

During the funeral, Dre faces the gold-colored casket, the young artist in it, his birth and stage names listed on the crate. Soon he and producer Denaun Porter are talking. He tells Porter where he's at. "Yo, I'm working on my shit."

Porter lets him know he's tired of Detroit. "I'm out of here."

Dre says he's thinking of using three Porter tracks. "You good for my album." Then he invites the producer to work exclusively for Aftermath. No more freelancing. Stable money. Porter accepts the offer and a way out of this city. "He's done with Busta's record and he's jumping back into it," Porter says of *Detox*.

Back home, Dre juggles numerous projects, really devoting most of his time to Bishop's album, since it's coming first, then hears an Interscope employee named Karen pitch Joell Ortiz, a Puerto Rican rapper known for witty lyrics, battle raps, popular mix-tapes, and online journals. "I think she had hooked it up or whatever," Ortiz says. "But he flew me out and it was crazy." He's still looking for rappers who have the right look and demeanor, and great voices. "And we have to be able to get along." He's tired of rappers arriving in awe then resenting him when he doesn't drop everything to work on their music. He also wants rappers who bring their share of ideas to the studio. He can't, and won't do it all; not with his own album to write.

During their meeting in May, Dre sits and listens to Ortiz's music. After fifteen minutes, he says, "Yo, I'm feeling you."

Ortiz is ecstatic. "Yo, what the dilly, yo?"

"Yo, you wanna be Aftermath?"

"You're damn right I wanna be Aftermath!"

After signing Ortiz, Dre keeps working steadily on *Detox* right into November 2006, when Game's back in the media. *The Documentary* has sold just under two and a half million copies, and in addition to feuding with 50 and G-Unit, Game also fell out with his brother Fase and members of his crew, Black Wall Street. He moved into a big house near the pop rock group Good Charlotte and kept alternating between dismissing Dre's production and calling him his hero during interviews to promote his second album, *The Doctor's Advocate*. Now, he shamelessly tells reporters about a new title track with Dre's producer friend J.R. Rotem and Busta, in which he drunkenly apologizes for letting Dre down. "Dre, I ain't mean to turn my back on you," he cries on the song. "I owe you my life." Then: "I told you, you were like a father to me. I meant that." Whether Dre believes this is sincere or just another of Game's marketing ploys is unclear, but Game keeps trying to tie his name to his on many of this album's songs. He mentions him so much even the ever-supportive *Los Angeles Times* notes, "Dr. Dre's presence looms large on almost every song on *Doctor's Advocate*."

December 2006 finds Dre avoiding the media, focusing instead on the work. And while he sits and crafts drums—probably abandoning the dull style he's been stuck in since Tha Dogg Pound—D.O.C. tells a reporter they want *Detox* done by Summer 2007. He also says sessions feel like they did in the beginning. "He's really able to concentrate on making these drums work, and I sit in there and try to concentrate on making these words work."

With everyone claiming *Detox* will never see release, Dre takes a minute to join Bishop Lamont in a homemade video online. He's still nervous about failing in public, but he looks fitter, younger than ever in his white golf shirt. And while Lamont promises *Detox* in September 2007, he simply moves from one foot to the next near a mix board. Then the camera's turned off and he gets back to work.

◆ ◆ ◆

Nothing out there really inspires him or catches his ear. Everyone's trying to sound like each other and it's boring fans and ruining sales. "There's nobody doing or saying anything that I haven't heard before." He keeps lining up his five MPC3000's, and spending hours on the drums. He uses the same sound on each song, but they sound different since he equalizes them. He cleans them up before sampling, then does it again once they're loaded in the computer. He also keeps using the same old school keyboards and avoiding samples because he wants to be free to remove or insert a bass line during a mix. He still loves Curtis Mayfield, Isaac Hayes, and P-Funk, but has new influences that include orchestras, music theory lessons, and sixties' rock by the Doors, among others. And, with someone teaching him piano, he's really getting into structuring chords.

He takes his time now, when he writes melodies. He sits and applies everything he's learned in music theory or piano class, placing notes at the right place, trying new rhythms, experimenting with timing and chord changes and arrangements.

He keeps working on songs until he feels they're right. He can't explain it. The feeling usually arrives during a mix. He'll suddenly know something's done. Some songs take weeks to work out, and even then, they don't work. Others are knocked out quickly, within hours, and could potentially be singles. Either way, since he's in charge at Aftermath, "Nothing leaves this studio until I get that feeling."

He still avoids the clubs. There's nothing out there for him anymore. He's happily married, with kids and into working out again. He gets to the studio at three and stays for as long as the ideas flow. There, he feels as young and alive as he did when he started over twenty years ago. After all this time, all of the attacks from haters, and even the incident at the VIBE Awards, "I still feel it, I love music."

Detox will be the last one. And he'll miss rapping, even though he tells people he sees himself mainly as a producer. He loves making music. It's his life's work. And when *Detox* is done, it'll be different, just standing behind the board, watching others do it.

Now, he no longer worries about his age. Rap isn't a young man's game. If you have hot music and put it together in an exciting way, fans will buy an album. "If you feel old, it's going to turn out like that." He can be fifty, he told *Scratch Magazine* over a year ago, "and still make a hot hip-hop record." It won't be him up there at that age, but someone that old can still be behind the scenes, producing, if they make good music. They can be seventy and still at it if they're creating the type of stuff people want to hear. "If people are talking about somebody being too old, that means that sound is getting too old. It's time to start your game over, reinvent yourself or something."

For *Detox* he'll reinvent himself. Do the same thing and people get bored, he feels. And with so many people imitating his newest sound, that makes it die out even faster, so he'll have to keep changing. Maybe since he won't rap anymore, he'll have time to finally create that black rock album he talked about since leaving Death Row. If he finds the right lead singer, he can find the band later. He'll also see if he can finally leap into scoring a film. This is why he keeps studying music theory. He doesn't have it down yet—another two or so years and he will—but he wants to conduct a full orchestra and be the best at this, too. He'll also keep making rap records with hot new artists. And in the end, when all is said and done, he hopes people will remember he didn't coast. He could have, but instead kept trying to create better music each time he entered the studio. He wants people to remember he really cared about his music and wanted to entertain people. He wants them to view him as having been talented. "I just want to be remembered as being the shit," he says.

Acknowledgments

I'd like to thank my agent, Jim Fitzgerald, for his continued support and encouragement during this latest project, which found me sifting through about seven years of research and adding even more at the last minute.

DR. DRE DISCOGRAPHY

WITH N.W.A.

N.W.A. AND THE POSSE
Ruthless Records
Release: November 6, 1987
Certified gold: April 19, 1994

STRAIGHT OUTTA COMPTON
Priority Records
Release: January 1, 1989
Certified double platinum: March 27, 1992

100 MILES AND RUNNIN'
Ruthless Records
Release: August 16, 1990
Certified platinum: September 16, 1992

EFIL4ZAGGIN

Priority Records
Release: May 28, 1991
Certified platinum: August 8, 1991

GREATEST HITS
Priority Records
Release: July 2, 1996
Certified gold: February 14, 2002

THE DEATH ROW YEARS

THE CHRONIC
Death Row
Release: December 15, 1992
Certified triple platinum: November 3, 1993

DOGGYSTYLE
Death Row/Interscope
Release: November 23, 1993
Certified 4 times platinum: May 31, 1994

ALL EYEZ ON ME
Death Row/Interscope
Release: February 13, 1996
Certified 9 times platinum: June 18, 1998

MURDER WAS THE CASE
Death Row/Interscope
Release: October 14, 1994
Certified double platinum: April 5, 1995

THE AFTERMATH YEARS

DR. DRE PRESENTS . . . THE AFTERMATH
Interscope Records

Release: November 26, 1996
Certified platinum: September 12, 1997

2001
Aftermath/Intercope
Release: November 16, 1999
Certified 6 times platinum: November 21, 2001

DR. DRE AS PRODUCER FOR EMINEM

THE SLIM SHADY LP
Aftermath/Interscope
Release: February 23, 1999
Certified 4 times platinum: November 14, 2000

THE MARSHALL MATHERS LP
Aftermath/Interscope
Release: May 23, 2000
Certified 9 times platinum: February 12, 2004

THE EMINEM SHOW
Shady/Aftermath/Interscope
Release: May 28, 2002
Certified 8 times platinum: March 13, 2003

ENCORE
Shady/Aftermath/Interscope
Release: November 12, 2004
Certified 4 times platinum: December 17, 2004

CURTAIN CALL—THE HITS
Shady/Aftermath/Interscope
Release: December 6, 2005
Certified double platinum: January 27, 2006

DR. DRE AS PRODUCER FOR EMINEM AND D12

DEVIL'S NIGHT
    Shady/Interscope
    Release: June 19, 2001
    Certified platinum: September 13, 2001

D12 WORLD
    Shady/Interscope
    Release: April 27, 2004
    Certified double platinum: September 9, 2004

DR. DRE AS PRODUCER FOR 50 CENT

GET RICH OR DIE TRYIN'
    Shady/Aftermath/Interscope
    Release: February 6, 2003
    Certified 6 times platinum: December 9, 2003

THE MASSACRE
    G-Unit/Shady/Aftermath/Interscope
    Release: March 3, 2005
    Certified 5 times platinum: December 16, 2005

DR. DRE AS PRODUCER FOR 50 CENT WITH G-UNIT

BEG FOR MERCY
    G-Unit/Interscope
    Release: November 14, 2003
    Certified double platinum: December 16, 2003

SOUNDTRACKS

DEEP COVER
    Epic Records
    Release: April 14, 1992

FRIDAY
Priority Records
Release: April 11, 1995
Certified double platinum: June 4, 1996

GET RICH OR DIE TRYIN'
G-Unit/Interscope
Release: November 8, 2005
Certified platinum: December 21, 2005

DR. DRE FILMOGRAPHY

1993

"Yuletide in the 'hood" (TV)
Voices of: Dr. Dre, Tommy Davidson, T.K. Carter, Patrick Ewing, Whoopi Goldberg, Orlando Jones, Dawnn Lewis, Ed Lover, Reginald VelJohnson

1994

"A Cool Like That Christmas" (TV)
Voices of: Dr. Dre, Boys II Men, T.K. Carter, Tommy Davidson, Whoopi Goldberg, T'Keyah Crystal Keymáh, Phil LaMarr, Dawnn Lewis, Tone Loc, Ed Lover, Ron Taylor, Reginald VelJohnson
Warner Brothers Television
Executive Producers: David Cohen, Quincy Jones, Phil Roman, David Salzman, Roger Shulman
Directors: David Feiss, Swinton O. Scott III
Screenplay: David Cohen, Roger Shulman

1996

Set it Off

Dr. Dre (Black Sam), Jada Pinkett, Queen Latifah, Vivica A. Fox, Kimberly Elsie, John C. McGinley, Blair Underwood, Vincent Baum, Van Baum, Chaz Lamar Shepherd, Thomas Jefferson Byrd, Charles Robinson, Ella Joyce, Anna Maria Horsford, Samantha MacLachlan, Samuel Monroe Jr.

New Line Cinema
Executive Producers: F. Gary Gray, Mary Parent
Director: F. Gary Gray
Screenplay: Takashi Bufford, Kate Lanier
Cinematography: Marc Reshovsky

1999

Whiteboyz

Dr. Dre (Don Flip Crew #1), Danny Hoch, Dash Mihok, Mark Webber, Piper Perabo, Eugene Byrd, Bonz Malone, Rich Komenich, Annabel Armour, Lisa Jane Todd, Brooke Byam, Diane Rinehart, Mark Swanson, Rick Snyder, Jacqueline Williams

Fox Searchlight Pictures
Executive Producers: David Peipers, John Sloss
Director: Marc Levin
Screenplay: Garth Belcon, Danny Hoch, Mark Levin, Richard Stratton
Cinematography: Mark Benjamin

2001

Training Day

Dr. Dre (Paul), Denzel Washington, Ethan Hawke, Scott Glenn, Tom Berenger, Harris Yulin, Raymond J. Barry, Cliff Curtis, Snoop Dogg, Macy Gray, Charlotte Ayanna, Eva Mendes, Nick Chinlund, Jaime Gomez, Raymond Cruz

Warner Brothers Pictures
Executive Producers: Bruce Berman, Davis Guggenheim
Director: Antoine Fuqua

Screenplay: David Ayer
Cinematography: Mauro Fiore

The Wash

Dr. Dre (Sean), Anthony Albano, Tic, Lamont Bentley, The Bishop Don Magic Juan, Bruce Bruce, Thai Buckman, Frank Chavez, Tommy Chong, Angell Conwell, Mark Cooper, Joseph Davis, Tray Deee, Louis Deron-Davenport, D.J. Pooh

Lions Gate Films

Executive Producers: Dr. Dre, Snoop Dogg, Kip Konwiser, Tom Ortenberg, Michael Paseornek

Director: D.J. Pooh

Screenplay: D.J. Pooh

Cinematography: Keith L. Smith

SOURCES

While preparing *Dr. Dre: The Biography* I turned to a few sources (besides original interviews conducted while preparing earlier works about him). And the following sources proved invaluable. Not only did they provide details about his remarkable journey through this tumultuous and somewhat tarnished industry, they also helped me avoid delivering some *Have Gun Will Travel* retread (something I've no interest in doing). Before describing the sources and how they helped, I'd like to say each book was well written, the articles are enlightening, and the web sites employ many talented reporters; and that all can provide more information for anyone interested in the subjects of Dre, Aftermath Entertainment, Interscope, Jimmy Iovine, and the people Dre worked with at each stage of his storied career, as well as what he might include on his upcoming, *Detox* (he's vowed to release it September 2007).

For books, I turned to my own *Have Gun Will Travel* first (New York: Doubleday, 1998). Not only because I wrote it, but because I wanted to look at it with a fresh eye and sort of see things as Dre would have. I also looked through Randall Sullivan's *Labyrinth* (New York: Grove Press, 2002) and felt he did a wonderful job of reporting on controversies surrounding various murders and investigations. There would have been more of that in this book but Dre's never concerned himself with that sort of stuff, so I wanted to be true to how he'd see and approach things. I then turned to 50 Cent's *From Pieces to Weight* (New York: MTV Books, 2005) to learn how 50 viewed things. 50's not the villain of the piece, but neither is he the hero. He is simply, like Dre and like most rap artists today, a businessman. And he certainly has his own view of things and opinions. I then looked through Verna Griffin's *Privileged to Live* (California: Milligan Books, 2005) and while she doesn't get into her son's music much, her work did provide a few surprising insights that helped me report on Dre's development and evolution as an aspiring producer. Other works I found enjoyable and helpful include S.H. Fernando's *The New Beats* (New York: Anchor Books. 1994) and also Alex Ogg and David Upshal's *The Hip Hop Years* (London: Channel Four Books, 1999). Both took me down memory lane in terms of how the industry, and the culture, then both combined, used to be; and reminded me even more of how far its come, for better or worse. Since the deadline for this was almost as tight as the one Dre faced for *The Wash* soundtrack, I didn't get to read many other rap works; and it's probably for the better. The rap-related book has gone to the dogs and with this, I'd like to think I'm restoring a little dignity to the reportorial side of a once-proud industry.

Other sources that proved helpful were various articles written by many fine journalists and cultural critics over the years. Josh Tyrangiel did a hell of a job covering Dre's *The Wash* for *Time* magazine's September 15, 2001, edition, and Dre himself in other stories, as did Christopher John Farley in two 1993 articles about Snoop's *Doggystyle*. The people at *Scratch* meanwhile—Jerry Barrow, Josephine Basch, my colleague Alvin Blanco, and Thomas Gianopoulos—delivered an impressive cover story about *Detox* in their magazine's September/October 2006 issue. And while Dre didn't say much, others around him provided further insight into who he's become. Then there was reporter Jonathan Gold's classic *Rolling Stone* cover story, "Dre Day," and Chuck Philips and Robert Hilburn's coverage of Dre and Death Row in the *Los Angeles Times*. And *The Source*, despite recent tumult, ran some rather interesting stories about Dre and Aftermath, including "Before & Aftermath." Jesse Washington's story about Jerry Heller, meanwhile, printed by the

Associated Press on September 4, 2006, was also amusing. Then there were a
number of web sites that ran some interesting interviews with some of the
characters involved in this tale. They include:

Aftermathmusic.com

Alleyezonme.com

Allhiphop.com

Answers.com

Ballerstatus.net

Billboard.com

Donmega.com

Dubcnn.com

Findarticles.com

Forbes.com

Imdb.com

Laweekly.com

Montereycountyweekly.com

MTV.com

Music.yahoo.com

Newsweek.com

Prefixmag.com

Rapindustry.com

Rapnews.net

Rapnewsdirect.com

Raptism.com

Rockonthenet.com

Rollingstone.com

Xxlmag.com

Scratchmagazine.com

Sixshot.com

Thesmokinggun.com

Sohh.com

Songwriteruniverse.com

Southcoasttoday.com

Streetgangs.com

Thaformula.com

The411online.com

Ukmusic.com

Vibe.com

Westcoast2k.net

Wikipedia.org

INDEX